Ulrich Klinge

Success in Essay Writing

Gymnasiale Oberstufe

TRAINING

Klett Lernen und Wissen

Bibliographische Information Der Deutschen Bibliothek
Die Deutsche Bibliothek verzeichnet diese Publikation in der Deutschen Nationalbibliographie; detaillierte bibliographische Daten sind im Internet über http://dnb.ddb.de abrufbar.

Auflage 4. 3. 2. 1. | 2009 2008 2007 2006
Die letzten Zahlen bezeichnen jeweils die Auflage und das Jahr des Druckes.
Dieses Werk folgt der reformierten Rechtschreibung und Zeichensetzung. Ausnahmen bilden Texte, bei denen künstlerische, philologische oder lizenzrechtliche oder andere Gründe einer Änderung entgegenstehen.

Internetadresse: www.klett.de
Umschlaggestaltung: VIER FÜR TEXAS Ideenwerk, Frankfurt/Main
Satz: Klaus Bauer, Bondorf
Redaktion: form & inhalt verlagsservice Martin H. Bredol / Linda Strehl
Reproduktion: Meyle + Müller, Medien-Management, Pforzheim
Druck: Mediahaus Biering GmbH, München
Printed in Germany.
ISBN-10: 3-12-927066-3
ISBN-13: 978-3-12-927066-0

9 783129 270660

Was Sie in diesem Buch finden

Der vorliegende Trainingsband enthält **zwölf Übungs- und Musterklausuren** zu wichtigen Themen der Oberstufe, wie sie im Fach Englisch in den Jahrgangsstufen 12/13 und im Abitur gestellt werden. Für jede der zu bearbeitenden Textaufgaben gibt es ausführliche Beispiellösungen. Darüber hinaus werden in diesem Buch die wichtigsten Techniken für das Schreiben englischsprachiger Essays erklärt und systematisch geübt.
Die Übungsklausuren mit Musterlösungen sind nach dem Prinzip steigender Schwierigkeit (vom Leichteren zum Schwereren) angeordnet. Sie bieten reichhaltiges Material sowohl für die Vorbereitung auf die schriftliche Abiturprüfung in Englisch nach 8 wie auch nach 9 Jahren.

Was Sie in diesem Buch lernen können

Eine Vielzahl von Übungen macht Sie auf die häufigsten Fehler im Englischen aufmerksam und hilft, sie in Zukunft zu vermeiden. Besonderer Schwerpunkt liegt dabei auf der Verbesserung des Ausdrucksvermögens und der Aufsatztechnik im Englischen. Sie erhalten zahlreiche Hilfen, um das fremdsprachliche Transport- und Klausurvokabular zu erweitern, und lernen die geforderten *writing skills* (Textaufbau, kommunikative Textgestaltung) kennen und beherrschen.

Wie arbeiten Sie mit diesem Buch?

Sie können dieses Buch vom ersten Kapitel an systematisch durcharbeiten, alternativ jedoch auch bestimmte Kapitel heraussuchen, um einzelne Aspekte direkt zu bearbeiten.
Die *study-* und *practice*-Teile kommen in einigen Kapiteln *vor* den Klausuraufgaben. Bearbeiten Sie diese auch zuerst, denn diese *pre-essay writing exercises* sollen Sie an spezifische *text skills* erinnern und helfen, diese beim Beantworten der Textaufgaben anzuwenden. In der Regel sind die vorbereitenden Sprachübungen auf den folgenden Text genau zugeschnitten. Sie können sie für eigene Essays ebenso nutzen wie die *translation exercises:* Beide enthalten nützliches Themenvokabular für Ihre Antworten.

In anderen Kapiteln sind die sprachpraktischen Übungen *hinter* den Textaufgaben angeordnet. Hiermit sollen die *text* und *language skills* im Allgemeinen verbessert werden.
In dem kleinen Glossar am Ende des Buches finden Sie Formulierungshilfen, die Sie beim *essay writing* unterstützen.
And now, take heart: Viel Erfolg beim Lösen der Aufgaben!

Ulrich Klinge, im Juni 2006

1 Survival of the Prettiest

1.1 Elizabeth Montebello Is the Prettiest Girl in School

"Elizabeth Montebello is the prettiest girl in school." That's what I wrote in my diary last night.

I keep track of what E. M. is wearing each day in my diary. I do this because she has a lot of great clothes. Her dad is on TV – he's the commentator for the Channel 9 news.

Elizabeth Montebello is tall and skinny, and she smells like lavender. Sometimes I watch her opening her locker. Our lockers are on the same row. One time she forgot her combination, and she had to call the guard. I could really be her stalker[1] if she let me, but I try to leave her alone.

My name is Doreen Kleinzahler. I'm fat, not really fat, but maybe she'll[2] grow out of it fat, and my face is all broken out[3], and I don't know how to dress at all. My dad says I could be anything I want to be. I think maybe he's a little naïve.

My dad thinks it's great that I'm going to summer school. He doesn't understand what it's like to be 16. He thinks it's great to be wearing recycled clothes. He gives all our money away.

E. M. is only in summer school because she's graduating early, and she's already got early admission to college. I'm here because I failed PE. I signed up for a swimming class and just forgot to show up.

E. M. and I are in Social Studies together this summer. I sit across from her, because in summer school that shit doesn't matter as much. Otherwise she'd be sitting with her boyfriend, whose name is Hal.

I often exchange knowing glances with her during class, whenever the teacher fucks up[4], and once I caught her looking over at my paper during a test. I wanted more than anything in the world to be able to give her the answer, but I didn't know it either.

Today is August 11. E. M. spoke to me today, in the hall. She said, "Hey, nice book bag, Doreen."

(I've got a Hello Kitty book bag. It's the nicest thing I own.)

"Hey, thanks," I said, as if we were total equals and I'd expected her to say that.

Maybe I'll try and talk to her tomorrow. Maybe I ought to rehearse.

(380 words)

1 someone who follows and watches another person over a period of time in a way that is very annoying or threatening – **2** read: maybe-she'll-grow-out-of-it-fat, i.e. what grown-ups say to soothe her – **3** if you break out in spots etc., they appear on your skin – **4** *(taboo, spoken)* to make a mistake or do something badly

1.1.1 How to Refer to the Text for Proof

Study

Whether you answer comprehension questions on the text, analyse or comment on a relevant aspect related to the text, you will be expected to **refer to** or **quote from** the given text to prove your point. Read the suggested answer to the following question studying how **text reference** is provided.

Question

Why does 16-year-old Doreen so desperately want to be friends with Elizabeth Montebello?

Answer

There are several reasons why the 16-year-old narrator of the story is eager to associate with the star of her class. For one, her classmate corresponds to the teenage beauty ideal of our time and is well-groomed ("she smells like lavender", l. 8). For another, she seems to be very popular with boys and has a boyfriend called Hal (l. 29). Furthermore, "E. M.", as Doreen calls her in her diary, seems to be an "A" student. This can be traced in ll. 24–25 where it says that she has already an admission to college. Most importantly, perhaps, she can afford "a lot of great clothes" (ll. 5–6), which she seems to change daily and which make her look very attractive in Doreen's eyes. So, Elizabeth Montebello seems to be privileged in every imaginable way. She represents a role model, whom the unhappy Doreen discreetly follows around and whose dealings are the main topic in the diary she writes.

How to refer to the text: five options

(1) … and has a boyfriend called Hal (l. 29)	→ *refer to the line(s) in brackets*
(2) Her classmate corresponds to the teenage beauty ideal of our time and is well-groomed ("she smells like lavender", l. 8).	→ *quote key words + line(s) in brackets*
(3) Most importantly, perhaps, she can afford "a lot of great clothes" (ll. 5–6).	→ *work the quote into your sentence + line(s) in brackets*
(4) In ll. 1–2 the narrator mentions that Elizabeth Montebello is the prettiest girl in school.	→ *use a "reporting verb" + that-clause*
(5) "E. M." […] seems to be an "A" student. This can be traced in ll. 24–25 where it says that she has already an admission to college.	→ *state the point in your own words (paraphrase); give evidence in the following sentence*

Practice

Find the corresponding text references below and fill them into the gaps.

"gives all our money away" (l. 23). ("my face is all broken out", l. 16).

This can be traced in ll. 14–15. ("I'm here because I failed PE", l. 25)

she "do[es]n't know how to dress at all" (ll. 14–15). (l. 1–5).

Doreen compares herself unfavourably with "E. M." ______________________

____

Her father appears to favour an alternative lifestyle and ______________________

____

The fact that she cannot afford to buy the clothes she craves makes her feel

that ____

And, finally, she apparently does not "sail through" school. ______________________

____

Unlike the famed Elizabeth, Doreen, for another, feels ugly, she describes herself as fat. ______________________________

She worries about her facial skin problems ______________________________

____

TIP As you launch into your comprehension questions and analysis, make sure that **text references** and **quotes** are part of the package that you will deliver!

1.1.2 How to Express Meaning

Study

Students are supposed to read texts to understand their **meaning.** When asked to analyse texts, they will have to elicit significant **facts** *(Textdetails ans Licht bringen, herausfiltern)* and draw **conclusions** as to what these facts – within the context of the narrative or non-fictional text – **mean.** What we have, on the one hand then, is the **text** as its author has chosen to shape it. We do have, on the other, the **reader** who "deconstructs" the text according to his private systems of thought *(seine persönlichen Überzeugungen, sein Wissen über die Welt)*:

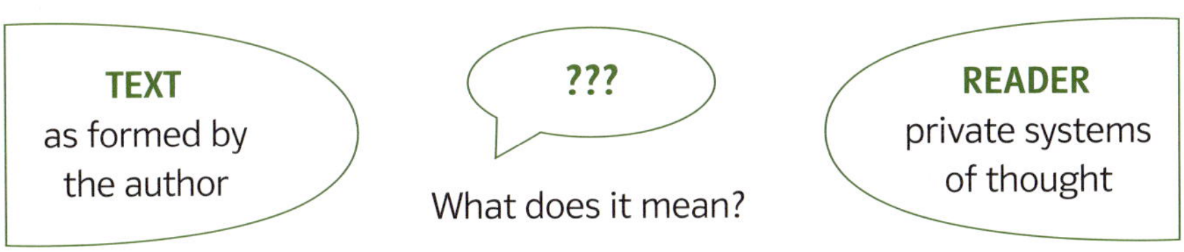

What the reader does is to fit his findings in the text into his private systems of thought. To make that process explicit in essay writing, one needs **verbs** that express **meaning:**

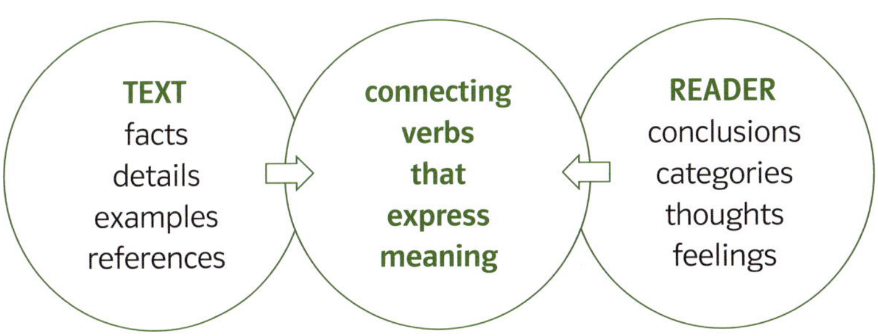

Practice 1

Read the short passage on the protagonist of text 1.1 and underline the connecting verbs that express meaning.

In the story "Elizabeth Montebello Is the Prettiest Girl in School" Doreen portrays herself as a hopeless 16-year-old high school student. The way she describes her own shortcomings suggests that she is not very self-confident. The school's star, Elizabeth Montebello, seems to have it all: she is said to be an attractive girl, very popular among her peers and, on top of that, what we call an "A" student.
Unlike Elizabeth, Doreen comes across as somebody who complains about her looks and her clothes. This clearly reveals that she is very unhappy with her personal situation.
As regards her shyness and reserve, we view her as the type of girl who is commonly known as a wallflower. It should, however, be mentioned that she will have her chance: will she live up to it?

Study

Read the following sentences: "In ll. 4–5 Doreen says that she carefully writes down what E. M. is wearing each day. **This means that** Doreen is jealous of Elizabeth's clothes and looks."

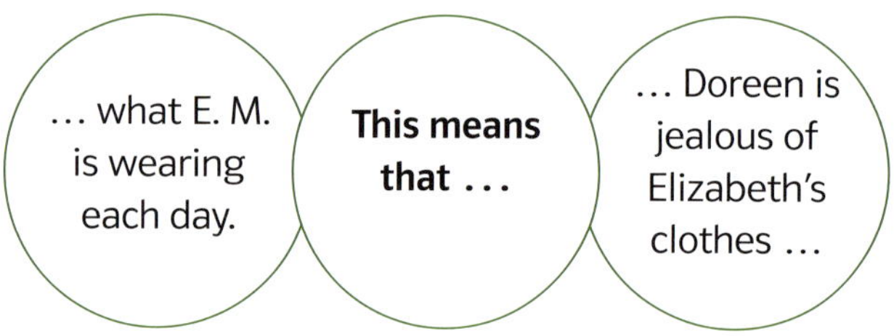

The almost "classic" phrase "This means that ..." indicates what the reader concludes from ll. 4–5. German learners of English tend to overuse this expression. You are encouraged to enlarge your vocabulary of text analysis beyond this phrase!

Practice 2

Find the corresponding phrases in the box below and fill the gaps.

borders on   can be put down to   comes across as

I come to the conclusion that   is indicative of   suggests

it is no coincidence that   there is some evidence to suggest that

it is true that … but   my explanation is that   to put it bluntly

this is due to the fact that   this clearly reveals that

it is hardly surprising, therefore, that   it is safe to say that

Unlike Elizabeth, Doreen **(„kommt rüber als")** ______________________________ ______________ somebody who complains about her looks and her clothes.

(Dies spiegelt deutlich, dass) ______________________________ she is very unhappy with her personal situation.

The way her father treats his daughter **(grenzt an)** ______________________________ ______________________________ neglect.

The fact that he "gives all our money away" (l. 23) **(deutet hin auf)** ______________ ______________________________ his out-of-touch attitude.

(Um es drastisch zu sagen) ______________________________, he seems to be a deluded ideologist.

(Es ist daher kaum überraschend) ______________________________ ______________________________ Doreen feels left alone.

(Meine Erklärung dafür ist, dass) ______________________________ ______________________________ Doreen's father has never been young.

(Es gibt einige Belege dafür, dass) ______________________________ ______________________________ Doreen is not an insensible girl.

The fact that she plans to talk to Elizabeth the following day **(legt nahe, dass)** ______________________________ she has "guts".

(Es scheint gesichert, dass) ______________________________

______________________________ Doreen will come to grips with her life.

(Es ist kein Zufall, dass) ______________________________

______________________________ Doreen admires E. M.

(Zwar) ______________________________ she is full of self-pity

(aber) ______________________________ she will grow up one day.

Her present unhappiness (lässt sich zurückführen auf) ______________

______________________________ false ideals within our society.

(Ich komme zu dem Schluss, dass) ______________________________

______________________________ Doreen is very unhappy.

(Dies kommt daher, dass) ______________________________

______________________________ she does not feel understood at all.

1.1.3 Assignments

A) Comprehension

1

Why does 16-year-old Doreen so desperately want to be friends with Elizabeth Montebello?

2

How does Doreen – in her own eyes – compare with "E. M."?

3

What is it that, finally, gives Doreen an "opening" to approach the object of her worship?

B) Analysis/Comment

1
Study the style in which the story is told. Why could the narrator's thoughts and feelings be diary entries?

2
Growing up in a baffling teenage world: How much do "cool clothes", does a "cool outfit" matter?

3
"Maybe I'll try and talk to her tomorrow" (l. 39). Write a diary entry of how Doreen has summoned all her courage and approached "E. M.". It might be a good idea to imagine how she rehearses *(proben)* for her approach.

C) Translation

Translate the following passage into German.

Why Beauty Spas Thank Heaven for Little Girls

Mothers taking daughters as young as five for facials and manicures have created a booming new market

Laura Lilly's favourite thing in the world is climbing trees. The seven-year-old is proud of her skills: she can climb higher up the apple tree in her back garden than any of her friends.

But she won't be climbing trees in the next few days – on Friday her mother took her to her local spa and treated her to a manicure and pedicure. "After I have had spa treatments, I like to behave like a grown-up and be careful of myself," she said. "My mother says I come out like a little lady, so that is how I like to behave."

Small girls have always been drawn by the lure of the make-up bag, but are scaling up their ambitions. More mothers who want the best for little Chloë or Gemma are seeking out spa treatments and their daughters have begun to demand salon care for beauty problems they might once have never even noticed.

Sensing a valuable new market whose business, once captured, can be relied upon for decades, pre-teen spas have begun springing up across Britain, with even the most traditional centres introducing treatment lines for children as young as five.

Experts worry that the trend will exacerbate the increasingly troubled relationship between women and their self-image: a survey by the Social Issues Research Centre at Oxford found female dissatisfaction with their appearance begins at a very early age. “Human infants begin to recognize themselves in mirrors at about two years old and female humans begin to dislike what they see only a few years later,” the report said.

A survey of more than 2,000 teenage girls by “Bliss” magazine found 92 per cent were unhappy with their bodies and one in four had had an eating disorder.

(310 words)

1.1.4 Keep Your Language Errors in Check – Verb Watch

Verb forms are a major problem in your “Kursarbeiten”.

Practice

The following short text calls your attention to some of the most common errors. The verb forms printed in colour are incorrect. Correct them in the right column.

Sixteen-year-old Doreen felt deeply misunderstood	
by her father. He **made her clear** that she could be	*made it clear to her*
anything she wanted to be. He **wanted that she**	______
wore recycled clothes and he still **trys** to teach her	______
what counts in life. “We **aren’t be allowed to** waste	______
our natural resources,” he **sayed**. Doreen did not	______
know what that **was meaning**. She **had heared**	______
about environmentalists but she did not share	______
her father’s alternative views. She **didn’t be afraid**	______
of the future. She **thought to be** her mother’s	______
daughter.	

Like her mother, Doreen has different ideals.
Her attention **is catched** by the pretty Elizabeth Montebello. She **didn't have seen** a girl like her before. Elizabeth Montebello is the girl to make her fellow students **feeling** envious. Elizabeth **can not** imagine how shy she makes girls like Doreen when they are face to face.
Doreen **is send** to summer school where she meets Elizabeth again. Elizabeth compliments Doreen on her Hello Kitty bag. That is the moment Doreen **has been waited** for. Will this be the beginning of a wonderful friendship?
In this story, the author **has showed** us how important "cool" looks and smart clothes are for young girls. This text **can be understand** as a warning against the hype that is presently made about people's outward appearance.

____

____

____

____

____

____

____

____

1.1.5 Writing Skills – How to Organize Your Thoughts

Practice

Read this model essay. Then read it again to study how introduction, main body and conclusion are handled here. Find out how the main body is built: listing, antithetical, or climactic?

Growing Up in a Baffling Teenage World: How Much Should "Cool Clothes", Should a "Cool Outfit" Matter?

There is no question that the clothes young people choose to wear must be regarded as an important means of self-expression. However, is the hype that is presently being made about what to wear a good thing?

← *introduction*

← *discourse markers: controversial topic*

To begin with, in an age which values "cool" looks, personal attractiveness and, consequently, expensive clothing styles, the worries about "how do I look" do not come as a surprise, especially among the young – and among those who do not want to grow old. The role models are everywhere: In films, on TV, in the glossy magazines that spill out of the racks. But do I really express myself when I copy or even ape *(nachäffen)* the style dictated by trendsetters and showbiz celebrities? I am not convinced.

What is more, there is nothing to be said against "communicating through the clothes I wear" and what statement I want to make about myself.

Equally, "feel good" clothes certainly help to boost one's well-being and, therefore, one's self-esteem.

Yet can we *really* agree to the idea that a

dressingstyle "makes" the person? Must we not insist that it matters where a person "stands", i.e. a person's mind, views and attitudes, and not how the person is "decorated"? What counts is substance – rather than styling.Last but not least, what do we think about incidents – as reported in the papers – in which the violation of a particular dress code accounts for "freezing out" the person that does not conform? To my mind, it is intolerable that a person is rejected solely for wearing the wrong piece of clothing, or for being unable to pay for the right brand. Here a point is reached where "expressing oneself" and "communicating through clothes" are overdone and where hype turns into harm.

No doubt, the issue of how to dress up for the occasion and of how "to fit in" matters. It often decides about being "in" or being "out". The point is, though, that the present trend clearly overrates the importance of clothes.

1.2 The Tyranny of Slenderness

"Sometimes I think it's called 'The Club' because they hit me over the head with body guilt."

What we need to ask is *why* our culture is so obsessed with keeping our bodies slim, tight, and young that when 500 people were asked what they feared most in the world, 190 replied, "Getting fat".

Needless to say, the vast majority of those 190 were … women. In the 1950s, by contrast, with middle-class women once again out of the factories and safely tucked up in the home[1], the dominant ideal of female beauty was exemplified by Marilyn Monroe – hardly your athletic, adolescent body type. At the peak of her popularity, Monroe was often described as "femaleness embodied"[2]; last term, a student of mine described her as a cow[3]. So, too, we need to explore the fact that it is women who are most oppressed by what is sometimes called "the tyranny of slenderness".

Most strikingly, body-builders put the same emphasis on *control:* on feeling their life to be fundamentally out of control, and on the feeling of accomplishment[4] derived from[5] total mastery of the body. That sense of mastery, like the anorectic's, appears to derive from two sources.

First, there is the view that one can overcome all physical obstacles, push oneself to any extremes in pursuit of one's goals[6] (which is a characteristic motivation of compulsive runners, as well).

Second, and most dramatic (it is spoken of time and again by female body-builders), is the thrill of being in total control of the shape of one's body. "Create a masterpiece," says "Fit" magazine. "Sculpt your body into a work of art." As for the anorectic – who literally cannot *see* her body as other than what her inner reality dictates and who is driven by an ideal image of extreme slenderness – so for the body-builder a purely mental conception comes to have dominance over her life: "You visualize what you want to look like … and then create the form." "What a fantasy, for your body to be changing! … As I work out I keep a picture in my mind of what I want to look like and what's happened to me already." Dictation to nature of one's own chosen design for the body is the central motive for the body-builder, as it is for the anorectic.

The sense of security derived from the attainment of this goal[7] appears, first of all, as the pleasure of control and independence. "Nowadays," says Michael Sacks, associate professor of psychiatry at Cornell Medical College, "people no longer feel they can control events outside themselves – how well they do in their jobs or in their personal relationships, for example – but they can control the food they eat and how far they can run."

(from: Susan Bordo, Unbearable Weight. 450 words)

1 i.e. after the war, they could concentrate on being housewives who cared for their husbands and raised the children – **2** *Verkörperung des Weiblichen* – **3** negative term implying that a woman is unattractive and stupid – **4** *Leistung, Vollkommenheit* – **5** *zurückführen auf, herleiten von* – **6** *in Verfolgung seiner Ziele* – **7** *Erreichen dieses Ziels*

1.2.1 Keep Your Language Errors in Check – Spelling

The pre-writing practice will remind you of some of the most common spelling errors made by German students and present two more text skills to prepare you for the essay questions.

Practice 1

Examine the verbs and spot the spelling mistakes.

1. When asked what they feared most, many people answerd, "Getting fat".
2. Susan Bordo speakes of "the tyranny of slenderness."
3. She talkes of anorectic people and bodybuilders in the same context.
4. 14-year-old Betty carefully watchs her weight.
5. Bordo discribes both anorectics and bodybuilders as control freaks.
6. I can not but agree with her.
7. I havn't made up my mind whether to agree or not.
8. On the matter of starving oneself to perfection opinions were devided.
9. "Bodytalk" is a website that reachs millions of people all over the world.
10. Have you heared about "Bodytalk"?

Practice 2
Remember Doreen Kleinzahler from text 1.1? Examine the sentences and spot the spelling mistakes.

1. She realy wanted to be like Elizabeth Montebello. ________________
2. She thought her clothes were awfull. ________________
3. And she allways tried to watch her weight. ________________
4. Her father refused to fullfill her most urgent wishes. ________________
5. Doreen thought he was a naïve charakter. ________________
6. Her parents had decided to seperate. ________________
7. In reality, Doreen was a nice girl. She looked better ________________
   then she thought. ________________
8. She did not belive that Elizabeth would talk to her. ________________
9. In summer school Doreen had to change her ________________
   oppinion. ________________
10. They exchanged knowing glances about there ________________
    summer school teacher. ________________

1.2.2 How to Express the Author's Intention

You will be required not only to understand the text itself but also to grasp the author's intention. You may want to enlarge your vocabulary in this field.

Practice 1
Translate into English by making use of the appropriate verbs in the box.

assert that	assume that	be convinced that
conclude that	disapprove of the fact that	maintain that
point out that	underscore that	warn of

1. Viele Autoren **warnen vor** einer Entwicklung, die gefährlich werden kann.
2. Brad Adams, ein New Yorker Fotograf, **behauptet**, dass 100 % aller Modefotos retuschiert sind *(to be retouched)*.
3. Er **versichert**, dass gewöhnlich die Augen und Zähne weißer gemacht, Make-up und Hautprobleme korrigiert und die Haare glänzend gemacht werden.
4. Er **missbilligt** die Tatsache, dass man Models, die schon dünn sind, noch dünner aussehen lässt.
5. Er ist **überzeugt von** der Idee, dass Models trotz Diät und der Hilfe persönlicher Trainer immer noch nicht gut genug für die Industrie aussehen.
6. Eine andere New Yorker Fotografin **nimmt an**, dass auch Filmstars eine „digitale Diät" erhalten.
7. Sie **unterstreicht** die Tatsache, dass sogar Schnappschüsse von Berühmtheiten, wie sie im Magazin „People" erscheinen, retuschiert werden.
8. Sie **legt dar**, dass „Photoshop", ein weit verbreitetes Software-Programm, Hüften digital schmaler erscheinen, den Busen größer machen und jede Veränderung realistisch aussehen lassen kann.
9. Sie **schlussfolgert** daraus, dass alles ein Schwindel ist *(a fake)*.

Practice 2

Do not translate from German word by word. Check the wrong phrases printed in colour and supply a suitable English version.

Bordo's text **shall** *(soll)* give the reader a clear idea of why some people go to great lengths to be slim.
→ *Bordo's text is meant to give the reader ...*

1. She **wants that** *(will, dass)* her readers understand the reasons for our obsession with thinness.

   ____

2. She **argumentates** *(argumentiert)* that it is all about controlling one's own body.

   ____

3. Bordo **brings a good argument** *(bringt ein gutes Argument)* when she says that people wish to "design their own bodies".

   ____

4. Especially young girls **are desperated** *(sind verzweifelt)* when their bodies become heavier.

___

5. **It gives no chance** *(es gibt keine Möglichkeit)* to talk them out of their negative body image.

___

6. The website "Bodytalk" **brings facts** *(bringt Fakten)* concerning that issue.

___

7. Another website **describes detailed** *(beschreibt detailliert)* how extreme diets and compulsive workouts can lead to health problems.

___

8. Bordo **takes this problem very serious** *(nimmt ... ernst).*

___

9. Referring to a survey and to a statement by a student of hers, she **becomes very concrete** *(wird konkret).*

___

10. When she discusses the problem, she **remains rather abstract** *(bleibt abstrakt).*

___

1.2.3 How to Express Meaning

Study

Take another look at the diagramme in chapter 1.1.2. Let us do some more work on this: Good essay writing makes sure that the three levels, i.e. (1) **text reference,** (2) your **own thoughts** and **conclusions**, and (3) **connecting verbs** and **discourse markers** are well balanced.

Practice 1

Consider the following example and underline which of the three levels the parts of the sentence printed in colour belong to.

And, **characteristically**, it is a fashion item that arouses the other girl's interest: Doreen's "Hello Kitty" book bag, the "nicest thing" (l. 36) she possesses.	*text reference?* *reader's conclusion?* *discourse marker?*
And, characteristically, it is a **fashion item that arouses the other girl's interest**: Doreen's "Hello Kitty" book bag, the "nicest thing" (l. 36) she possesses.	*text reference?* *reader's conclusion?* *discourse marker?*
And, characteristically, it is a fashion item that arouses the other girl's interest: Doreen's **"Hello Kitty" book bag, the "nicest thing" (l. 36) she possesses.**	*text reference?* *reader's conclusion?* *discourse marker?*

Practice 2

This is about Doreen Kleinzahler again. Take three different colour text markers and highlight (1) quotes and text references, (2) the reader's thoughts and conclusions, and (3) discourse markers and connecting verbs.

There is no denying that Doreen herself compares unfavourably with "E. M.". She feels she is at a disadvantage because, for one, she has a father who is at odds with her own outlook on life and who, evidently, does not recognize her wishes and needs: he appears to favour an alternative lifestyle and "gives all our money away" (l. 23). Unlike the famed Elizabeth, Doreen, for another, feels ugly, she describes herself as fat, though not obese (ll. 14–15) and worries about her facial skin problems (l. 16). The fact that she cannot afford to buy the clothes she craves makes her feel that she "do[es]n't know how to dress at all" (ll. 16–17). And she apparently does not "sail through" school since she has to make up for a failed PE course in summer school. So, it can be said that Doreen seems to miss precisely what she finds in her admired peer.

Practice 3

Insert the missing connecting verbs as you think fit.

be equated	contains	fine-tunes the issue
is called	is concerned with	points out that
proceeds to discuss	understands	which indicates that

The opening sentence of Bordo's text _contains_ the word *why* (in italics), ______________________ the author ______________________ ______________________ finding the reason(s) for the interviewees' preoccupation with "getting fat" (l. 7). In the second paragraph, Bordo ______________________ she is going to tackle ("So, too, we need to explore that fact that", l. 17). By "exploring" she ______________________ finding the causes for the effect that "it is women who are most oppressed by what sometimes ______________________ the "tyranny of slenderness" (l. 18). In the following, she ______________________ the wish to gain control over one's body "derives from two sources", l. 22). The word "source" can ______________________ with causes. Having established her pattern of thought, Bordo ______________________ the two sources in detail.

1.2.4 Assignments

A) Comprehension

1
Which facts does the author Susan Bordo propose to explore?

2
Which reasons are given to help explain the present "tyranny of slenderness"?

3
Study the pattern of thought that Bordo uses in her text. Show how she arranges her ideas in a cause-and-effect order.

B) Analysis/Comment

1
Do you personally subscribe to the explanation Bordo gives in her text, or do you think her answer is a little far-fetched?

2
You have logged on to a chatroom where visitors are discussing the topic of slimming. You read this statement: "In the transition to high school I kind of got lost. I wanted to be a part of things, and I felt like everybody around me was thin, so I thought if I got thin like they were, everything would be perfect. I linked having the perfect body to being liked by other people." – Charlie's Angel

Write a spontaneous message under the pen name of "Charlie's Angel 2".

3
Is the preoccupation with slimness and fitness a healthy sign or a symptom of a society that has become "sick"? Give a personal comment.

C) Translation

Translate the following passage into German.

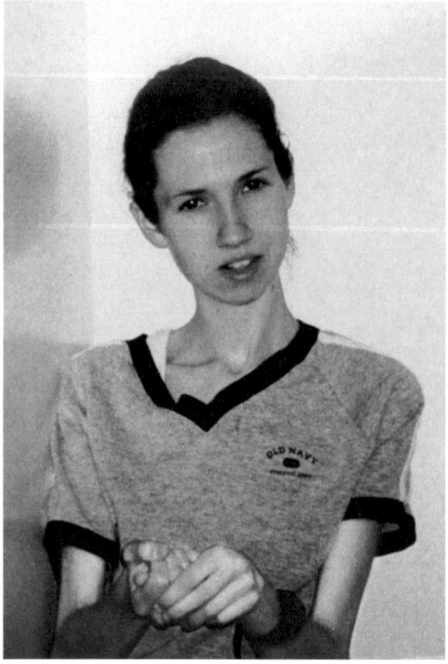

Mass Media and the Female Body

Adolescent girls are experiencing more changes today than 15 years ago. There are more opportunities for deviant behavior, which is also more dangerous than ever before. Dr Pipher explains that young girls are hampered by their desire to fit into society, which often conflicts with their desire to be themselves. When girls hit puberty, they begin to distance themselves from a body they feel is betraying them; growing hips and gaining weight without permission. This is contradictory to the images given them in the media: an almost pre-pubescent figure with no hips or extra weight at all. Pipher also believes that girls are required to be feminine by the society they long to be a part of, often at the cost of their humanity. In a personal interview, Jeff Morrison said that he believes adolescent girls attempt to fit into society by rejecting their most visible authorities (parents and teachers) and modeling themselves after media figures who also rejected authority, such as Madonna.

Current beauty standards are very tough to live up to: the "number one wish" for girls ages 11–17 is "to be thinner," and a young woman between 18 and 34 has a whopping 1 % chance of being as slim as a supermodel. As stated by Karen

Schneider of "People" magazine, current standards of beauty are just short of starvation for most women. So who is to blame for creating such standards of "beauty"?

When asked to watch television with an eye toward how women are portrayed, Dr. Pipher's client, 15-year-old Cayenne, found that TV rarely features women who are elderly, heavy, or plain. Women who are doctors could also grace the pages of Playboy, and female characters are more likely to be victims of violence than men. According to a research study by Mediascope, the average woman has seen over 250,000 commercial messages over the media by the time she is 17. In a study of Saturday morning cartoons, researchers found that 50 % of the commercials targeted towards young girls spoke about being attractive; other studies have found that 50 % of advertisements in teen magazines use beauty as an appeal to buy the product. Mediascope also found that advertisers deliberately market impractical ideals because it drives up profits. The diet industry is currently generating $ 33 billion per year in revenue, which attests to the success of such a campaign.

(400 words)

2 Two Glimpses of the American Dream

2.1 Arriving at the Monopark 5000 Hotel

When he reached Atlanta he had some problems locating the hotel in the city's daunting[1] system of one-way streets. He could see it, three or four blocks away, an impressive slab[2] of steel and reflecting glass, but he seemed able only to circle it: no street led directly there – it hovered out of reach, a massive illusion. Eventually he parked the pickup and attempted to make his way there on foot. He saw signs for the "Monopark Complex", then "Monopark 5000 Hotel". He went through an arch beneath a shopping mall, up a dark ramp of a corridor and pushed through swing doors at the far end.

He found himself in a tall brilliant lobby. Thick wands[3] of sunlight shone through vast overhead windows onto a marble floor. There appeared to be numerous entrances. The one through which he had emerged was clearly not the most significant. Various doormen and bellboys stood around in stylised cavalry uniforms: boots, hats, gold epaulettes[4], even dinky[5] sabres at their belts. At the rear of the lobby was what appeared to be a dense wood of twenty-foot high trees. In front of this forest was a long reception desk. This Henderson approached with due reverence and awe. The experience was, he thought, akin to appearing at Heaven's gate with the sin-virtue equation[6] still in balance.

"Dores," he said to the tanned cavalryman. "D, O, R, E, S. I have a reservation."

"Good afternoon, sir," he said. "Welcome to Monopark 5000." He tapped out the name on a computer keyboard. There was a whirring and clicking and the machine fed out a piece of plastic with holes punched in it.

"What's this?" Henderson asked. "A credit card?"

"Your key, sir. Need some help with your case?" The smile never budged.

"No thanks. I can manage."

"You are in suite 35 J. Follow this path," he gestured at an opening in the forest wall, "go through the atrium and take the scenic elevator to the thirty-fifth floor. Enjoy your stay at Monopark 5000."

"Right." Henderson picked up his bag and looked dubiously at the path which was signposted "To the atrium". He felt like an explorer leaving base camp. "Goodbye," he said to the man and set off.

He had imagined that the trees were merely a decorative screen but he was wrong. He found himself in a copse[7], a grove[8], a veritable spinney[9] of weeping figs[10], silver birches, and stands of bamboo. A soft greenish light filtered down from above, xylophonic music burbled from hidden speakers. Other paths bifurcated from his. "Convention Reservation", he saw, "To the Indian village" and "Swimming Creek". These signs were deliberately "olde West": chunks of varnished[11] wood with the message burnt on with a branding iron. The frontier theme was enhanced by the sudden appearance from behind a tree of a waitress in fringed buckskin[12] waistcoat and miniskirt. Henderson gave a shrug of alarm. There were stripes of warpaint on her cheeks and forehead.

"Cocktails, sir?" she asked. "At the Indian village."

"What? Oh, no. I'm looking for the atrium."

"Keep right on to the end of this path." She slipped away into the trees.

He followed her instructions and broke into a towering atrium some twelve or fourteen stories high. Before him stretched a lake, blocking his way, some thirty yards across, dotted with islands furnished with seats and sprouting plants. Over on the left of the far bank was a cluster of wigwams which on closer inspection turned out to be a large restaurant and bar area. On the balconied far wall, a dozen scenic elevators rose up and down, some of them disappearing into holes in the roof like silent glass scarabs[13].

Henderson let out a spontaneous gasp of surprise. He had heard of this new breed of American hotel: the hotel as wonderland, as secular cathedral, as theme park – but his imagination had been deficient. Plants grew everywhere, fountains splashed, the light was pale, neutral and shadow-free.

A cowboy wandered over and handed him a wooden paddle.

"Good God, what's this for?"

"For the canoe, sir."

Henderson looked to his right. Sure enough, a dozen canoes were tethered to[14] the concrete bank.

"Do you mean I've got to paddle myself across to the elevators?"

"I can do it for you, sir, but a lot of our guests like to make their own way."

He saw an intrepid[15] couple set off, little shrieks of delight coming from the wife.

"Oh. Right."

The cowboy let him down to a canoe, deposited his bag in the bow and helped him in. Henderson settled down.

"Listen, are you sure these things are stable? Perhaps you'd better – "

The cowboy pushed him off. "Enjoy your stay at Monopark 5000, sir."

Henderson found himself drifting into the middle of the lake. He looked about him. The various islands were linked to the far bank by large round stepping stones. Indian maidens tripped across these carrying drinks from the huge gloomy bar area. Hesitantly, Henderson dipped his paddle in the water and performed a couple of gentle strokes.

(from: William Boyd, Stars and Bars. 850 words)

1 frightening in a way that makes you feel less confident – **2** a thick flat piece of a hard material such as stone – **3** a thin stick you hold in your hand to do magic tricks; a tool that looks like a thin stick – **4** small pieces of cloth attached to the shoulder of a coat or shirt, especially on a military uniform – **5** (AE) too small and often not very nice – **6** *Sündenregister* – **7** a group of trees or bushes growing close together – **8** *Hain* – **9** a small area of trees and bushes – **10** *eine Feigenart* – **11** *lackiert* – **12** *Hirsch- oder Ziegenleder* – **13** *eine Käferart* – **14** tied to a post – **15** willing to do dangerous things or go to dangerous places

2.1.1 Keep Your Language Errors in Check – Word Order

Study

The pre-writing practice this time reminds you of another difficulty faced by German students, i.e. word order. It also teaches you how to emphasize what you want to say.

When struggling with the text under discussion some students tend to translate straight from the German language into English. This frequently leads to errors in **sentence building** since the **word order** in the English sentence is different.

0	**1**	2	**3**	**4**	5
adverb(ial)	**subject**	adverb	**verb (V)**	**object (O)**	adverb(ial)/ other parts

A special reminder:

- **The "V-O-block": No adverb or any other part of the sentence "goes" between the verb and the object.**
- **When using adverb(ial)s you have three options: front-position (0), mid-position (2), or end-position (5).**

Practice

Translate into English.

1. Im Text wird gesagt, dass das Hotel wie ein *theme park* aussieht.

   ~~(In the text is said)~~ ______________________________

   ____

2. Jeder assoziiert mit Las Vegas Spielcasinos.

   ~~(Everybody associates with Las Vegas)~~ ______________________________

   ____

3. Diese Welt kann man eine große Illusion nennen.

   ~~(This world can you call)~~ ______________________________

   ____

4. Das Problem lösen sie, indem sie einen Cowboy zur Hilfe für die Gäste an den See stellen.

   ~~(That problem solve they)~~ ______________________________

   ____

5. Diese Aussage kann man in Zeile 45 finden.

   ~~(That statement can you in line 45 find.)~~ ______________________________

   ____

6. Zum Beispiel schreibt der Autor, dass die Türsteher als U.S. cavalrymen verkleidet sind.

   ~~(For example writes the author that)~~ ______________________________

   ____

7. Im zweiten Teil ist Hendersons Suche nach seinem Hotelzimmer beschrieben.

   ~~(In the second part is Henderson's search for his hotel room described.)~~

   ____

8. Er steigt am Ende in das Kanu.

   ~~(He climbs in the end)~~ ______________________________

   ____

9. Er würde alles versuchen, um nicht in dem Hotel übernachten zu müssen.

   ~~(He would everything try not to)~~ ______________________________

   ____

10. Diesen Text schrieb der Autor William Boyd im Jahre 1984.

    ~~(That text wrote the author)~~ ______________________________

    ____

11. In dem Text werden die guten und schlechten Seiten amerikanischer Hotels präsentiert.

    ~~(In that text are presented)~~ ______________________________

    ____

12. Im ganzen Text werden nur Fakten gegeben.

    ~~(In the whole text are only facts given.)~~ ______________________________

    ____

2.1.2 How to Emphasize What You Want to Say

Study

Four examples

(1) The hotel episode, **therefore**, carries what I would call a satirical undertone.	deshalb, daher ← *emphasizes what you* ***conclude***
(2) **Besides**, "firewater" has not gone down too well with Indians in their native villages, or has it?	außerdem ← *emphasizes the* ***next point*** *in your argument*
(3) **Unfortunately**, this is standard with international hotel chains.	leider ← *emphasizes that you have* ***objections***
(4) **Curiously/paradoxically**, the historical frontier was not noted for its easy-going, risk-free life.	seltsamerweise ← *emphasizes that you call an* ***argument*** *into question*

Practice

Check the following list of sentence adverbs and choose from them as you translate the sentences below into English.

admittedly	zugegeben, zwar
amazingly	erstaunlicherweise
finally	schließlich
generally (speaking)	allgemein gesagt
however	hingegen, jedoch
interestingly	merkwürdigerweise
ironically	ironischerweise
presumably	vermutlich
sadly	bedauerlicherweise
strangely enough	seltsamerweise
strikingly	erstaunlicherweise
undeniably	unbestreitbar
undoubtedly	zweifellos
yet	hingegen, jedoch
though	allerdings

1. Er entscheidet sich **schließlich**, seinen Wagen zu parken und zu Fuß zum Hotel zu gehen.
2. Was Henderson **allerdings** beunruhigt, ist etwas anderes.
3. **Ironischerweise** kann der Hotelgast den „alten amerikanischen Westen" noch einmal erleben *(relive)*.
4. **Erstaunlicherweise** laufen auch einige indianische Mädchen in Miniröcken herum und servieren Drinks.
5. **Merkwürdigerweise** gibt es Räume, die „Convention Reservation" oder „Swimming Creek" heißen.
6. Das Ganze *(the whole arrangement)* ist **zweifellos** eine große Illusion.
7. **Allgemein gesagt** sieht das Monopark 5000 aus wie ein Las-Vegas-Spielcasino.
8. Die Hotelgäste müssen etwas wagen, **jedoch** stellt eine Schar *(host)* von Angestellten sicher, dass die untrainierten Gäste nicht zu Schaden kommen *(come to harm)*.

TIP Add these sentence adverbs to your active vocabulary!

2.1.3 Assignments

A) Comprehension

1

What problems does the narrator have to face when he tries to locate his hotel in Atlanta (first paragraph)?

2

Once inside the hotel, Henderson feels caught up in a paradox (a situation that seems strange because it involves two ideas or qualities that are very different). Explain.

3

How does the narrator himself react to that unexpected environment? Select two examples from the text to support your view.

B) Analysis/Comment

1

If not in Atlanta, where in the U.S. would you rather expect and indeed find such hotels? Give reasons.

2

America and its future-minded optimism ("The best is still ahead of us"): Explain and comment on the clashing *(widersprüchlich)* attitudes that characterize the American "lifestyle" as illustrated in Boyd's text. For further evidence you may draw on your knowledge of the country and its people.

3

The satire has been defined as a literary manner which points up the fundamental incongruity *(Unvereinbarkeit)* of an action or situation and makes it appear laughable and ridiculous: Does "Arriving At The Monopark 5000 Hotel" - according to you - contain clues that the narrator's adventure has a satirical undertone? Discuss.

C) Translation

Translate the following passage into German.

The Four Most Successful Boom Regions

The four most successful boom regions according to a survey conducted by "Inc. Magazine" – Atlanta, Georgia; Riverside, California; Las Vegas, Nevada; San Antonio, Texas – are Republican territory, all of them. And of the 100 communities in America, which have the fastest growth, Bush has won no less than 97. Five years ago many of these settlements haven't even been there. They are instant-communities, urban ready-mades. In his new book "On Paradise Drive", David Brooks, the New York Times columnist and "favoured conservative of the liberals", has dubbed them "Exurbia".
Without even mentioning Bush or Iraq, Brooks portrays Exurbia's residents, the growing reservoir of voters. These people perpetually live "in the future" as the catchy subtitle of Brook's book suggests. Their gaze is firmly focussed on the future, on the trail ahead: Hovering "over-mums", ambitious mothers, who already expose their unborn children to Mozart to make sure they will be ahead in music school; college students, who, because of their involvement with learning programmes and extracurricular activities, find no time anymore to fall in love; people in middle management, who collect bonus miles like mad and who are prepared to dedicate their lives to perfectioning a single tiny, profitable innovation.

(200 words)

2.2 George W. Bush: the Second Inaugural Address, Jan. 20, 2005

At this second gathering, our duties are defined not by the words I use, but by the history we have seen together. For a half century, America defended our own freedom by standing watch on distant borders. After the shipwreck of communism came years of relative quiet, years of repose, years of sabbatical – and then there came a day of fire.

We have seen our vulnerability – and we have seen its deepest source. For as long as whole regions of the world simmer in resentment and tyranny – prone to ideologies that feed hatred and excuse murder – violence will gather, and multiply in destructive power, and cross the most defended borders, and raise a mortal threat. There is only one force of history that can break the reign of hatred and resentment, and expose the pretensions of tyrants, and reward the hopes of the decent and tolerant, and that is the force of human freedom.

We are led, by events and common sense, to one conclusion: the survival of liberty in our land increasingly depends on the success of liberty in other lands. The best hope for peace in our world is the expansion of freedom in all the world.

America's vital interests and our deepest beliefs are now one. From the day of our founding, we have proclaimed that every man and woman on this earth has rights, and dignity, and matchless value, because they bear the image of the maker of heaven and earth. Across the generations we have proclaimed the imperative of self-government, because no one is fit to be a master, and no one deserves to be a slave. Advancing these ideals is the mission that created our nation. It is the honorable achievement of our fathers. Now it is the urgent requirement of our nation's security, and the calling of our time.

So it is the policy of the United States to seek and support the growth of democratic movements and institutions in every nation and culture, with the ultimate goal of ending tyranny in our world.

This is not primarily the task of arms, though we will defend ourselves and our friends by force of arms when necessary. Freedom, by its nature, must be chosen, and defended by citizens, and sustained by the rule of law and the protection of minorities. And when the soul of a nation finally speaks, the institutions that arise may reflect customs and traditions very different from our own. America will not impose our own style of government on the unwilling. Our goal instead is to help others find their own voice, attain their own freedom, and make their own way.

The great objective of ending tyranny is the concentrated work of generations. The difficulty of the task is no excuse for avoiding it. America's influence is not unlimited, but fortunately for the oppressed, America's influence is considerable, and we will use it confidently in freedom's cause.

My most solemn duty is to protect this nation and its people against further attacks and emerging threats. Some have unwisely chosen to test America's resolve, and have found it firm.

We will persistently clarify the choice before every ruler and every nation: the moral choice between oppression, which is always wrong, and freedom, which is eternally right. America will not pretend that jailed dissidents prefer their chains, or that women welcome humiliation and servitude, or that any human being aspires to live at the mercy of bullies.

We will encourage reform in other governments by making clear that success in our relations will require the decent treatment of their own people. America's belief in human dignity will guide our policies, yet rights must be more than the grudging concessions of dictators; they are secured by free dissent and the participation of the governed. In the long run, there is no justice without freedom, and there can be no human rights without human liberty.

(650 words)

2.2.1 Rhetorical Devices

Study

Public addresses by American presidents are rhetorically well crafted. An inaugural address is written to be heard, not read. This means that easy intelligibility is a major concern so that the listening span is not strained. A sentence written to be heard should be simple, direct, and short. The speechwriter thus faces the challenge of finding words that convey the speaker's meaning clearly, but that also draw on spoken English. Complex sentences can be clarified by repeating key words and using simple connections. By numerous rhetorical techniques, the speaker states, restates, and states again in different ways, the central themes of the speech. The given extract from Bush's Second Inaugural Address is no exception to the rule.

Major rhetorical devices used by speech writers are:

- **parallelism:** The linkage of similar words or ideas in a balanced construction that repeatedly uses the same grammatical form to convey parallel or coordinated ideas: "Bigotry has no head and cannot think; no heart and cannot feel".
- **antithesis:** A common form of parallel structure comparing and contrasting dissimilar elements. For instance, "Give me liberty, or give me death", "Ask not what your country can do for you, ask what you can do for your country".
- **rhythmic triads:** The grouping of words into patterns of three can lead to a memorable effect, provided the device is not overused. Some notable examples from classic oratory include: "Veni, vidi, vici", "Never … was so much owed by so many to so few".
- **alliteration:** The repetition of initial sounds in a series of words to give emphasis. For instance, "the nattering nabobs of negativism …".
- **anaphora:** This is the repetition of the same word or words at the beginning of successive clauses or sentences, for example, "We shall fight on the beaches, we shall fight on the landing grounds …".
- **rhetorical questions:** The speaker leads the audience to the conclusion he hopes they will draw by asking a question that makes his point: "Is peace a rash system?", "Is life so dear or peace so sweet as to be purchased at the price of chains and slavery?"
- **imagery:** No speech will sound fresh and vivid if it is not animated by imaginative imagery, by metaphor in its many forms: "the hatred of entrenched greed", "Democracy is the healthy lifeblood which circulates through the veins and arteries of society …"

2.2.2 Assignments

A) Comprehension

1

"…and then there came a day of fire": Which event in recent American history does the speaker refer to? Do a quick internet research and give a 60–80 word summary of that event.

2

Presidential speeches are said to mark America's place in time. Point out President George W. Bush's view of America laid out in this part of his speech.

3

The following are considered to be typical elements of speeches delivered by American presidents on occasions such as the Inauguration:

(1) identification of the speaker with his audience by alluding to experience shared by speaker and audience
(2) look back in history
(3) appeal to patriotism (emotion)
(4) reference to the Bible/to religion
(5) expression of the belief that America has a mission to fulfil
(6) expression of the will to make sacrifices
(7) emphasis on the triumph of democracy
(8) evaluation of the speaker's own position (devaluation of the opponent's position)

Trace four of these elements in the extract above. You may want to revise the exercise on how to refer to texts in chapter 1.1.1 before you set out to answer this and the following questions.

B) Analysis/Comment

1

Analyse how Bush tries to make this part of his speech effective. Pay particular attention to the use of rhetorical devices (see chapter 2.2.1).

2

Comment on the role George W. Bush claims for the United States. In doing so, you may draw on your knowledge of what is commonly called the American Dream.

3

Your school takes part in an exchange programme with an American high school. You are to prepare for a debate with American host students on America's role. Write an introductory statement from the point of view of a German participant.

C) Translation

Translate the following passage into German.

America's Democratic Deficit

Is the United States truly a democracy? The question may seem absurd, and almost impertinent for anyone on this side of the Atlantic to raise. The U.S. constitution begins with the words "We the People", locating power clearly as something that flows from the bottom up, not from the top down.
Yet half its own population has so little interest in its supposedly democratic system that it rarely bothers to vote.
Moreover, many millions of Americans are disenfranchised not only because they are now in prison at rates far above those in any western European country, but also because, in some states, a past conviction, even for a non-violent drugs offence, is enough to remove a person from the franchise for life. Such people, needless to say, are disproportionately poor and black.
In other respects, too, the U.S. is less democratic than it looks. If freedoms of press and information laws are stronger than in Europe, other freedoms, such as workers' rights to organize in unions, are weaker.
The gravest and most fundamental flaw in America's democracy is that its politicians and parties are, by all normal standards, corrupt. This truth is largely obscured by the openness of the system; there is no real secrecy about campaign donations or interest-group lobbying and, therefore, prosecutions are rare. But a politician is no less bought for being bought openly.
Jonathan Freedland, in his book "Bring Home the Revolution", enjoined the British to learn from America's attachment to liberty, law and elections. But lessons should travel the other way, too. In the U.S., constitutional issues are hardly ever discussed. The U.S. written constitution has remained virtually

unchanged since the 18th century. And its central inadequacy for the 21st century becomes increasingly apparent: that, despite their admirably advanced principles, the founding fathers, being affluent, slave-owning property owners, distrusted not just executive power but mass democracy itself.

(310 words)

2.2.3 Keep Your Language in Check

Verb Watch

Practice 1

Check the verbs, spot the mistakes and correct the sentences.

1. The speaker wants to make his listeners clear that America can not sit back and wait.
2. His mentioning Sept 11 made us leaving the grandstand *(Haupttribüne)*.
3. The speaker wants that his listeners approve of the role he outlines for America in the years to come.
4. At the end of his address he thought to have won his listeners over.
5. That was the moment the audience had been waited for. They gave him a standing ovation.
6. "One thing," a listener said, "I don't agree to: that the government trys to develop new guidelines on gun control because of homeland security."
7. Homeland Security's plan is that citizens without a serious reason aren't be allowed to carry a gun.
8. "I am used to carry a gun when I feel like it," said another.
9. His neighbour from the West Coast said him to keep quiet.

Adjective or Adverb?

Study

The tricky thing is that, in German, we do *not* formally make a distinction between adjectives and adverbs whereas the English do (→ "-ly"-rule!). Before you carry on, you may want to turn to your grammar book to check on the most important facts concerning

- the comparison of adjectives/adverbs,
- the main word classes that are modified by adverbs,
- the verbs that take an adjective, not an adverb or both ("he looked suspiciously at his opponent" vs. "he looked pale").

Practice 2

Can you comment on the obvious errors in the following sentences? Correct them.

The hatred felt by Arab countries towards the Americans is **much more greater** than the U.S. would have expected.	______________________ ______________________
For the U.S. the region is **extreme difficult** to deal with.	______________________ ______________________
We should explore every option possible to resolve the Middle East crisis **peaceful**.	______________________ ______________________
The Bush Administration will have to send **much more troops** to pacify the region than are prepared to do.	______________________ ______________________

Practice 3

Translate into correct English. Pay special attention to the question of whether to put adjective or adverb.

1. Allgemein ist der Mensch ein geselliges Wesen.
2. Das ist allgemein zutreffend.
3. Allgemeine Wahlen finden bei uns alle vier Jahre statt.
4. Diese Tatsache ist allgemein akzeptiert.
5. Im Allgemeinen gehe ich zur Wahl.
6. Was du sagst, ist einfach falsch.
7. Sie schreibt in einem klaren und einfachen Stil.
8. Sag es so einfach, wie du kannst.
9. Zu der Bush-Rede gab es extrem unterschiedliche Reaktionen.
10. Es gibt extreme Unterschiede zwischen den Gegnern und den Befürwortern.
11. Bushs Hinweis auf die "expansion of freedom in all the world" ist nicht ironisch, sondern ernst gemeint.
12. Bush liegt hier klar falsch.
13. In seiner Antrittsrede wird er nicht sehr detailliert, was die politischen Maßnahmen seiner Administration betrifft.
14. Aus verständlichen Gründen bleibt er sehr allgemein.

2.2.4 Writing Skills – Expressing Degrees of Certainty or Doubt

Study

Read these examples and the following table.

It **is not** known, and **will probably never be** known, when George W. Bush decided to launch his political career.	→ *positive* → *very likely*
The reasons for it **can almost certainly be** found in the larger Bush family and, **perhaps**, in the fact that his wife Laura helped him get a grip on his life.	→ *strong* → *less strong*
It appears that the money he made in oil management in Texas gave him the financial basis for his plans.	→ *personal assumption (uncertain)*

Degrees of certainty/doubt

positive/assertive	**is (not)** **will (not)** **must (not)**	**certain(-ly)** **definite(-ly)** **clear(-ly)** **undoubtedly**
(very) likely	**can/cannot** **should (not)**	**probably (is)** **presumably**
partially likely	**could (not)**	**likely/unlikely**
less likely	**may (not)** **might (not)**	**possibly (not)** **perhaps (not)**
unlikely	**is (not)** **will (not)** **must (not)**	**certain(-ly)** **definite(-ly)** **clear(-ly)** **undoubtedly**
personal assumption (uncertain)	**It is said that …** **It appears that …** **There is evidence to suggest that …**	**apparent(-ly)** **evident(-ly)**

Practice 1

In the table below on the left, there are a number of assertive statements. Your task is to make them more tentative *(vorsichtiger)*.

There is no doubt that many German students need to improve their standard of English.	→ *less likely:* It may be the case that many German students need to improve their standard of English.
German students will not improve their language skills unless they work hard.	→ *unlikely:* ______
Students who work intelligently rather than hard will experience the most success.	→ *very likely:* ______
German students will not improve their language skills unless they work hard.	→ *personal assumption:* ______

Practice 2

Translate into correct English using suitable expressions from the table below.

IN CONGRESS.

The unanimous Declaration

I am in two minds about

doubtless (adverb!)

I can see the point, yet I wonder

I have gnawing/serious doubts

incredibly

I simply cannot believe that

it stands to reason that

it is more than doubtful that

there is no denying that

1. **Es lässt sich nicht leugnen, dass** Amerika behaupten kann, die älteste Demokratie auf der Welt zu sein.
2. **Zweifellos** haben die Amerikaner allen Grund, stolz auf ihre Unabhängigkeitserklärung und ihre Verfassung zu sein.
3. **Ich kann einfach nicht glauben, dass** die Hälfte seiner Bevölkerung so wenig Interesse an Washington hat, dass sie es nicht der Mühe für Wert hält, zur Wahl zu gehen.
4. Sicherlich ist Washington weit weg, sagen sie. **Ich kann das verstehen, aber ich frage mich,** ob jene Nichtwähler begreifen, was Demokratie ist.
5. **Ich habe ernste Zweifel,** wenn ich lese, dass Millionen Amerikaner nicht wählen dürfen, nicht weil sie im Gefängnis sitzen, sondern weil sie in der Vergangenheit für kleinere Vergehen verurteilt wurden.
6. **Meine Meinung ist gespalten zu** der Rolle, die Spenden und Geld bei den amerikanischen Wahlen spielen.
7. **Es ist unglaublich, dass** Politiker von Interessengruppen gekauft werden.
8. **Es ist mehr als zweifelhaft, dass** Kandidaten, die nicht durch die großen Industrien unterstützt werden, keine Chance im Rennen um die Präsidentschaft haben.
9. **Es leuchtet ein, dass** die Amerikaner gut beraten wären, ihr System, den Präsidenten zu wählen, zu ändern.

2.2.5 Writing Skills – Text Comprehension

Study

When asked to elicit and explain significant details from a text you have to study, you will need **connecting verbs** to express what a(n) author/speaker does. Go back to chapter 1.1.5 Writing Skills – How to Organize Your Thoughts. Revise what you have learned there.

Practice 1

Read the following sentences about the given passage from Bush's Inaugural Address and translate the expressions printed in colour into German.

From the very start, the speaker tries to evoke	______________________
common experiences shared by speaker and	
audience:	
He briefly recalls what (most of) his listeners	______________________
have witnessed during their lifetime.	
It is his reference to the terrorist attacks on	______________________
America (9/11) that serves to strengthen the	______________________
emotional bonds to his audience.	
This mission was proclaimed by other presidents	______________________
before him and reiterated by Bush.	______________________

Practice 2

Presidents' public addresses are rhetorically well crafted. Choose the appropriate connecting verbs from the box and fill in the gaps.

can be found in	to add emphasis to	a case in point
can be traced in	makes ample use of	states
a particularly effective stylistic means	occurs	
provides further examples of	abounds in examples of	
may be quoted here	underscores	

Two of the most effective devices used by Bush to add emphasis to his words are parallelism and antithesis. An example of syntactic parallelism __________ l. 6 ("We have seen our ... and we have seen its ..."). The speech transcript __________ semantic parallelism in ll. 25, 30, and 46. Equally, the speaker __________ antithesis: in ll. 1–2 he __________ that "our duties are not defined by the words I use, but by the history we have seen together". In ll. 33–35 Bush __________ the idea of American power and influence by antithesis. The most obvious example, however, __________ in ll. 44–45 when Bush elevates America's moral superiority and devaluates her enemies' moral stance ("eternally right vs. always wrong"). The speech extract also __________ __________ parallelism and antithesis combined. Ll. 13–14 are __________: "The survival of liberty in our land ... depends on the success of liberty (parallelism) in other lands" (antithesis). Further examples of parallelism + antithesis __________ ll. 18–19 and in ll. 21–22. Rhythmic triads are __________ to balance spoken sentences. The speaker repeatedly uses this device in the passage under review. His reference to "years of relative quiet, years of repose, years of sabbatical" __________ ll. 4–5. While this appears to be a rather simple triad, there are more complex triads to be found, too: "... violence will gather and multiply ... and cross ... and raise ..." (ll. 8–9) and "Freedom must be chosen ... and defended ... and sustained ..." (ll. 29–31).

2.2.6 Writing Skills – How to Emphasize What You Want to Say

In essay writing, sentences must be properly linked so your message comes across effectively. Besides, a text will go down well with the reader (and your English teacher!) if there is sufficient contrast and emphasis to guide him. This occurs when you respect some simple rules as to how to achieve **emphasis** and **contrast** in your sentences.

The Sweeping Sentence

Study

A sweeping or clincher sentence is a sentence that makes it clear that no objection is allowed. Read the following examples.

Baseball is competitive, it allows you to judge the performance of each player and, besides, its pros are highly paid. **Those are the three reasons why I like baseball.**	→ *a weak and unnecessary concluding sentence: you'd better drop it*
The disrespect for the views of others is all-pervasive. **Anything goes!** Change your body, tone up your breast muscles, have your butt tucked in. **You'll feel a lot better afterwards.**	→ *very effective: a sweeping sentence makes the point*

Practice 1

Add a sweeping sentence of yours to clinch the point.

1. George W. Bush's Second Inauguration ceremony was an early highlight of the year 2005. It provided a patriotic moment and everyone was in high spirits.

   ____

2. The terrorist attacks on New York and Washington D.C. on September 11, 2001, came as a shock.

   ____

3. Anorexia and bulimia are the twin sisters of a misguided body cult in our time. Girls and young women are made to believe that their careers are enhanced by chest and waist measurements and that they can cash in on their physical assets.

   ____

4. Men brutalize women, they take advantage of them in every conceivable way and they expect them to turn the other cheek.

   ____

5. However hard we try, our English teacher is never satisfied with what we achieve.

   ____

TIP While varying sentence length is certainly the "spice" of good writing, you should be warned against "overkill". **Basic rule:** Do not overuse the sweeping sentence according to the motto: complex sentence/sweeping sentence/complex sentence/ another sweeping sentence. You should not tack on a clincher artificially either and avoid weak sweeping sentences. Nevertheless such a "killer" sentence at the end of a paragraph now and then comes across nicely!

Parallelism and Contrast

Study

Read the following examples.

The author explains the present situation and **that he is convinced of** a hopeful outlook into the future. What he said and **the things he meant** were not the same.	→ *faulty: unlike grammatical forms are paired here!*
If, in the present climate of fear and mistrust, **the liberals have to rethink their policies, so do the conservatives.**	→ *balanced parallel structure emphasizes that both elements are equal in rank*
The young have been taught that they should **not** think of the views of others **as false, but only as different.**	→ *parallel structure emphasizes the contrast*

Practice 2

Try your hand at the game of parallelism and contrast by adding a suitable element to each of the following sentences.

1. Robotics may be a **new** technology but the ______________ rules still apply.
2. For many millions in the developing countries the outlook **will not be better,** for many it ______________________.
3. Girls are often discouraged from taking science and math – **not just by their teachers** but **by** ______________________ **as well.**
4. According to my teacher, my composition revealed **that I have exceptional creative ability but that** ______________________.
5. The new film was praised **more for its style than for its** ______________.

6. He recommended **both the food and the** ______________________
   in the small hotel.
7. The U.S. citizen is assumed to have **responsibilities as well as** ____________, **duties as well as** ____________.
8. Americans take great pride in their country. This must **be understood** when one **visits the U.S.** and it must ______________________ when one ______________________________________.
9. To the unthinking person war may be a **romantic** and ____________ adventure; to the wise person it may be a **foolish** and ____________ business.
10. The young have been taught that they should never think of the views of others **as false but only as** ________________; they have been taught that to suggest that someone who is wrong is **at best** rude and ________________ immoral.

TIP As with your preference for the sweeping sentence, don't overdo the "parallelism-stuff". **Basic Rule:** Look for coordinate ideas (and words!) that are equal in rank. It is a nice move to first negate an idea and confirm its opposite or vice versa.

The Rhythmic Triad

Study

Read the following examples.

All this is fine in a **democratic, ordered and stable country**. We look to the future **with fear, not with hope or with confidence**.	→ *careless: most relevant element first!* → *careless: relevant point comes unprepared!*
All this is fine in an **ordered** (1), **stable** (2) and **democratic** (3) country. When we look to the future, it is **not with hope** (1), **still less with confidence** (2), **but with fear** (3).	→ *balanced and emphatic: the three elements ("triad") are arranged so as to suggest a climactic order* → *the two negative elements prepare for and emphasize the third element of the triad*

Practice 3

The greatest challenge in this section! Expand the following (debatable) statements by supplying the missing element(s).

1. "... that they are endowed by their Creator with certain unalienable Rights, that among these are ____________, **liberty**, and ____________."
2. "America's promise is that **everyone belongs**," i.e. that whoever comes first ____________ an opportunity and needn't fear ____________.
3. For some people, hating is **easier**, ____________ and ____________ than loving.
4. If the family is breaking down, **it's men's fault**; if there is a traffic jam on the German Autobahn, ____________ and if the next Aldi store around the corner has run out of pizzas, ____________, too.

5. The young simply want to assert themselves and are prepared to oppose their elders; they are given to **lying**, to ________________ and to ____.

6. Considering the degree of involvement that some of our teachers normally display, we cannot overlook that **some take their jobs rather easy**; we cannot forget that ______________________________________ and, most of all, we do not want to accept that ________________________ ____.

TIP A final warning: Use your rhetorical means wisely and use them sparingly, i.e. when the right moment has come. It's quality, not quantity that counts!

3 Future Images of Man

3.1 The Coming Merging of Mind and Machine

***Note:** This text was written in the 1990s. The author Ray Kurzweil is CEO of Kurzweil Technologies, Inc. He led teams that built a pioneering print-to-speech reading machine, the first omni-font ("any" font) optical-character-recognition system, etc.*

Sometime early in the next century, the intelligence of machines will exceed that of humans. Within several decades, machines will exhibit[1] the full range of human intellect, emotions and skills, ranging from musical and other creative aptitudes[2] to physical movement. They will claim to have feelings and, unlike today's virtual personalities, will be very convincing when they tell us so.

By 2019 a $ 1,000 computer will at least match the processing power of the human brain. By 2029 the software for intelligence will have been largely mastered, and the average personal computer will be equivalent to 1,000 brains.

As this happens, there will no longer be a clear distinction between human and machine. We are already putting computers – neural[3] implants – directly into people's brains to counteract Parkinson's disease and tremors from multiple sclerosis. A retinal[4] implant is being developed in the U.S. that is intended to provide at least some visual perception for some blind individuals, basically by replacing certain visual-processing circuits[5] of the brain.

By 2030, instead of just phoning a friend, you will be able to meet in, say, a virtual Mozambican game preserve[6] that will seem compellingly real. You will be able to have any type of experience – business, social, sexual – with anyone, real or simulated, regardless of physical proximity.

By the third decade of the 21st century, we will be in a position to create complete, detailed maps of the computationally relevant features of the human brain and to re-create these designs in advanced neural computers. We will provide a variety of bodies for our machines, too, from virtual bodies in virtual reality to bodies comprising swarms of nanobots[7]. In fact, humanoid robots that ambulate and have lifelike facial expressions are already being developed at several laboratories in Tokyo.

Such possibilities prompt a host of intriguing issues and questions. Suppose we scan someone's brain and reinstate the resulting "mind file" into a suitable computing medium. Will the entity that emerges from such an operation be conscious? This being would appear to others to have very much the same personality, history and memory. For some, that is enough to define consciousness. For others, such as physicist and author James Trefil[8], no logical reconstruction can attain human consciousness, although Trefil concedes that computers may become conscious in some new way.

At what point do we consider an entity[9] to be conscious, to be self-aware, to have free will? How do we distinguish a process that is conscious from one that just acts as if it is conscious? If the entity is very convincing when it says, "I'm lonely, please keep me company," does that settle the issue?

If you ask the "person" in the machine, it will strenuously[10] claim to be the original person. If we scan, let's say, me and reinstate[11] that information into a neural computer, the person who emerges will think he is (and has been) me (or at least he will act that way). He will say, "I grew up in Queens, New York, went to college at MIT[12], stayed in the Boston area, walked into a scanner there and woke up in the machine here. Hey, this technology really works." But wait, is this really me? For one thing, old biological Ray (that's me) still exists. I'll still be here in my carbon, cell-based brain. Alas, I (the old biological Ray) will have to sit back and watch the new Ray succeed in endeavors that I could only dream of.

But New Ray will have some strong claims as well. He will say that while he is not absolutely identical to Old Ray, neither is the current version of Old Ray, since the particles making up my biological brain and body are constantly changing. It is the patterns of matter and energy that are semipermanent (that is, changing only gradually), while the actual material content changes constantly and very quickly.

Will the new entity be capable of spiritual experiences? Because its brain processes are effectively identical, its behavior will be comparable to that of the person it is based on. So it will certainly claim to have the full range of emotional and spiritual experiences that a person claims to have.

Before the next century is over, earth's technology-creating species – us – will merge with our own technology. And when that happens, we might ask: What is the difference between a human brain enhanced a millionfold by neural implants and a nonbiological intelligence based on the reverse-engineering of the human brain that is subsequently enhanced and expanded?

(760 words)

1 show – **2** abilities – **3** *Nerven…* – **4** *Netzhaut…* – **5** *Schaltkreise* – **6** *Wildreservat* **7** microrobots – **8** known for his writing and his interest in teaching science to non-scientists – **9** *Wesen, Ding* – **10** *hartnäckig* – **11** "feed" – **12** Massachusetts Institute of Technology, one of the world's leading research institutions in science and technology

3.1.1 Assignments

A) Comprehension

1

What does Ray Kurzweil predict – in general as well as for the different decades in the first half of our century?

2

Which "issues and questions" are – according to the author – raised by his predictions?

3

Do a little internet research to find short, workable definitions of (1) "artificial intelligence" (AI), (2) "Turing test", and (3) "nanobots". Write them down.

B) Analysis/Comment

1

In which respect does the text break into two distinct parts? Do we have what we may call a cause-and-effect pattern here?

2

Show that Ray Kurzweil, while being convinced of his "factual" predictions, answers the questions he raises on a more cautious note.

3

"Issaquah, Wash. (AP) – A 43-year-old man was coaxed out of his home by police after he pulled a gun on his personal computer and shot it several times, apparently in frustration."

Comment on this news item.

4

Does the scenario imagined by the author reassure you or does it make you feel concerned about the future of artificial intelligence (AI)? Give a personal comment.

C) Translation

Translate the following passage into German.

Will Computers Ever Achieve a State of Consciousness?

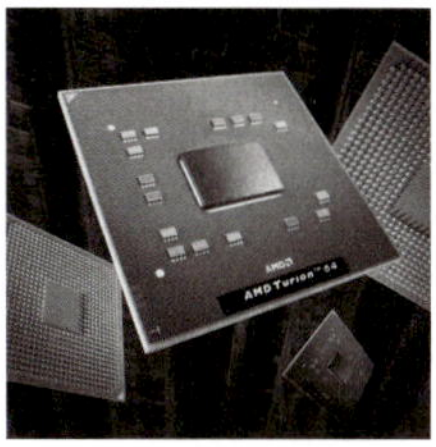

Certainly computers will continue to get smarter, as the defeat of the world chess champion Garry Kasparov by IBM's Deep Blue reminds us. Today's computers can converse in English on restricted topics, they have control of mechanical arms that weld and spray paint, and they can duplicate human expertise in dozens of areas, from prescribing drugs to diagnosing equipment breakdowns. Still, today's computers are not even close to a four-year-old human in their ability to see, talk, move or use common sense. One reason is sheer computing power. It has been estimated that the information processing capacity of even the most powerful supercomputer is equal to the nervous system of a snail – a tiny fraction of the power available to the "supercomputer" inside the bloated human skull. But the kinds of processing are different, too.

Computers find it easy to remember a 25-digit number, but find it hard to summarize the gist of Little Red Riding Hood; humans find it hard to remember the number but easy to summarize the story. One reason for the difference is that computers have a single, reliable processor (or a small number of them) working very, very fast; the brain's processors are slower and noisier, but there are hundreds of billions of them, each connected to thousands of others. That allows the human brain to recognize complicated patterns in an instant, whereas computers have to reason out every niggling detail one step at a time.

Human brains also have the advantage of sitting inside human beings, and can soak up terabytes of information over the years as humans interact with other humans and with the environment. Brains also have the benefit of a billion-year R & D (research and development) effort in which evolution equipped them with cheat sheets for figuring out how to outmanoeuvre objects, plants, animals and other humans.

So, how well will tomorrow's machines do? Technological progress is unpredictable. When it comes to replacement parts for the body, who knew that artificial hips would become commonplace and artificial hearts elusive? When it comes to the performance of duplicates of the mind, the most reasonable answer is that computers will probably do a lot better than they do now, for some kinds of thinking, and they will probably not do as well as a human being, for other kinds.

(400 words)

3.1.2 Keep Your Language Errors in Check – Future and Conditional Tenses

Study

There are several ways to use verbs to talk about the **future** in English. Check this table:

I'll write her a letter tonight.	***will + infinitive****: information about the future or possible events which are not already decided or obviously on the way*
I'm leaving for Ireland tomorrow.	***present progressive****: events that have some present reality, or which have already been planned or decided*
I am not going to answer that letter. She is going to have a baby.	***going to + infinitive****: the firm intention or plan to do something, or an event believed to be inevitable*
The ferry to Dover leaves at 5:15.	***simple present****: events in the future that are part of a timetable or a regular schedule*
My cats will be waiting for me when I get home.	***future progressive****: an event or situation that will be in progress at a particular time*
The milk is about to boil over. Take it off the hotplate.	***to be about + infinitive****: a future event that is very close*
Sort it out when you have time. If you see something interesting, tell me about it.	***present tense*** *(not: ~~will-future~~): reference to future events in subordinate clauses*

Practice 1

Decide which of the future forms fit into the following sentences. Sometimes there will be more than one solution!

1. Most areas ______________________ (be) sunny tomorrow and we ______________________ (have) intermittent showers in many areas.
2. We ______________________ (find) a cure for the HIV virus, but in the meantime this disease ______________________ (claim) thousands of victims every year.
3. Secretary: "Professor Kurzweil ______________________ (be busy), I'm afraid. He ______________________ (give) two lectures in the morning and another one in the afternoon. ... Tomorrow Mr Kurzweil ______________________ (leave) for New York at 5:30 in the morning. ... Oh, sorry, I see Mr Kurzweil ______________________ (leave) this minute."
4. ______________________ (get up) or ______________________ (stay) in bed all Sunday?
5. In case you ______________________ (get up), don't go outside. It ______________________ (be) very cold later in the day. You ______________________ (be aware of) the low temperatures the minute you ______________________ (step) outside.
6. By this time next year we ______________________ (travel) the U.S. and Canada. – When you ______________________ (go) to the States or Canada, you ______________________ (meet) a lot of friendly people there.
7. When __________ you ______________________ (book) your flight ticket with American Airlines? – I have already done that. My plane ______________________ (leave) at 7:30 from Frankfurt International Airport next Sunday.

Practice 2

Read this letter addressed to Ray Kurzweil and decide which of the future forms from the box below goes to which sentence.

are we assessing	are we going to regard	will be discussing	
is going to be	will be capable of	is going to interfere	
will be	will always be	will be limited	will match

Dear Mr Kurzweil,

I need to write to you since I'm rather concerned about what you predict about the intelligence of future machines on your KurzweilAI.net.
So, according to you, there is little doubt that artificial machines ________________________ intelligent thought in the near future. You have set up a truly horrifying timetable. In 2019, you say, computers ____________ the power of the human brain, and you are convinced that software for intelligence ____________________ more powerful than 1,000 human brains. My mind boggles at reading that "we ________________________ in a position to create virtual bodies with artificial intelligence". Wow!
Even the most powerful machine intelligence _______________________.
This limit of machine intelligence is known to researchers as narrow intelligence. One of your critics says that computers "merely manipulate formal symbols according to rules in the program" (Mr Searle). __________________________ an intelligent computer as having the attributes of personhood and dignity just like us? Does he (or it?) have the right to choose, or is he merely a machine without any rights? How __________________________ the problem of a computer's consciousness when the moment has arrived? We ________________________ these questions for many years to come.
Are you not afraid that God ____________________________________

with your ambitious plans? Human specialness is symbolized in the metaphor that humans are created in the image of God, not in the name of computer scientists. This has been so and ______________________ so. Constructing a machine with human-like intelligence, to me, is blasphemy. Yours respectfully, …

Practice 3

Read ll. 40–46 of text 3.1 again to complete the following conditional clauses.

1. How do we distinguish a process that is conscious from one that ________ ____?
2. If the entity is very convincing when it says, "I'm lonely, please keep me company," ____ ____.
3. If you ask the "person" in the machine, ______________________________ ____.
4. ____ ______________________________ the person who emerges will think he is (and has been) me (or at least he will act that way).

Practice 4

Check these conditional clauses and correct the errors.

1. What would you do if you would be asked to take part in experiments connected with artificial intelligence?

   ____
2. If your parents didn't allowed you to play the guinea pig *(Versuchs-kaninchen)* in any artificial intelligence experiment, you'd have to say no.

   ____
3. If you'll tell me why you are worried about the future of machine intelligence, I can try and explain to you why this is completely harmless.

   ____

4. It would be much better if scientists can research as they please.

____

5. If scientists had been more open-minded, we would been better informed.

____

6. Your household robot were come if you had asked it more politely.

____

7. It had done the job you wanted it to do if you had pressed the right button.

____

3.1.3 Keep Your Language Errors in Check – Modal Auxiliaries

Study

How do you express German **"sollen"** in English? Look at the following table.

man sollte eigentlich … *(moralische Verpflichtung)*	one **ought to** … / one **should** …
wir sollen („es wird erwartet, dass") …	we are **expected to** … / we are **supposed to** …
jemand soll („wie man sagt") …	somebody is **said to** … / somebody is **reported to** …
soll ich („möchtest du, dass") …?	**shall** I …?
soll … *(dahinter stehende Absicht)*	is **meant to** …

Practice 1

Translate into correct English.

1. Man sollte die Wahrheit sagen.
2. Er soll ein berühmter Mann gewesen sein.
3. Sollen wir heute etwas später kommen?
4. Der Text soll ausdrücken, was ich denke.
5. Was soll das bedeuten?

6. Der Leser soll aufgestachelt werden.
7. Der Arzt soll sofort kommen.
8. Sie soll als Fotomodell für „Vogue“ gearbeitet haben.
9. Ich sollte eigentlich heute Abend meine Eltern anrufen. (2x!)

Study

Check out the auxiliary forms of **"must"**, **"mustn't"** and **"needn't"**.

must	→ have/has to, had to, had had to, will have to	müssen
needn't	→ don't/doesn't have to, didn't have to, won't have to	brauchen
mustn't	→ is/are not allowed to, was/were not allowed to, will not be allowed to	dürfen

Practice 2

Choose the correct auxiliary or "Ersatzverb" to fill the gaps.

1. You ______________ park your car here. Can't you see the sign over there?
2. You ______________ walk all the way home. I'll give you a lift.
3. I ______________ do the shopping every day because my girlfriend is bed-ridden.
4. I ______________ take a taxi at the airport. My friend met me there.
5. You ______________ wash the car. My son has already done it.
6. He ______________ go to work on Sundays because he couldn't make ends meet.
7. You ______________ learn all the words. The vocabulary will be essential for your coursework.
8. You ______________ go to the chemist's. I can do without the prescription.
9. We ______________ to use his iPod. We might break it.

Study

Check out how German **"lassen"** is expressed in English.

let us …	lass(t) uns … *(einen Vorschlag machen)*
let sb. do sth.	jemanden etwas tun lassen („erlauben“)
leave sb./sth.	jemanden zurücklassen / etwas unterlassen
have sb. do sth./ **make** sb. do sth.	jemanden veranlassen, etwas zu tun
have sth. done	etwas erledigen lassen

Practice 3

Translate into English.

1. Lasst uns darüber reden.
2. Er ließ die SchülerInnen viele Vokabeln lernen.
3. Der Unfallflüchtige ließ den Verletzten auf der Straße liegen.
4. Meine Eltern lassen mich fernsehen, solange ich will.
5. Der Zollbeamte ließ uns sämtliche Koffer öffnen.
6. Lass uns in Ruhe.
7. Er ließ seinen Wagen stehen.
8. Was hat dich deine Meinung so schnell ändern lassen?
9. Sie ließ den Motor laufen. Sie wollte nur einen Brief einstecken.
10. Lassen Sie sich Zeit.
11. Der Arzt ließ den Patienten ins Krankenhaus bringen.
12. Er ließ uns eher nach Hause gehen.

3.1.4 Keep Your Language Errors in Check – False Friends

Study

You do not use "make" when you talk generally about action, rather than mention a particular action. Talking **generally** about action you use **"do"**. You do not say, for example, "I don't know what to ~~make~~," you say, "I don't know what to **do**."

Practice 1

German "machen": Decide whether to insert *do* or *make*.

1. We have ____________ the homework we have been assigned.
2. What you are saying does not ____________ sense.
3. I must have a new dress ____________.
4. You'll have to ____________ the complete set of exercises, I'm afraid.
5. You should not say one thing and ____________ something else.
6. Let me just show you: this is the way it is ____________.
7. They ____________ him captain of his team.
8. What does Peter ____________ for a living?
9. Can you ____________ that for me?
10. Can you ____________ *(es schaffen)* it for 8 p.m.?

Practice 2

Beware of false friends.

excited ↔ exciting	We were all very __________________ when we discussed the __________________ class trip to London.
accept ↔ except	When the teacher asked the class, all ____________ one ____________ his idea.
put into practice ↔ realize	We had to ________________________, though, that his idea was quite difficult for us to ________________________.
eventually ↔ possibly	When we ________________ put the idea to the vote, our teacher said we could ________________ plan for a five-day trip.

lay ↔ lie	I was ______ in bed when our family doctor ______ the prescription on the bedside table where it ______ until my mother got the medication.
fewer ↔ less	Our doctor was quite old. He worked ______ hours, for which he got ______ pay, a fact he liked ______ and ______ .
sensible ↔ sensitive	She was a ______ girl who had ______ views on family planning.
self-conscious ↔ self-confident	She is rather ______, but she might learn to become more ______.
sympathetic ↔ likeable	I am ______ to her situation because she is a ______ girl.
lose ↔ loose	Why are you not setting your dog ______? Are you afraid of ______ him?
economical ↔ economic	How do you feel about our ______ system? Should our politicians not be more ______ when spending the taxpayer's money?
critic ↔ criticism ↔ critique	The ______ was very harsh in his ______ of government policy. His ______ was very harsh.

Practice 3
Translate into English and beware of false friends.

1. Er hat keine **eigene** Meinung.
2. **Im Gegensatz zu** mir hast du einen Job.
3. Ich möchte Dir trotzdem **einen guten Rat** geben.
4. Wir erhielten eine Menge nützlicher **Informationen**.
5. Ich möchte Dir den Grund dafür **detailliert** erläutern.
6. Das ist eine **sinnvolle** Entscheidung.
7. **Es gibt** noch viel zu diskutieren.
8. Du **bekommst** ein schönes Geschenk.
9. In seinem Artikel **bringt** der Autor viele Fakten.
10. Er argumentiert **konsequent**.
10. Das ist **typisch für** dich: niemals etwas zugeben!
12. Ihre Lebensumstände sind schlicht **unmenschlich**.

3.1.5 Get a Grip on Your Sentence Building – Adverbial Clauses

Study
Let us focus on the special case of adverbial clauses.

Now that Tom has graduated, he will start his career as a journalist. **After** Tom handed in a sampler of his articles, he was accepted as a volunteer.	***temporal clauses:*** *after, as, as long as, as soon as, before, now that, once, since, until, when, whenever, while*
Wherever Tom was placed, he found out he had a lot to learn about journalism.	***spatial clauses:*** *where, wherever*
Tom was ready to commit himself to the job **because** he wanted to become a journalist.	***causal clauses:*** *because, since, as*
If Tom had not written successful articles for his school paper, he might never have considered becoming a journalist.	***conditional clauses:*** *if, provided that, supposing that, in case, unless*

Even though Tom had little experience, he soon became a welcome colleague.	***concessive clauses:*** *although, even though, even if*
Tom applied himself **so that** he made good progress.	***purposive clauses:*** *so that, in order that*
Tom considered becoming a journalist **so** he applied for an apprenticeship.	***resultative clauses:*** *so … that, such … that, so*
Tom writes interesting articles **while** his brother is into computer games.	***contrastive clauses:*** *while, whereas*

Practice 1

Try to complete the following sentences checking whether the concept of time, space, reason, condition, concession, purpose, result or contrast makes sense.

1. ______________ the Euro has been around for some time now, it is not very popular.	concession
2. Quite a few holidaymakers welcome the Euro ______________ they don't need to change money when going to other European countries.	______________
3. Twelve European countries have joined the new European currency ______________ Britain, Denmark and Sweden have so far rejected the Euro.	______________
4. The Euro "starter kits" were sold out ______________ they were issued in December 2001.	______________
5. The spokesman for the European Commission announced that, ______________ the new Euro bills were "safe", it would be impossible to forge the new bank notes.	______________

6. "We need the new currency," he was quoted as saying, " ________________ European firms can become more efficient." ____________

7. Britain, Denmark and Sweden will eventually join the new currency, too, ________ they realize that the Euro turns out to be a monetary success. ____________

8. Consumers in Europe wereconfident about the new currency ________ they did not fear the monetary change would be used to raise consumer prices. ____________

9. __________the Euro has been established as the new currency, people won't miss their old money. ____________

10. The Euro has been controversial precisely __________ it engages vast political ambitions. ____________

11. The Euro won't be a success ____________ all European countries join the new currency. ____________

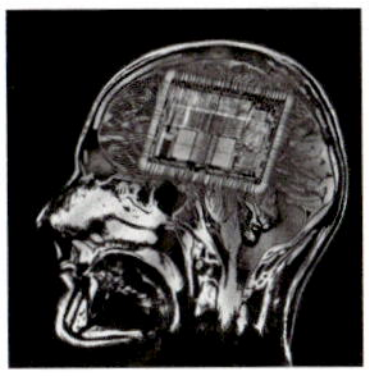

Practice 2

Join each sentence pair by forming a conditional or a concessive clause.
(a) conditional clause: *if/in case/unless/supposing that*
(b) concessive clause: *although/despite the fact that/in spite of*

1. Think positive. The merging of man and machine predicted by Kurzweil will be a breakthrough.
2. Ray Kurzweil delivers on his promise. Otherwise he will make a fool of himself.
3. We may believe in the possibility of an intelligent computer. It is hard to imagine the possibility of a conscious computer or a computer with a free will.
4. A smart robot can be like us one day. It will not be accepted by humans as

one of us, i.e. as a person.
5. It will be possible to call the new neural computers intelligent on one condition. We redefine our idea of intelligence.
6. We ought to stop AI research now. Otherwise it might be too late.
7. I read all of Kurzweil's articles on machine intelligence. I remain unconvinced.
8. Ask the machine. It will vehemently claim to be person with consciousness.

Practice 3

Connect these sentence pairs by expressing either antithetic or concessive contrast:

(a) antithetic contrast: *but / by (way of) contrast / instead / by comparison / on the contrary / alternatively*

(b) concessive contrast: *yet / however / still / besides / all the same / nevertheless / after all / at the same time*

1. I didn't ask her to leave. I tried to make her stay for another hour.
2. He has been here for two weeks only. He has achieved more than we expected.
3. The hotel caught fire. No hotel guest was killed.
4. Don't be so aggressive. You shouldn't be too timid.
5. He doesn't listen. He just sits and day-dreams.
6. She hadn't slept for days. She managed to look as fresh as a daisy.
7. So far the weather has been bad indeed. We are enjoying our stay.

3.1.6 Writing Skills – The Paragraph as a Unit of Its Own

Study

A **paragraph** can be regarded as a unit which develops one particular idea or a group of closely related ideas. Each paragraph should express **one central idea (topic sentence)** which is then developed, illustrated or amplified **(supporting sentences)** and, sometimes, finished with a **concluding sentence.**

English paragraphs usually vary in length between 50 and 250 words, with an average of 100 words. A sequence of paragraphs that are longer than that is considered as long-winded *(langatmig)*, a succession of shorter paragraphs as "choppy" *(abgehackt)* style. Read the following paragraph discussing the modern-day "macho".

Modern-day "Macho"

For starters, I should like to take a look at a type of male that you may often come across in public as well as in private life these days – the macho. He likes to present himself as an irresistible "lady-killer". We will never see his hair undone, which will shine brighter than the sun because of the tons of hair gel he has applied. The typical macho is packed with muscles ("washboard stomach"), which he knows how to present and use if necessary. He will drive a car that fits him and that underscores his exhibitionism. I can imagine a macho sitting in a convertible, his left arm casually resting on the door and exuding *(verströmen)* a cloud of perfume. All this is supposed to impress a woman and make her "melt in his arms".

(From an essay submitted by 12-grader Ina Neb, Gymnasium Zum Altenforst, Troisdorf)

Teacher comment

The above English student certainly knows how to write effectively. Her paragraph is a coherent piece of writing. It opens with two topic sentences, which are followed by a number of illustrating example sentences. The concluding sentence provides the necessary emphasis. Note the skilful use of tenses throughout the paragraph:

For starters, I should like to take a look at *a type of male* that you may often come across in public as well as in private life these days – *the macho.*	← *topic sentence 1 states the theme of the paragraph.*
He likes to present himself as *an irresistible "lady-killer".*	← *topic sentence 2 makes the point*
We will never see his *hair* (1) undone, which will shine brighter than the sun because of the tons of hair gel he has applied. The typical macho is *packed with muscles* (2) ("washboard stomach"), which he knows how to present and use if necessary. He will *drive a car* (3) that fits him and that underscores his exhibitionism. I can imagine a macho *sitting in a convertible* (3), his left arm casually resting on the door and exuding a cloud of perfume.	← *developing sentences expand and illustrate the main idea of the paragraph:* *(1) hairstyle* *(2) build* *(3) status symbol*
All this is supposed to *impress a woman* and make her "melt in his arms".	← *final sentence sums up main point*

Practice 1

"Unscramble" this version of a paragraph from a student's essay submitted by an 11-grader from Kalkuhl-Gymnasium, Bonn. Try to put the sentences in the right order: Which is a suitable opening sentence, which are supporting or developing sentences and which sentence is appropriate to close the paragraph?

sentences scrambled	unscrambled
(A) You want to impress your friends and, obviously, the clothes you wear can help a lot to accomplish that.	☐
(B) If your parents cannot afford to spend money on designer clothes, you'll be faced with a problem.	☐
(C) For one, it is a plain fact that clothes matter.	1.
(D) So you enter into a competition that is not only time-consuming but also upsets your parents.	☐
(E) You have to be trendy in order to belong and to feel accepted.	☐

Practice 2

Here you'll find a number of debatable statements (topic sentences) that you may or may not agree to. It is your task to support each topic sentence by providing two pro-arguments or developing sentences.

Good Looks: Many people today worry about the role of physical beauty, and indeed our television culture has grossly exaggerated its importance.

supporting argument 1: …
supporting argument 2: …

Car Crazy: The symbolic role that the automobile has come to play in American life means that for an adult, especially a male, not to have a license and wheels is synonymous with being less than human.

supporting argument 1: …
supporting argument 2: …

Technological Change: Historically, the evidence that technological change has been gathering speed is clear at a glance.

supporting argument 1: …
supporting argument 2: …

Practice 3

Read and criticize the following student paragraph. These questions may be your guideline:
How long do we have to wait for the topic sentence?
How is the topic sentence supported in the following?
Does the paragraph have a thematic unity?

Artificial Intelligence

There is no denying that computers will become more and more complex and that their abilities will grow massively.	←	________________
		________________
They can support us in lots of daily things. You can say that, today, nobody can live without computers.	←	________________
When I read Pinker's article, I'm not much afraid of the future.	←	________________
But there are other people who see the development of robots in another way.	←	________________
Maybe in a few years AI will surpass human intelligence. It is my view that mankind should begin to worry then.	←	________________
Because, if robots are in charge, humans are capable of controlling them.		________________

(From a student essay submitted by a 12-grader at the Gymnasium Zum Altenforst, Troisdorf)

3.2 The Satisfied Customer

Melvin blinked slowly and scratched himself as he watched the brain-numbing[1] flow of mild radiation streaming out of his television set. It was well after three in the morning and infomercials[2] ruled the mighty tube.

Channel eleven offered a free, five-minute, psychic reading. Madam Ursula guaranteed her accuracy and authenticity while "for entertainment purposes only" stood in fine print underneath the number. He had called Madam Ursula on several occasions before, taking full advantage of his free five minutes. She had assured him on numerous accounts that he would soon have the job of his dreams, a beautiful wife, and a bright future. Madam Ursula was a liar.

Channel two explained why Melvin didn't have to be bald[3]. Through vigorous research and advanced technology, renowned scientist Edwin Sponk had discovered a way to facilitate hair growth by electronic stimulation. For only $ 39.99 you could purchase a set of electrodes that when attached to your scalp were guaranteed to rebuild a healthy mane.

Melvin glanced to his dresser where the electrodes were stashed away in a drawer. He grimaced as he recalled the uncomfortable shocks that seemed to pinch into his head when he tried them, and the twitch in his left eye that never went away. He reminded himself that he still needed to get his full refund[4] before his thirty days were up.

He clicked the down arrow one more time, he was supposed to return to channel thirteen on his cable-less TV but instead landed on channel "00". Melvin frowned, he didn't know double zero was a channel. He scratched at his receding hairline as he watched the never before seen infomercial unfurl[5]. A man dressed in a white lab coat stood in front of a spinning, vertigo[6] backdrop and spoke to the camera with intense eyes.

"Are you tired of being ripped off? Lied to? Taken for a ride[7]?" said the man.

Melvin nodded absent-mindedly as he leered into his screen.

"Has your life not panned out[8] as you had expected? Are you searching for an escape? Would you give anything just to relieve yourself of the hassle life brings and live on in personal freedom?"

Melvin leaned forward in anticipation as the man continued.

"Consider lobotomy[9]. Now you can leave behind the pressure of real life and live on in a state of continuous, internal bliss. My method of hypnotic brain alteration is guaranteed and can be administered directly over the phone. A small fee of only $ 199.99 can be charged to your major credit card, or be automatically charged to your phone bill if you have direct deposit[10]. After the procedure the price will be the very last thing on your mind as you find yourself unable to comprehend even the smallest troubling thought."

As if in a trance Melvin reached for his phone and slowly began to dial the

number on the screen. After two rings an operator picked up.
"Hypnotic Lobotomy, thank you for calling. Do you have direct deposit for your phone bill?"
"Y…yes I do."
"Okay sir, please accept the charges to your local phone bill by stating your name and saying 'I accept' at the tone please."
A short beep followed.
"M…Melvin Duncan … I accept."
"Thank you sir, your request has been processed. Stay on the line and a doctor will be with you shortly."
Two minutes later Melvin dropped the phone and leaned back on his couch his mouth agape and his eyes vacant. He was found that way two days later by a neighbor and taken to a nearby hospital. No official explanation was ever determined for his mentally disconnected state. But Hypnotic Lobotomy INC. knew he was simply another satisfied customer.

(Nathan Carter, The Satisfied Customer. 620 words)

1 making sb. unable to feel, think or react in a normal way – **2** mix of info + commercials – **3** having little or no hair on the head – **4** a sum of money that is paid back to you because you returned goods to a shop/store – **5** *here:* play – **6** screen background of moving pictures (vertigo: *Schwindel*) – **7** to cheat or trick sb. – **8** *(of events or a situation)* to develop in a particular way – **9** a medical operation that cuts into or takes away part of a person's brain in order to treat mental illness – **10** a bank account

3.2.1 Assignments

A) Comprehension

1
What indicates that the story "The Satisfied Customer" appears to be set in the future?

2
Which needs felt by Melvin Duncan and the people living in his world do the (nightly) TV channels mentioned in the text claim to cater to *(bedienen)* and why can Melvin himself be described as a man leading an "unhappy" life before he stumbles upon channel "00"? What is he like after receiving treatment through Hypnotic Lobotomy INC.?

3
What distinguishes the service provided by channel "00" from the other two channels mentioned and what does the unusual channel number suggest about its policy?

4
Is the author to be taken seriously or can we discover satirical overtones as he unfolds his story? What is he poking fun at?

B) Analysis/Comment

1
Write a personal e-mail to *hypnolobotomy@aol.us* congratulating the company on their consumer-oriented services or protesting against their practice.

2
As we step into the 21st century, are *we* travelling down Melvin Duncan's road? Consider present-day tendencies such as our obsessive shopping habits („Geiz ist geil"), the wellness craze, or of your own choice.

C) Translation

Translate the following passage into German.

Real Fun

His wife in the TV parlour paused long enough from reading her script to glance up.
"What's on this afternoon?" he asked tiredly.
"Well, this is a play that comes on the wall-to-wall circuit in ten minutes. They mailed me my part this morning. They write the script with one part missing. It's a new idea. The home-maker, that's me, is the missing part. When it comes time for the missing lines, they all look at me out of the three walls and I say the lines. Here, for instance, the man says, 'What do you think of this whole idea, Helen?' and he looks at me sitting here center stage, see? And I say, I say –"
She paused and ran her finger under a line in the script. "'I think that's fine!' And then they go on with the play until he says, 'Do you agree to that, Helen?' and I say, 'I sure do!' Isn't that fun, Guy?"
He stood in the hall looking at her.
"It's sure fun," she said.
"What's the play about?"
"I just told you. There are these people named Bob and Ruth and Helen."
"Oh."
"It's really fun. It'll be even more fun when we can afford to have that fourth wall installed. How long you figure before we save up and get the fourth wall torn out and the fourth wall-TV put in? It's only two thousand dollars."

(235 words)

3.2.2 Keep Your Language Errors in Check – False Friends

Study

As you bring your ideas and thoughts to paper, you may tend to translate them word by word into English. This is not considered a good strategy generally since quite a number of similar-looking words have a different meaning in English: They are **false friends.** Beware of false friends, for example:

Meinung ≠ meaning: I share your ~~(meaning)~~ **opinion** in every way.
machen ≠ make: You should not say one thing and ~~(make)~~ **do** something else.
erinnern ≠ remember: This song ~~(remembers)~~ **reminds** me of the Beatles.

TIP Start a list of your "favourite" false friends!

Practice 1

Translate these sentences into correct English.

see	catch sight of something or someone, often quickly or for a short time; understand what is meant
look	set eyes on something or someone
watch	set eyes on and pay attention to; look at something or someone continuously

1. Siehst Du oft *Infomercials* im Fernsehen?
2. Kannst du verstehen (sehen), was mit Melvin nicht stimmt?
3. Egal, wie Du es siehst, Melvin ist selbst schuld.
4. Wenn ich das richtig sehe, hätte Melvin woanders nach Hilfe ausschauen sollen.
5. Sieh mal dorthin, was kannst Du sehen?
6. Hast du den Film gesehen, in dem Truman Burbank (Jim Carrey) von der ganzen Welt beobachtet wird?
7. Ich wollte wegsehen, aber ich konnte nicht anders, als den Unfall mit anzusehen.

Practice 2

Check the words in the left column carefully, then fill the gaps in the right column.

rise ↔ raise	The man in the white lab coat ____________ his voice when he addressed the viewers. Melvin didn't ____________ from his chair, he leaned forward.
who's ↔ whose	Madam Ursula, ____________ readings had proved fruitless, was a liar! ____________ the one to blame in Melvin's case?
topical ↔ actual	The ____________ state Melvin is in resembles that of vegetable. His case is of ____________ interest for us.
at last ↔ at least	He is a satisfied customer ____________. ____________ we can say that he is not very smart.
hardly ↔ hard	Melvin has to face a ____________ life. It is ____________ surprising therefore that he seeks help.
interesting ↔ interested	Is this an ____________ story? Are you ____________ in discussing its implications?
meaning ↔ opinion	What in your ____________ is to you the ____________ of the short story? Does it possibly have more than one ____________?
ready ↔ finished	Sorry, I haven't ____________ my essay but I'll be ____________ to listen in a minute.
let ↔ leave	He ____________ himself be talked into undergoing the treatment. Hypnotic Lobotomy INC. ____________ nothing to chance. Let's ____________ it at that for the moment.

3.2.3 Get a Grip on Your Sentence Building – Conditional Clauses

Study

There are a few other options, of course, but you should stick to the basics first:

Bedingung	***if*-clause**	**main clause**
erfüllbar (Typ I)	present tense	*will*-future
unwahrscheinlich (Typ II)	past tense	*would* + infinitive
nicht mehr erfüllbar (Typ III)	past perfect	*would have* + past participle

Practice 1

Examine the use of tenses in the following sentences and correct the errors.

1. What would you do if somebody would give you a ticket for a flight to China?
2. Your father said no, didn't he? If you had asked him nicely, he had perhaps said yes.
3. If you had performed better at school, your father had allowed you to fly to China.
4. If you'll tell me what is worrying you, I might try and help you.
5. She were come if you had asked her personally.

Practice 2

Complete **(a)** and rewrite **(b)** the sentences below.

a) More *ifs*

1. If I were more fortunate, I ______________________ **(certainly make it)**.
2. I would certainly have made it if I ______________________ **(be more fortunate)**.
3. Should I be as fortunate as you have been, I ______________________ **(let you know)** at once.
4. If I ever pass that test, I ______________________ **(be most fortunate)**.
5. If nothing helps, some people ______________________ **(turn)** to religion.

b) Melvin Duncan's *ifs*

1. Melvin Duncan stumbled across channel "00". He got interested in Hypnotic Lobotomy INC.'s brain treatment. → If he …, he … not …
2. He got interested in Hypnotic Lobotomy INC.'s brain treatment. He rang up their number. → If he …, he … not …
3. He rang up their number. He accepted their charges to his local phone bill. → If he …, he … not …
4. He accepted their charges to his local phone bill. He was lobotomized a few minutes later. → If he …, he … not …

Practice 3

The *ifs* of our contemporary lifestyle. Translate into English. Be careful about the tenses you use!

1. Wenn wir den Tatsachen des Lebens ins Auge blicken wollen, müssen wir unsere Lebensweise ändern.

____

____

2. Wir würden vernünftiger handeln *(act more sensibly)*, wenn wir nicht dem Ideal der ewigen Jugend nachliefen.

____

____

3. Wir wären auch viel zufriedener, wenn wir nicht immer das besitzen wollten, was wir nicht haben.

4. Wenn wir nicht Angst vor dem Altern hätten, würden wir in Würde *(in dignity)* alt werden.

5. Wenn wir uns nicht so viel vormachten *(delude ourselves)*, würden wir den Versprechungen der Wellness-Industrie nicht glauben.

6. Wenn wir glauben, wir bräuchten nur einfach ein Wochenende in einem Wellness-Hotel zu buchen, liegen wir falsch.

7. Wenn wir wüssten, dass Schönheitsoperationen nicht ohne Risiko sind, wären wir zurückhaltender *(more reluctant)* in dieser Hinsicht *(in this respect)*.

8. Wenn wir uns auf die wahren Dinge im Leben konzentrierten, wäre unser Leben nicht eine solche Hetze *(hassle)*.

3.2.4 Writing Skills – Comparison and Contrast

Study

In your "Kursarbeiten" you'll often be asked to compare and contrast texts or views and opinions adopted by various authors. Examine how **comparison** and **contrast** are accentuated in these two short passages:

On Sports and Practice

All the top *private schools* insist on lots of compulsory practice and boast of their *sports facilities*. *State schools*, **by contrast**, are selling off *playing fields* at a disgraceful rate despite this government's promise to stop them.	← *element 1: private schools* ← *element 2: state schools* ← *discourse marker: contrast*

On Cosmetic Surgery

Many people say that only *women* are keen on changing their outward appearance in order to look more attractive. This is, in fact, only **partly** true. Let us admit that there are still more women than men who go under the knife. **But** more and more men are also beginning to change their appearance with the help of cosmetic surgeons. Cosmetic surgery is of course the easiest and fastest way to change your looks. **However,** following the newest trends in cosmetic surgery may eventually (schließlich!) become problematic. People may "win" beauty **but** they will lose one very important thing: their self-esteem.	← *element 1: women* ← *downtoner* ← *element 1 specified* ← *discourse marker: contrast* ← *argument 1* ← *discourse marker: contrast* ← *argument 2* ← *discourse marker: contrast*

(From an essay submitted by 12-grader Konstantin Pietrek, Gymnasium Zum Altenforst, Troisdorf)

Practice 1

Check the following list and choose the most suitable words and phrases as you fill in the gaps in the passage comparing two famous dystopian novels below.

similarity	difference
conjunctions:	
	while whereas
adverb(ial)s:	
likewise similarly so is/are equally	on the one hand on the other yet *(am Satzanfang)* however *(zweites Wort im Satz)* though *(am Satzende)* by comparison by contrast conversely
prepositions:	
compared to in comparison with in proportion to	unlike in contrast to as against
phrases:	
is/are/look just like resembles has a strong resemblance to are very much alike are comparable have something/a lot in common there is little to choose between there is some similarity between there is a strong parallel between	is/are very different indeed differ greatly are very dissimilar are very much opposed to each other is the very antithesis of there is no comparison between contrast sharply with is/stand in marked/sharp contrast to something have nothing in common bears no relation to are worlds apart that is a far cry from

We are in Utopia

A. Huxley's "Brave New World" can be called a welfare tyranny **(im Gegensatz zu)** ______________________ G. Orwell's "1984", which is based on sheer violence and terror. In "Brave New World" **(jedoch)** ______________________ drugs play an important part.

The rulers of "1984" are not reluctant to use intimidation and torture, **(wohingegen)** ______________________ the system in "Brave New World" genetically manipulates their citizens and conditions their reflexes.

The two novels are **(in der Tat sehr unterschiedlich)** ______________________ ________________. **(Anders als)** ______________________ "Brave New World"-citizens, the people in "1984" have to face a miserable existence with few joys and hardly any pleasures.

On might say that life in "Brave New World" is **(das genaue Gegenteil von)** ____ that in "1984".

(Einerseits) ____________________________, "Brave New World's" world controllers provide their citizens with all they need, **(andererseits)** _________ ______________________ the people have their lives run for them.

Practice 2

Read the following compare-and-contrast essay and fill in the gaps using appropriate expressions of comparison and contrast from the box below.

aren't similar in every respect	more different
as well as	quite similar
be compared to	similarly
the biggest difference between	the only difference being
both	unlike
in the first place	whereas

Some people say that German television can easily ____________________ ____________________ American TV. They ____________________ ____________ put advertising and entertainment before information and both can be accused of attaching too much importance to "ratings". Is that all there is?

____________________, there can be no doubt that advertising time on German ____________________ on American TV is excessive, ____________________ that over here advertising intervals are rather long while in the U.S. the intervals are shorter but come more often.

____________________, in both countries entertainment is the order of the day. Even the news shows, sometimes poorly disguised, are expected to have a high entertainment value. Hence the term "infotainment".

____________________ German anchors, however, their American counterparts are more professional and entertaining.

However, German and American TV ____________________ ____________________. In a few key ways, they are ____________________ ____________________ than they are the same.

____________________ the major German channels run at

least some informative programmes, in the U.S. TV the human interest angle is central. Finally, ____ the two countries is that, in America, TV is generally free of charge, while in our country there is a competition between commercial TV and fee-paying TV stations.

Given that TV in both countries can appear to be ____________________ ____________________, it makes sense to draw attention to one or two significant differences between them that cannot be denied.

TIP Add the words and phrases expressing similarity and contrast to your active vocabulary!

"We interrupt this rubbish to give you another chance to switch off."

4 Genetic Engineering

4.1 Cloning As a Valid Reproductive Choice

Note: *James Hughes at the time he published his web column "Better Humans" taught health policy at Trinity College in Hartford Connecticut, and served as secretary of the World Transhumanist Association, a non-profit organization devoted to encouraging the use of technology to transcend the limitations of the human body.*

The timing and kind of children we bear are some of the most personal and life-changing decisions we can make, which is why our reproductive freedoms are so important. The right to use cloning, once safe, should be another reproductive choice to be protected along with contraception and abortion.
Not long ago, bad science fiction movies and religious dogmas were arrayed against "test-tube babies[1]." Today in-vitro fertilization is an accepted, mundane, widely used tool. Just as with in-vitro fertilization, opponents of reproductive cloning deploy a dozen tenuous, hypothetical scenarios in which society or the clones would be harmed by cloning. But none of these makeshift[2] reasons are weighty enough to deny people the right to control their own reproduction.
Francis Fukuyama[3], of the President's Council on Bioethics, warns that fathers will lust after daughters cloned from their mothers, since they will resemble the mother as a young girl. Yet this is really an argument for adoption, because many girls resemble their mothers.
Opponents worry about a "brave new world" or "designer babies" and the supposed slippery slope to totalitarianism. But the problem with reproduction in the novel "Brave New World" was precisely that control over baby making had been taken away from parents and given to the state. There is no slippery slope from parents freely choosing to use cloning to totalitarianism, and dictators don't need to clone armies when they can build them more cheaply and quickly the old way[4].
Opponents also fret that clones will face inordinate expectations from their parents. But if clones are harmed by their parents' expectations – especially the expectation that kids have the same tastes, values and abilities as their parents – then very few people should have children at all.
Some oppose cloning on the grounds that it will only be available to the wealthy and is a waste of resources that could be better used. But that is also true of fertility treatments in general. The way to give more people more access to quality health care is by creating national health insurance systems, not by banning elective, out-of-pocket[5] services.

Finally, some argue that people will be harmed by not being biologically unique. Of course, no one's DNA should be used without permission. But where does the harm come from in having a twin? Most twins appear to value their closeness. As annoyed as we can be by our similarities to our parents, they are also important to the parent-child bond. Clones will simply be delayed twins and beloved children, with all the rights and burdens of any child.

The right to have a cloned child, like the right to wear a red hat, is not an important right in the scheme of things. But if we take away this right because of irrational fears, we will have lost a small measure of our freedom for no gain.

(480 words)

1 The first test-tube baby, Louise Brown, was born in Britain in 1978. – **2** *here:* not serious, not valid – **3** F. Fukuyama has written widely on issues relating to questions concerning democratization and international political economy. His most famous book is "The End of History and the Last Man" (1992). – **4** i.e. by indoctrinating and training them for their job – **5** that cannot be paid for by everybody

"And then they perfected stem cell embryos"

4.1.1 Get a Grip on Your Vocabulary – the Cloning Debate

Practice 1

Check if the following phrases and expressions suggest a pro or a contra attitude as regards cloning. Put a "P" or a "C" behind each item.

1. Children are given to us, they are not our property.	☐
2. Cloning is the answer to many medical questions, and to a better quality of life.	☐
3. The catch is …	☐
4. Should we travel the road to the brave new world that science and technology are taking us towards?	☐
5. It is clear that cloning has enormous potential.	☐
6. We are not playing God, we are merely using technology to improve our lives.	☐
7. It is a wonderful additional reproductive option.	☐
8. We will push the boundaries of science.	☐
9. It will be possible to make clones of exceptional people in hope that their gifts and talents can be passed on.	☐
10. A world driven by greed and power will abuse the technology.	☐
11. The very thought is repellent and disgusting.	☐
12. It is the beginning of a slippery slope.	☐
13. Being able to clone humans is a tantalizing idea.	☐
14. The technology will bring along life-saving treatments.	☐
15. I believe such a practice unethical.	☐
16. The impact will be profound, pervasive, and largely unpredictable.	☐
17. Every aspect of human culture will be affected.	☐
18. Nature has created the proper way to make babies and we shouldn't do it in a different way.	☐

Practice 2

Here is another pack of debatable statements (topic sentences) that you may or may not agree to. As in chapter 3.1.6 Practice 2, it is your task to support each topic sentence by providing two pro-arguments or developing sentences.

a) *debatable statement*: This era of ours is Frankenstein time.

supporting argument 1: ______________________________

____

supporting argument 2: ______________________________

____

b) *debatable statement:* The prime target for eugenics and genetic scientists is to produce the perfect baby.

supporting argument 1: ______________________________

____

supporting argument 2: ______________________________

____

c) *debatable statement:* A human clone will be genetically identical with another person.

supporting argument 1: ______________________________

____

supporting argument 2: ______________________________

____

d) *debatable statement:* Nature has devised the proper way to make babies, and we shouldn't do it in a different way.

supporting argument 1: ______________________________

____

supporting argument 2: ______________________________

____

Practice 3

Read this (slightly enhanced) essay submitted by a 12-grader from Gymnasium Zum Altenforst, Troisdorf near Bonn. Add the missing **discourse markers** from this list.

admittedly   to begin with   however   yet

moreover   therefore   more importantly

Biological Engineering On the Road to "Playing God": Should We Do What We Can Do?

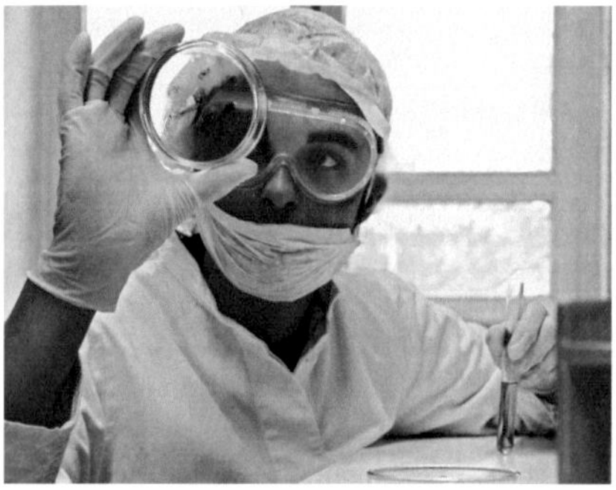

Within the last decades scientists have made great progress in genetic research, thus improving our prospects of making life for people healthier and more comfortable. To me, it is clear that this kind of research has enormous potential benefits and a few real negative consequences.

____________________, I have to admit that stem cell research is still too hazardous for its results to be applied in medical treatment. The possibility of dangerous gene mutation cannot be dismissed. ____________________, the time will come when medical science transcends those hazards. If scientists are be able to safely "breed" new parts of the body, it will be hard (or even impossible) to stop them from marketing the technology.

____________________, it is often said that the research on stem cells violates human dignity as these cells, with which scientists conduct their research, are or, rather, will become living human beings. That is why opponents of genetic research call it "murder".

____________________, these cells are potential embryos or babies but, at the time when scientists work with them one can hardly consider them already as living beings. It must be mentioned that these first cells are all of the same type and not yet specialised, i.e. skin, bone, blood cells or any other organ of a human body.

_________________________________, bearing in mind that immediately after the cerebral death of a hospital inmate all machines that have kept him alive are shut down without thinking of the other cells of his body living still, the question arises why people attach such enormous importance to human cells at the beginning of life but not at its end since cells clearly have more "human indications" before death than those pre-embryonic cells. To my mind, the ethical value of stem cells is overrated by critics.

_________________________________, that kind of cell research is a further step into the arena of reproductive cloning. Creating not only spare parts but entire human beings affects human uniqueness. This step might lead us in the wrong direction.

_________________________________, if the genetic research is not perfected to the risky point of cloning entire human beings, it will be a blessing for mankind that instils hope and enriches life.

4.1.2 Assignments

A) Comprehension

1

Point out what view James Hughes takes of reproductive cloning in his text.

2

Collect the arguments opposed to cloning that James Hughes addresses in his text.

B) Analysis/Comment

1

How does the author deal with the contra arguments raised by people who do not share his opinion? You may study the way he builds his paragraphs and his choice of words when characterising his opponents.

2

Write an e-mail to *j.hughes@changesurfer.us* in response to the view expressed by James Hughes.

C) Translation

Translate the following passage into German.

Cloning and Stem Cell Research

Cloning and stem cell research 1997 saw the birth of Dolly the sheep, the first animal cloned from an adult cell. This was a remarkable achievement which created world-wide debate on the ethical issues surrounding cloning. International organisations such as the European Parliament, UNESCO and WHO all declared that human cloning is both morally and legally wrong. However, we need to make a distinction between reproductive cloning and therapeutic cloning. Nowadays the idea of reproductive cloning – creating a copy of another person – is no longer interesting for researchers. Instead therapeutic cloning is creating excitement in the biotech world. Key to this technique are stem cells, which are master cells that have the potential to become any other kind of cell in the body, e.g. nerve cells, blood, heart muscle or even brain cells.

Stem cells themselves have generated a lot of controversy as it was believed that only human embryos could provide them. However, it now appears that adult stem cells offer the same possibility. This would mean that a patient who suffered a heart attack could provide doctors with his adult stem cells which could then be implanted back into his heart and used to create heart muscle, replacing the muscle that was damaged. As the genetic code is identical, there would be no problem of the body rejecting the implant as, unfortunately, happens with organ transplants. In the future, biotechnologists hope that stem cells could be used to grow entire organs. In this way biotechnology offers the hope of revolutionizing medical treatment.

(260 words)

4.2 The Ten Year Old Head

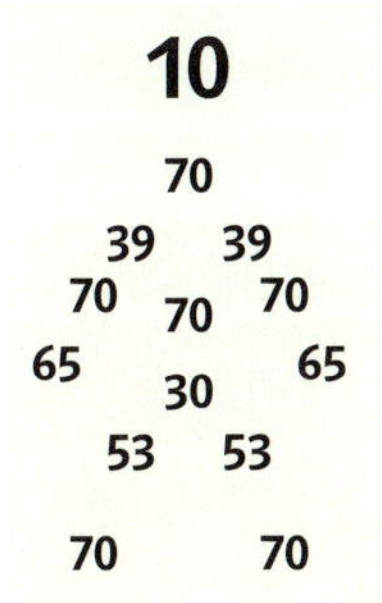

Julie died at seventy, but her head was only ten. Her breasts were close to forty, her buttocks fifty-three. Her waist was only thirty, while her hands pushed sixty-five. Her head was by far the youngest, although it, too, was fully dead. Still, had her head somehow managed to disengage in time from its neck, it seemed at least theoretically possible that it might still be alive.

But, alas, it hadn't, and so when Julie's heart went down at seventy, her head got pulled along.

Her husband died at seventy-one just as Julie passed out of her fifties. Her head by then was only twenty but her waist was fully sixty, a tragedy that bothered her almost as much as dear Henry's passing.

Until the age of forty, Julie's head and body had coexisted in perfect concordance, after which they began beating to the ticks of different clocks. By birthday forty-five, Julie's eyes were twenty-nine. By birthday fifty-two, her face was thirty-eight, a state at which it held rock steady for the next seven years. It was not till fifty-nine that her breasts shed[1] a decade and then almost overnight.

Henry left behind a generous inheritance, a home with no mortgage[2], and a reliable monthly pension. By the time of Julie's death, however, her bank balance in dollars was only slightly larger than the total circumference of her arms, thighs, and waist in inches.

Daughter Anne, long irritated by her mother's morphing[3] corpus, had ceased all communication a decade earlier, just after Julie's torso passed over the big six-0[4] and her head nose-dived into its twenties. Anne's hysterical parting words had to do with Julie one day attaining the chronological age of eighty, at which time her head seemed firmly on course to reach zero, a point from which it could only go negative.

But, of course, no such biological perversion came to pass[5] because Julie's heart gave out at seventy when her head was still a positive ten.

Happily, Julie's mind aged in concert with her head and grew blissfully unaware of both her daughter's callous[6] abandonment and the state of her squandered[7] finances. After all, by the time of Julie's death, her head of ten was half its way to nine.

Attendance at the funeral was sparse, just four worried men in long starched white coats, all of whom had loved the lady dearly and would miss her far more than she could have ever imagined.

Dressed in pink chiffon and surrounded by frilly satin, Julie looked as darling as a little girl. All that showed of her was her perfect face – eyelids tight, cheeks without jowls, skin like finest porcelain.

Saddened to learn of her impending cremation, each man secretly fought back the urge to yank sweet Julie free from her coffin, peel away her gown, and admire the results of his life's finest work.

(Jimi Five, The Ten Year Old Head. 480 words)

1 grew younger – **2** arrangement by which you borrow money from a bank or similar organization in order to buy a house, and pay back the money over a period of years – **3** developing a new appearance – **4** sixty years of age – **5** took place – **6** not caring that other people are suffering – **7** carelessly wasted

4.2.1 Keep Your Language Errors in Check – Collocations

Practice 1

Complete these collocations.

1. **(Der Wunsch)** ________________ to **(bewahren)** ________________ one's youth or event to become younger again is strong in many.
2. Many people lead a **(vollkommen normales)** ________________ life.
3. Old age **(kommt)** ________________ near, as senses **(lassen nach)** ________________ and organs begin **(zu versagen)** ________________.
4. The body clock **(läuft herunter)** ________________.
5. Old age makes life no longer **(lebenswert)** ________________.
6. We experience years of **(des Niedergangs)** ________________.
7. We enjoy the years of **(Gesundheit)** ________________ and **(Produktivität)** ________________.
8. We must learn to grow old **(in Würde)** ________________.
9. We are **(zerstört)** ________________ by age and, finally, **(sterben)** ________________ away.
10. We should think twice before we **(herumbasteln an)** ________________ ________________ the God-given human condition.

11. Many scientists say we should **(ergreifen)** ____________________ the opportunity.
12. Cracking the DNA code has **(gebahnt)** ____________________ the way for a bright future.
13. The **(Heilerfolg)** ____________________ may turn out to be a **(Fluch)** ____________________.
14. We are **(in der Lage)** ____________________ to eventually decide about our lives.
15. Genetic treatment may be **(hilfreich)** ____________________ in some fields but **(schädlich)** ____________________ in others.
16. We are **(gut beraten)** ____________________ to pause and think again.
17. Biotechnology **(gibt)** ____________________ hope in some but **(löst aus)** ____________________ fears in others.
18. Progress **(eröffnet)** ____________________ enormous possibilities for treatment of age-related illnesses.
19. What we know so far **(erweist sich als)** ____________________, at least for the time being, regenerative medicine to be an illusion.
20. I **(lehne ab)** ____________________ any dehumanizing treatment.
21. A genetic **(Veränderung)** ____________________ of your genetic make-up is dangerous.
22. We will be able to **(kontrollieren)** ____________________ and even to **(umkehren)** ____________________ the ageing of human cells.

4.2.2 Assignments

A) Comprehension

1

Explain the arrangement of the numbers in the illustration placed in the text.

2

Is there any logic behind the parts of Julie's body that age and those that grow younger?

3

What has become of the "generous inheritance" (l. 18) that her late husband has left behind for Julie?

4

Who are "the four worried men" (l. 34) at Julie's funeral and why are they mourning her death?

B) Analysis/Comment

1

Study the narrator's choice of words as he describes the stages that Julie's head goes through. What do they suggest?

2

Tragedy or farce? What personal view do you take of Julie and the likes of her?

3

"We can make cells 'immortal' without changing their genes art all. It turns out that ageing is not a matter of having the wrong genes. We can reset *(neu einstellen)* cell ageing so completely that your cells never age. We can even take old cells and make them young again without altering the genes at all, without changing their environment, without hormones, and without any special diet. Maybe you live in interesting times …"

Do you? State your case for or against genetic or other anti-ageing treatment.

C) Translation

Translate the following passage into German.

Happy 150th Birthday? New Era Looms for Ageing

High-tech Medicine Expected to Increase Life Expectancy, Experts Predict

Oxford, England, March 16, 2006 – Modern medicine is redefining old age and may soon allow people to live regularly beyond the current upper limit of 120 years, experts said Wednesday.

It used to be thought there was some built-in limit on life span, but a group of scientists meeting at Oxford University for a conference on life extension and enhancement consigned that idea to the trash can.

Paul Hodge, director of the Harvard Generations Policy Program, said governments around the world – struggling with pension crises, graying work forces and rising health-care costs – had to face up to the challenge now.

"Life expectancy is going to grow significantly, and current policies are going to be proven totally inadequate," he predicted.

Just how far and fast life expectancy will increase is open to debate, but the direction and the accelerating trend is clear. Richard Miller of the Michigan University Medical School said tests on mice and rats – genetically very similar to humans – showed life span could be extended by 40 percent, simply by limiting calorie consumption.

Translated into humans, that would mean average life expectancy in rich countries rising from near 80 to 112 years, with many individuals living a lot longer.

Aubrey de Grey, a biomedical gerontologist from Cambridge University, goes much further. He believes the first person to live to 1,000 has already been born and told the meeting that periodic repairs to the body using stem cells, gene therapy and other techniques could eventually stop the ageing process entirely.

(265 words)

4.2.3 Get a Grip on Your Sentence Building – Appearance vs. Reality and Truth

Study

Authors have a lot to gain from the interplay of deceptive appearance and underlying truth in their texts. When reading a text, you may be completely certain or less certain, or you may even venture a bold hypothesis as to what you infer from the text itself.

from appearance ...	... to reality
At first sight, – we are under the impression that ... – it seems that ... – it looks as if ... – we take it for granted that ... – we are led to think that	But in fact, / But actually, – we realize that ... – we are made to understand that ... – the writer takes great care to show that ... – we gradually become aware that ...

Practice

Translate using the expressions from the box below.

looks	**is not what it seems**
comes across as	**seems**
deep down	**didn't strike me as**
it is undeniable that	**the reality is that**
gives the appearance of	**there is some solid evidence that**
gives the impression of	**there's more to it than meets the eye**
in reality	**the truth is that**
look as if	**underneath**

1. Geldmangel **scheint** das Hauptproblem zu sein.
2. Du **siehst aus, als ob** Du die ganze Nacht nicht geschlafen hast.
3. In Interviews **erscheint** sie naiv, aber in ihrem Job ist sie sehr gut.
4. **Es ist unbestreitbar, dass** sie ein intelligentes Mädchen ist.
5. Es **sieht** alles sehr leicht **aus**, aber **die Wahrheit ist, dass** ich sehr hart arbeite.
6. Er **erweckt den Eindruck,** dass er schüchtern und bescheiden ist, aber **darunter** ist er ein Schläger.

7. Sie **kam mir nicht vor wie** jemand, die Lehrerin werden wollte. Aber **tief innen** hatte sie das immer gewollt.
8. Die Situation in unserer Schule **ist nicht, was sie scheint**: **Es gibt starke Anzeichen, dass** den meisten Schülern die richtige Haltung fehlt.
9. Viele Leute sagen, dass Lehrer streng sein müssen, aber **die Wirklichkeit ist, dass** einige überziehen (**overdo it**).
10. Mein Klassenlehrer **macht den Eindruck**, dass er alles unter Kontrolle hat, aber **da steckt mehr dahinter**: **In Wirklichkeit** ist er ziemlich hilflos.

4.2.4 Writing Skills – How to Add Emphasis to Your Sentences

Practice 1

Use the following words to emphasize or tone down the statements given.

emphasizers		downtoners	
definitely indeed simply frankly	completely absolutely entirely certainly	rather more or less somewhat partly	not at all not in the least to some extent barely

I don't know what he wants.
→ *I frankly/simply/definitely don't know what he wants.*

1. That's wrong. I can assure you.

   ____

2. I forgot about her birthday.

   ____

3. I enjoyed the show. It was exciting.

   ____

4. I enjoyed the show. Most of it was boring.

   ____

5. In the grammar test he failed. No correct answer.

   ____

6. In the grammar test he failed. Half his answers were wrong.

___

7. I agree. What you are saying convinces me.

___

8. I agree. I would perhaps add another point.

___

9. I can't follow you there. That's rubbish.

___

10. I can follow you there. You're right, that's rubbish.

___

Practice 2

Two good ways of achieving emphasis in your writing are a) end-focus and b) contrastive focus.

a) Rewrite the following sentences in passive using end-focus.

1. Who won World War II? **(the Allied Forces)**
2. What's the cause of cancer? **(among other things smoking)**
3. Was Columbus the first to discover America? **(the Norsemen in the 11th or 12th century)**

b) Rewrite the following sentences using contrastive focus.

1. I think I'll have red wine, not ___ today.
2. It was in the south of Germany, not ___, where I lived for 20 years.
3. This is a problem that a computer, rather than ___, could solve easily.
4. You won't make it by ___ but by working hard.

Practice 3

Another effective means to emphasize what you want to say is the **cleft sentence.** You begin your sentence with "It is …".

1. I want to watch the new free TV sports channel.

   ____

2. The class test took a long time to write because it raised many difficult questions.

   ____

   ____

3. The party got going after Peter and his friends had left.

   ____

4. The class speaker reported this incident to the headmaster *(three possibilities).*

   ____

   ____

   ____

5 A Taste of William Shakespeare

5.1 An Exhortation[1] Concerning Good Order and Obedience to Rulers and Magistrates (1547)

Almighty God hath[2] created and appointed all things in heaven, earth and waters, in a most excellent and perfect order. In heaven he hath appointed distinct and several orders and states of archangels and angels. On earth he hath assigned and appointed kings, princes, with other governors under them, in all good and necessary order. The water above is kept, and raineth[3] down in due time and season. The sun, moon, stars, rainbow, thunder, lightning, clouds and all birds of the air, do keep their order. The earth, trees, seeds, plants, herbs, corn, grass, and all manner of beasts, keep themselves in order: all the parts of the whole year, as winter, summer, months, nights and days, continue in their order. All kinds of fishes in the sea, rivers, and waters, with all fountains, springs, yea the seas themselves keep their comely[4] course and order. And man himself also hath all his parts both within and without, as soul, heart, mind, memory, understanding, reason, speech, with all and singular corporal members of his body, in a profitable, necessary, and pleasant order: every degree of people in their vocation, calling, and office, hath appointed to them[5] their duty and order. Some are in high degree, some in low, some kings and princes, some inferiors and subjects, priests and laymen, masters and servants, fathers and children, husbands and wives, rich and poor; and everyone hath need of the other; so that in all things is to be lauded and praised the goodly order of God, without which no house, no city, no commonwealth[6] can continue and endure or last. For where there is no right order, there reigneth[7] all abuse, carnal liberty[8], enormity, sin and babylonical confusion. Take away kings, princes, rulers, magistrates, judges and such states of God's order, no man shall ride or go by the highway unrobbed, no man shall sleep in his own house or bed unkilled, no man shall keep his wife, children, and possessions in quietness, all things shall be common[9]; and there must needs follow all mischief and utter destruction both of souls, bodies, goods, and commonwealths.

(355 words)

1 a serious attempt to persuade someone to do something; it is part of a homily which was read in church on Sundays throughout the reign of Elizabeth I – **2** has – **3** rains – **4** as it should be – **5** *bekommen vorgeschrieben und müssen respektieren* – **6** *Gemeinwesen, Gemeinschaft* – **7** reigns – **8** reference to sex outside marriage – **9** available to everybody

5.1.1 Get a Grip on Your Vocabulary – the Elizabethan World Picture

Study

As we said earlier, translating from German word-by-word produces "equal goes it loose"-English. This may sound funny but it will rarely get you the grades you need. You may want to pick up some more useful verbs and expressions.

"funny"	correct
In the main part the author *brings a lot of facts.*	In the main part the author **goes into detail.**
He has *engaged* himself for "Attac".	He has **committed** himself to "Attac".
We should not *look* too much TV.	We should not **watch** too much TV.

Practice 1

Find suitable verbs or expressions in English to fill the gaps below.

1. People in Shakespeare's time believed that the universe (God's creation) ____________________ **(darstellte)** a harmonious pattern that was based on a strict hierarchy.
2. Rebellion against the established order in one place ____________________ ____________ **(konnte zur Folge haben)** disturbances in other places.
3. The introductory first sentence of the entire paragraph **(liefert den Schlüssel für)** ____________________________________ our subdivision.
4. For emphasis the author **(verwendet)** __________________________ an adjectival triad: "in a profitable, necessary, and pleasant order" (l. 20).
5. Nature **(wurde so betrachtet als)** ________________________________ a visible expression of God's intentions.

6. In ll. 1–27 its author **(geht ins Detail)** ______________________ ______________________ about the order-disorder antithesis.
7. In ll. 19–25, however, **(ändert sich seine Perspektive)** ______________________ ______________________.
8. Here the author **(ist befasst mit)** ______________________ possible consequences that have to be faced.
9. The author's interesting choice of words **(dient dazu, zu unterstreichen)** ______________________ his religiously-tinged commitment *(religiös gefärbtes Engagement)*.
10. In fact *all* of Shakespeare's plays **(kreisen um)** ______________________ the order-disorder antithesis.
11. Let us **(als Beispiel anführen)** ______________________ the tragedy of "Macbeth" ______________________.
12. The doctrine of non-resistance and political thought at the time of the Elizabethans **(kann schwerlich genannt werden)** ______________________ ______________________ democratic.

Practice 2

Find smart translations for the words in brackets.

1. **(Wirklichkeit werden)** – We like to believe that our dreams may ______________________.
2. **(beruht auf)** – Success in life ______________________ talent, hard work, and luck.
3. **(uns auseinandersetzen mit)** – First we have to ______________________ the facts of life.
4. **(macht die Erfahrung)** – Everyone ______________________ that life is not a game.

5. **(hält sich an)** – The author of the "Exhortation" ______________________ the traditional Elizabethan world picture.
6. **(entspricht der Wirklichkeit)** – His view ____________________________ ____________________ of his times.
7. **(kontrastiert mit)** – The political system at the time __________________ ____________________ my own concept of democracy.
8. **(konstatiert)** – The writer of the "Exhortation" ______________________ that disturbances in one sphere might lead to chaos in others.
9. **(kritisiere an)** – What I ________________________________ this world picture is that modern human rights are entirely missing.
10. **(trägt bei zu)** – The author's choice of words ____________________ the provocative effect of the text.
11. **(bewirkt)** – What I believe is that the very existence of such a doctrine ____________________ a spirit of resistance and rebellion.
12. **(kommt mir vor)** – Such a doctrine ________________________________ very unrealistic.
13. **(ist zurückzuführen auf)** – Many historians say that it ________________ ________________ England's position of being surrounded by enemies.
14. **(wird deutlich)** – This _______________________ when you consider the political situation of the time.
15. **(Mit … ist gemeint, dass)** – The word "common" (l. 32) _______________ that everything is available to everybody.
16. **(ist voller)** – The text _____________________________ vivid examples.
17. **(bildet)** – The last paragraph ______________________ the climax of the text.
18. **(hat ihr Gutes)** – A perfect order _________________________, though.

5.1.2 Assignments

A) Comprehension

1
The above text is organized in *one* bulky paragraph. Subdivide it into smaller units as you think fit. Which are your criteria?

2
Which political (and cosmic) concept well known to 16th century Elizabethans does the text propagate and how is that concept justified?

3
How does the author's focus change in ll. 27–33 compared to what he points out in ll. 1–27?

B) Analysis/Comment

1
How does the author of the "Exhortation" try to elevate the idea he favours and how does he devaluate its antithesis? Consider his choice of words.

2
Does the doctrine of non-resistance, as it is frequently called, have any relevance for Shakespeare's plays? Refer to a Shakespearean drama you have studied.

3
From a modern point of view, what would you criticize about that belief? Comment.

C) Translation

Translate the following passage into German.

An Age of Invention, Discovery and Exploration

The Renaissance was an age of invention, discovery and exploration and perhaps the spirit of the age is best shown in the voyages of discovery. Christopher Columbus reached America in 1492, Vasco da Gama sailed round the Cape of Good Hope to India in 1498 and during the next century a host of Spanish, Portuguese and English sailors set off to explore the seas.

The reasons behind these voyages and the circumstances under which they were undertaken go a long way towards explaining what the Renaissance was. First of all, the Renaissance was an age in which man began to widen the horizons of his universe; the voyages of discovery were the geographical expression of this. Secondly, the Renaissance was an age of scientific invention and one of the most important inventions – although it had already been known to the Chinese for centuries – was the mariner's compass which allowed sailors to venture out into the open sea instead of following the coastline as they had done until then. Thirdly, the Renaissance was an age of growing trade between sovereign states; riches, until then unknown in Europe, were brought back from the Near and Far East and from the New World, as America was known at first. The city-states of northern Italy were the first to experience the new wealth (and, along with it, the power) which resulted from trade with the Near East. Capital was accumulated, banks were established and large-scale trading developed; this was the dawn of the Capitalist era. The circle is now full-drawn. Since the profits made from trade with the Near East were so great that not all the money was needed for re-investment in trade, money was also available for the arts and science.

The Renaissance, then, was the start of a new period of history; it was the beginning of our modern age. Profound changes took place in the economic system which, in turn, led to new developments not only in politics and diplomacy but also in culture and the arts. By the early 16th century, the Renaissance had reached its climax and was nearing its end in Italy, the country of its birth. In England, however, it had only just begun and it was to have its greatest influence there in Shakespeare's time.

(380 words)

5.1.3 Keep Your Language Errors in Check – False Friends

Practice 1

Translate into German.

1. My friend is a most **sympathetic** person.

   ____

2. If he is too much under pressure, he may **eventually** break down.

   ____

3. I've got another friend: he is the most **ordinary** chap I know.

   ____

4. At the same time he is very reticent and **self-conscious**.

   ____

5. His girlfriend is said to be a **sensible** girl.

   ____

Practice 2

Watch out for false friends.

1. **(Platz nehmen) –** Our host asked us to ______________________.
2. **(stattfinden) –** The exhibition was scheduled to ______________________ on Sunday.
3. **(auch keine) –** What you suggest is __________ a solution __________.
4. **(sinnvoll) –** I don't think that is ______________________ in this case.

Practice 3

Translate and beware of false friends.

1. Wir glauben, dass dieser Tag euch glücklich machen wird.
2. Er hat keine eigene Meinung.
3. Der Text lässt sich in fünf Hauptabschnitte unterteilen.
4. Im einführenden Teil stellt der Autor sein Thema vor.
5. Im Hauptteil bringt er viele Fakten.
6. Der Text soll den Leser beeinflussen.
7. Der Autor argumentiert einseitig.
8. Der Autor argumentiert konsequent.

5.1.4 Keep Your Language Errors in Check – Collocations

Study

Collocations are collections of words that "fit together", i.e. they are predictable patterns and phrases or groups of words that English speakers typically use together and that make a natural word partnership with each other.

that is to …	→ that is to **say**	das heißt
as it … to me	→ as it **appears/seems** to me	wie mir scheint
from my point …	→ from my point **of view**	von meinem Standpunkt aus
taking everything into …	→ taking everything into **account/consideration**	wenn man alles in Betracht zieht

Practice 1

Which verb fits best? Complete the following collocations.

a)

1. You are ______________________ things too seriously. Relax!
2. We need some more time. We'd like to ______________ our minds first.
3. He was a go-getter. He used every means to ______________ his aims.
4. Could you ______________________ the point now?
5. He is certainly the man to ______________________ that difficult situation.
6. She refused to comply. She ______________________ an attitude of defiance.
7. Hence it ______________________ that we are right.
8. The question ______________________ as to what can be done to help him.
9. A closer look ______________________ that things are not what they seem.

b)

1. You ______________________ an argument in a debate.
2. You ______________________ a solution to a problem.
3. You ______________________ proof of something.
4. You ______________________ a good/bad influence on another person.

5. You ____________________ a conclusion from something you see or read.
6. You _____________ an assumption as regards the outcome of something.
7. You _______ an explanation for something that is difficult to understand.

Practice 2

Translate these summative terminators.

zusammenfassend	**in** ____________________
um es kurz zu machen	**to cut a long story** ____________
mit einem Wort	____________________ **a word**
im Ganzen	**on the** ____________________
alles in allem	**(all) in** ____________________
kurz gesagt	**to put it in a** ______________
wenn man alles zusammen betrachtet	**all things** ________________

Practice 3

Fill the gaps to complete these collocations.

a)

1. **(tief beeindruckt)** – I was ____________________ by the author's main thesis.
2. **(mir lebhaft vorstellen)** – I could ____________________ the scenario he outlined.
3. **(deutet vage an)** – He ____________________ at the possibility of a new war.
4. **(kommentiert bitter)** – He ____________________ on the prospect of a new conflict.
5. **(weigere mich glatt)** – I ____________________ to accept our country's commitment.

6. **(erklärt präzise)** – The author ______________________________ what our options are.
7. **(immer schwieriger)** – It is becoming ______________________________ to negotiate peace.
8. **(völlig falsch)** – It is ______________________________ to stop working for a peaceful solution of the conflict.
9. **(nachdrücklich)** – I ______________________________ recommend listening to our political friends.
10. **(heftig; äußerst)** – I must object ______________________________; your proposition is ______________________________ unfair.

b)

1. **(überragend)** – Today's results are of ______________________________ importance to our team.
2. **(gering)** – For our opponents, on the other hand, they are of ______________________________ importance only.
3. **(sinnvoll)** – That's a very ______________________________ question to ask.
4. **(lebendig/anschaulich)** – He gave me a ______________________________ description of his father.
5. **(eng/vertraut)** – Here we have a very ______________________________ relationship among the members of the group.
6. **(angespannt)** – At home we can sense the ______________________________ atmosphere.
7. **(gemeinsam haben)** – A feature that both texts ______________________________ is their ironic undertone.
8. **(anständig)** – We are entitled to be treated ______________________________.

5.1.5 Writing Skills – Varying Sentence Length within a Paragraph

Study

Read the following paragraph: How does its author achieve an effect of coherence and emphasis?

Our Present Civilization

Our present civilization is a gigantic motorcar moving along a one-way road at an ever-accelerating speed. Unfortunately, as now constructed, the car lacks both steering wheel and brakes, and the only form of control the driver practices consists in making the car go faster, though in his fascination with the machine itself and his commitment to achieving the highest possible speed, he has quite forgotten the purpose of his journey. This state of helpless submission to the economic and technological mechanisms modern man has created is curiously disguised as progress, freedom and the mastery of man over nature. As a result, every permission has become a morbid compulsion.

Check the sentence-by-sentence break-up to see that, among other things, the author's skilful **variation of sentence length,** helps to create the effect of emphasis.

Our present civilization is a gigantic motorcar moving along a one-way road at an ever-accelerating speed.	← topic sentence (a debatable statement) = a short and straightforward main clause + a simple participle phrase
Unfortunately, as now constructed, the car lacks both steering wheel and brakes, and the only form of control the driver practices consists in making the car go faster, though in his fascination with the machine itself and his commitment to achieving the highest possible speed, he has quite forgotten the purpose of his journey.	← a longer complex developing sentence which consists of two "and"-linked main clauses (interspersed with a comparative clause and a relative clause) + an adverbial clause of concession (interspersed with an adverbial phrase)

This state of helpless submission to the economic and technological mechanisms modern man has created is curiously disguised as progress, freedom and the mastery of man over nature.	← fairly long developing main clause with a defining relative clause ← rhythmic triad
As a result, every permission has become a morbid compulsion.	← a sweeping main clause

Comment
It is indeed striking that the author, Lewis Mumford, prefers a very short (topic-giving) introductory and an even shorter (sweeping) concluding sentence. The two developing sentences that support his debatable statement are, by comparison, a lot longer and more complex. The effect of the writer's syntactic choices is doubtless one of unity and forcefulness.

Practice 1
Examine and comment on the syntactic choices of the following paragraph, which was submitted by an 12-grader, Gymnasium Zum Altenforst, Troisdorf. Pay special attention to the variety of sentences that the paragraph is composed of.

The Desire for Sensations I

The main reason that seems to drive people	______________
to watch daring and breathtaking events is	______________
their desire for sensations. Sensational events	______________
in general prove to be good material for	______________
conversations and chats. If, on a given day,	______________
one TV channel presents the pictures of	______________
someone jumping off a 150-feet cliff and	______________
diving into the water safely, this jump	______________
certainly will be the topic of conversations	______________
and chats on the other. Consequently people	______________
can brag about having seen it in the evening	______________

news, having watched the TV broadcast immediately after the jump or even having been at the scene of attraction itself, the cliff. By talking about a sensational event, one automatically draws attention to oneself. And this is something that few people can resist, of course.

Practice 2

Analyse and identify the sentence structures used in a paragraph submitted by another student that discusses why so many people seem to be interested in sensational events. Why does the paragraph make "poor reading"?

The Desire for Sensations II

Why are so many people drawn to events that are out of the ordinary? It is their longing to escape the dull and uneventful routine of their lives. The endless repetitiveness of their daily lives makes them hunger for a change now and then. This change should be sensational. It should also not be dangerous for themselves. They like excitement but it must not involve any personal risk for them. They like watching from the sidelines even better. They also do not mind watching catastrophes. Take the scene of an accident on the Autobahn, for example. You can see that car drivers in the opposite direction stop to get a good view of the damage done. They

block the traffic because they are curious. These are my reasons why I believe that ordinary people are highly interested in sensations.	

Practice 3

Feel like doing a little editing of your own? Rewrite the paragraph above to make it more readable.

Why are so many people fond of sensations whether they read them in the gutter press, watch them on TV or witness them with their own eyes?

They have been there and have a story to tell!

5.2 William Shakespeare, Henry V

Introductory note: ***Henry V*** *proposed to marry Catherine, daughter of the French King Charles VI, in 1415, demanding the old Plantagenet lands of Normandy and Anjou as his dowry (Mitgift). Charles VI refused and Henry declared war. The French war served two purposes – to gain lands lost in previous battles and to focus attention away from any of his cousins' royal ambitions. Henry possessed a masterful military mind and defeated the French at the Battle of Agincourt in October 1415, and by 1419 had captured Normandy, Picardy and much of the Capetian stronghold of the Ile-de-France.*
Before his war expedition to France to claim the French throne for himself, Henry V is afraid the Scots will exploit his absence to invade the north of England and dethrone him. The king's advisors ***Exeter*** *(Uncle to the King) and (the Archbishop of)* ***Canterbury*** *talk to the king about the risks of leaving England and going to war in France.*

Exeter: [...] For government, though high and low and lower,
Put into parts, doth keep in one consent[1],
Congreeing[2] in a full and natural close[3],
Like music[4].
Canterbury: Therefore doth heaven divide
The state of man in divers[5] functions,
Setting endeavour in continual motion;
To which is fixed, as an aim or butt[6],
Obedience: for so work the honey-bees,
Creatures that by a rule in nature teach
The act of order to a peopled kingdom.
They have a king[7] and officers of sorts;
Where some, like magistrates, correct[8] at home,
Others, like merchants, venture trade abroad,
Others, like soldiers, armed with their stings,
Make boot[9] upon the summer's velvet buds;
To the tent-royal of their emperor:
Who, busied in his majesty, surveys
The singing masons[10] building roofs of gold,
The civil citizens kneading[11] up the honey,

The poor mechanic porters[12] crowding in
Their heavy burdens at his narrow gate,
The sad-ey'd justice[13], with his surly[14] hum,
Delivering o'er to executors pale
The lazy yawning drone. I this infer,
That many things, having full reference
To one consent[15], may work contrariously;
As many arrows, loosed several ways[16],
Come to one mark; as many ways meet in one town;
As many fresh streams meet in one salt sea;
As many lines close in the dial's[17] centre;
So may a thousand actions, once afoot,
End in one purpose, and be all well borne[18]
Without defeat. Therefore to France, my liege[19].

(240 words)

1 agreement – **2** agreeing – **3** whole – **4** like an orchestra playing – **5** diverse – **6** target – **7** *read:* queen, head of the bee colony – **8** administer justice – **9** booty, prey, plunder – **10** workers – **11** *knetend,* i.e. forming wax – **12** hard-working labourers – **13** judge – **14** unfriendly, bad-tempered – **15** having full reference to one consent = being fully related by a common aim – **16** shot from different directions – **17** sundial, face on a clock – **18** well carried out – **19** lord

5.2.1 Some Clues as Regards English Style

Forcefulness and Fluency

Practice 1

Rewrite the following sentences to make them sound a) more forceful and b) more fluent.

William Shakespeare's use of metaphors is striking.
→ *William Shakespeare uses/employs a language rich in metaphors.*

1. The playwright has his character give a portrait of a bee colony.
2. By means of comparison a feeling of confidence is evoked in King Henry.
3. I am of the opinion that Canterbury's analogy is false.
4. The comparison between a bee colony and Henry's kingdom occurs in ll. 9–25.
5. In these lines the topic of order and obedience is enlarged on by Canterbury.
6. Later in the play, it is proved to Henry that his advisor has been right.

7. Shakespeare uses a rich metaphorical language, a fact which deserves to be mentioned since imagery is a typical poetic device the originality of which decides about the quality of the text, i.e. whether a piece of dialogue can be considered as interesting or boring.

Concreteness and Precision

concreteness:	Do not use vague or (too many) abstract nouns. Try to find exact words.
precision:	Exclude all unnecessary words. Try to connect your sentences by discourse markers. Try to stick to the tense you have chosen.

Practice 2

Rewrite the following sentences to make them sound a) more concrete and b) more precise.

a)

The character of Canterbury in the play "Henry V" **has some positive aspects**.

→ *The character of Canterbury in the play "Henry V" is that of a faithful and loyal subject.*

1. He behaves with a kind of deference to his King.
2. Comparing a beehive and the realm of England there are quite a few differences that should be mentioned.
3. The relationship between England and France is not a good one.
4. Canterbury describes England in a very positive way.

b)

1. He begins by describing the working of a beehive and, in the following, he **goes on to** encourage Henry.
2. The **final conclusion** can be found in l. 34.
3. Throughout his speech he **illustrates his point**.
4. The impression you get **is something like a discussion** between the king and his advisors.
5. **The ideas just mentioned** make me think of constitutional monarchy.

6. **The speaker's central problem can be expressed as** the question of whether to stay in England or to leave the country and go to war.
7. **According to his opinion** Henry's throne is safe.

Balance

You also should make sure that your sentences are balanced: Coordinated words/phrases take the same grammatical form. Parallel structures must be grammatically parallel.

Practice 3

Rewrite the following sentences by balancing them better.

1. The image in l. 12 not only suggests the bees' degree of organisation but also **that they have** a military to defend themselves.
2. The message Canterbury would like to impress on the King is **the safety of his throne** and that he need not worry about leaving his country.
3. What he says and **the things he means** are two different things.
4. He **both** praises England and its political stability.
5. By examining Shakespeare's imagery and **by the study of** his language in general you will understand the way he writes.
6. Canterbury explains the present situation and **that he is convinced that** Henry should go to war.
7. He expresses himself through vivid images but, sometimes, **abstract terms are used by him,** too.

Practice 4

German students' favourite verb is **"get".** Find a verb to replace "get" in each of the following sentences.

1. We **get to know** that Henry is about to leave England.
2. He tries to **get** some advice as to the wisdom of his mission.
3. As he speaks, Canterbury **gets** more and more involved.
4. Canterbury **gets** his message **across**.
5. This **gets** clearer as we read on.
6. Where can you **get** tickets for the Shakespeare play?

5.2.2 Assignments

A) Comprehension

1

Briefly state in your own words Henry's motive for going to war in France and his fears that make him hesitate to leave his country.

2

What is the advice that Exeter and Canterbury give their king and how do they try to dispel *(zerstreuen)* Henry's fears?

B) Analysis/Comment

1

Study the extended comparison that Canterbury draws and explain the cluster of images he uses. You may draw on your knowledge of the Elizabethan world picture.

2

Why can a bee colony perhaps be compared to the political system of a monarchy at the time of Shakespeare but not serve as a model for a modern western democracy like ours? Comment.

C) Translation

Translate the following passage into German.

Honeybees

Honeybees are social insects, living together in highly organized colonies. Each member has a specific job to do. A single honeybee cannot grow or survive by itself. The three distinct kinds of honeybees in a colony are queen, worker, and drone.

The queen is the longest bee in the hive but has the shortest wings. She is the mother of all the other bees. Her most important job is to lay eggs. Her productivity depends on the amount of food the workers bring in and the amount of brood space in the colony. She can lay more than 1,500 eggs a day.

Workers are smaller than the queen and drones, but there are lots of them. There might be only a few hundred during winter and early spring, but there are usually many thousands during summer when pollen and nectar are plentiful. A strong colony at full strength can have close to 100,000 workers. These bees keep the colony going. Workers' jobs change with their ages. Young bees, called house bees, do the hive chores. They produce wax and shape it into combs (structures of cells containing honey and brood) and use propolis (a gummy substance gathered from plants) to seal cracks or cover rough edges in the hive. House bees also fan their wings to ventilate the hive in summer, controlling temperature and humidity, and they provide heat in winter. Some guard the hive to keep out raiders. Many produce honey and royal jelly. A lot of time is spent feeding brood and cleaning and repairing cells. House bees also feed the queen, the drones, and each other. Older workers, or field bees, gather nectar, pollen, and water.

Drones are larger than workers but not as long as queens. A drone has large eyes that touch each other at the top of the head. Drones do not have stingers, pollen baskets on their legs, or glands for producing wax, and their mouthparts are too short to gather nectar. Moreover, they do not even do jobs they could like ventilating the hive. Their only function is to fertilize the queen, and they die in the process.

In many respects a honeybee colony is like a single animal. Individual bees and castes are like the cells and tissues. When one part is threatened, the whole colony reacts. If an essential segment of a colony becomes diseased or destroyed, the colony often can heal itself. It may divide and become two or more separate colonies.

(410 words)

5.2.3 Keep Your Language Errors in Check – a Mixed Bag

Practice 1

Check the verbs and correct the mistakes.

a)

The article can be understand as a warning against warmongers. ____________

Our attention is catched by the long list of gruesome facts about war reality. ____________

As always the author choses his words carefully. ____________

That war was a great risk; it has not payed off. ____________

The author has showed us which way to take in the years to come. ____________

b)

The text under discussion is about the problems our educational system faces with right now. ____________

Taken everything into consideration we'll have to make a complete U-turn. ____________

Nobody need to feel left behind if the financial stakes are raised. ____________

Success at school not depends on one's intelligence alone. ____________

The unexpected PISA results have made the school administrations' heads working. ____________

They did not understand what the results were meaning. ____________

They had heared about the Scandinavian countries top ranks. ____________

Practice 2
Correct the wrong word or expression in each of the following sentences.

Bend It Like Beckham?

In opposite to the members of her Indian family, ____________________
Jess loves football and worships David Beckham. ____________________
According to her family clan it gives no chance for ____________________
her to play for a local girls' team. ____________________
The prove can be seen in the way her mother ____________________
reacts when she learns that Jess plays football. ____________________
Jess argumentates with her mother but she has ____________________
to quit playing. ____________________
Jess gets to know her coach and she is fascinated ____________________
by his outlook. ____________________
When her team mate Jules finds out about Jess ____________________
and her coach, Jess has the baddest time of her ____________________
life. ____________________
Her sister's Indian wedding remembers her of ____________________
traditional Indian customs. ____________________
She feels she is old enough now and thinks she is ____________________
possible to stand on her own feet. ____________________
At one time in the movie there is nearly no ____________________
chance for her to continue playing on her local ____________________
team. ____________________
She is desperated until her father, who is more ____________________
understanding than the rest of her family, lets ____________________
her slip away to join her team and score the ____________________
winning goal with a Beckham-style free kick. ____________________

Practice 3

Find a synonym (word or expression of similar meaning).

1. The conflict needs to be **solved** now.	______________
2. That is certainly a **complicated** problem.	______________
3. He simply can't **make it clear to us** what he means.	______________
4. His unfriendliness **is due to** his lack of sensitivity.	______________
5. The author uses **pejorative** language.	______________
6. The protagonist's **way of speaking** is very offensive.	______________
7. **In sum,** the author supports monarchy.	______________
8. **The long and short of it** is that he won't be able to come.	______________
9. I can't agree. Your argument is **ill-founded.**	______________
10. Well. **I'm rather doubtful** if that is correct.	______________

5.2.4 Get a Grip on Your Vocabulary – Shakespeare

Practice 1

Complete the adjective phrases by adding the correct preposition.

1. Are you accustomed ____________ watching Shakespeare plays on stage?
2. I'm afraid I'm not familiar ____________ any of William Shakespeare's plays.
3. You are averse ____________ going to the theatre then?
4. I am still dependent ____________ my parents for my pocket money. I can't afford it.
5. Are you keen ____________ going to the movies?

6. That old guy Shakespeare in the movies? That information is new ___________ me.
7. Are you aware ___________ the fact that Shakespeare may be a guy from the past but that his plays are very modern?
8. He is concerned ___________ modern human conflicts such as love, hate, ambition and so forth.
9. I'm absolutely ignorant ___________ this fact.
10. And I am concerned ___________ your ignorance. He's especially good ___________ characterising people. He must have known a lot about us humans.
11. I am grateful ___________ you for telling me.

Practice 2

Check your spelling here.

1. A king is not ch_____sen but appointed.
2. He ch_____se the right life; he may ch_____se whether to keep the law or not.
3. My belie_____ is that man is independent; the belie_____s that were held at Shakespeare's time are outdated.
4. I belie_____e he is definitely wrong; belie_____ing is matter of faith; in my belie_____ that sounds odd.
5. He was afraid he might lo_____se his throne; and indeed he lo_____st it; winning is better than lo_____sing, right?
6. You fu_____fi_____ expectations; the text is fu_____ of images; I remember fu_____ well what it was like; a faithfu_____ friend; an awfu_____ experience; she has fu_____fi_____ed all my hopes.

Practice 3

Enlarge your vocabulary of analyzing Shakespeare.

a)

1. The author **(versichert)** ________________ / ________________ that disorder will result in chaos and destruction.
2. That can be **(kann interpretiert werden als)** ________________ / ________________ / ________________ as the manifestation of God's will.
3. Harmony will be **(zerstört)** destr______________; the end will be chaos and **(Zerstörung)** destr______________.
4. The author **(zählt auf)** ________________ / ________________ examples from all spheres of life.
5. Canterbury **(ermutigt)** ________________ Henry to trust his followers.

b)

1. Die Doktrin des Nicht-Widerstand-Leistens wurde nicht hinterfragt.

   ____

2. Dem Menschen wurde ein fester Platz in der Hierarchie zugewiesen.

   ____

3. Der Mensch ist zu komplex, um sich gehorsam in eine Hierarchie einzufügen.

   ____

4. Henrys Furcht davor, außer Landes zu gehen, sind tiefgreifend.

   ____

Practice 4

Do you remember these attudinal sentence adverbs?

1. **(Ganz klar)** ________________ the author supports the doctrine of non-resistance.
2. **(Zugegebenermaßen)** ________________, the Elizabethan world picture makes sense.

3. **(Zweifellos)** ____________________, Shakespeare must have been familiar with that doctrine.
4. **(Gerade herausgesagt)** ______________________________, I cannot agree.
5. **(Bedauerlicherweise)** ____________________, Henry is not very confident.
6. **(Offensichtlich)** ____________________, the Elizabethans understood very little about the world.
7. **(Sicherlich)** ____________________, Shakespeare is a master of language.
8. **(Nicht überraschend)** ____________________, Henry lets himself be persuaded to go to France.

Practice 5

Find a better version for the words and expressions printed in colour.

There are some **good points about** the Elizabethan world picture.	____________________
The "Exhortation" **shall** warn rulers and magistrates in Shakespeare's time of neglecting their duties.	____________________
As everything and everybody was assigned their firm place in the hierarchy, it was almost impossible for people to **get into a higher social position**.	____________________ ____________________
The doctrine was formulated to **get no conflicts** within the body politic *(Staat)*.	____________________
Chaos and destruction might **come up** if the laws were not respected.	____________________
A good king and ruler must **fight against** rebellion and unlawful behaviour in his realm.	____________________

6 The Changing Face of Britain

6.1 A Neighbourly Visit

Introductory note: ***Vic****, in his thirties, stocky*[1]*, broad shouldered, with large hands, and* ***Terry****, aged 17 or 18, his hair cropped to skinhead, dressed in regulation braces*[2] *and boots, are close friends ("blood brothers"). They occupy a groundfloor bedsitter*[3]*, which is sparsely furnished and decorated with some nude pin-ups and a German helmet and flag, together with a large picture of Hitler.*
Minutes before, they have played their radio with excessive loudness and stamped and banged the floor with their boots to disturb the second-year student ***Paul*** *who is living below them. Paul is gentle and slim, with longish hair and spectacles. Now Paul has knocked at their door to request them to be a little more quiet. He has been invited in.*

Vic: Now then … whatever you are. Do I understand that you're making a complaint of noise emanating[4] from this apartment?

Paul: No, not a –

Vic: Because, Mister Whatsit, if that is so, we shall have to look into the matter.

Paul: *(irritated)* Look, why don't we just forget it?

Vic: Ah, now then, that's not on, not on at all. We can't have blemishes[5] plastered all over our character at the drop of a hat, then just forget it. Hardly be democratic, would it?

Paul: I'm not accusing anybody. *(Paul stares at the floor, resigned and confused.)*

Vic: You see, Mister Terry Breedon and I have just dined out. Nothing extravagant or foreign, mind you, just a quiet tête-à-tête in the most discreet corner of a well-established English restaurant up West. Yes, top hole. A walk through the park, a taxi to the front door and into our apartment just in time to hear you slam – slam your door and pound up here to lodge this incredible complaint.

Paul: *(half moans, half sighs)* Ohh …

Vic: You tired?

Paul: No. I just want to go.

Vic: Good. So there was hardly time for us to … stamp, was it? And as for the radio … well, to put it in a nutshell, we haven't got one. So what do we make of that?

Paul: You know *damned well* what was going on!

Vic: Oh, language, please, please … Terry, do you know what to make of this gentleman's accusation?

Terry: Huh?

Paul: I want to go. *(Starts to turn but Vic is quickly on to him.)*

Vic: This may turn out to be a bother[6]. Eh?

Terry: Answer!

Paul: No.

Terry: No what?!

Paul: Thanks.

Vic: I did warn you, squire[7]. Mister Breedon's most particular, a dab hand at[8] good manners. Oh, yes. You'd be well-advised to tread carefully[9] in that direction … Apologise[10].

(Paul does not move.)

Terry: Let's bleeding[11] give him.

Vic: Gently, blood brother. I'm sure our guest will do the honourable thing. Apologise.*(Paul looks at Vic for guidance, points a finger back at Terry. Vic smiles and nods.)*

Paul: Sorry.

Vic: *(whispers confidentially)* Mister Breedon.

Paul: Mister Breedon.

Vic: Happy, Terry?

(Terry stares at the back of Paul's head.)

Paul: *(gestures helplessly with his hands before getting his words out)* I am just a student, second-year, living in the basement immediately below you. I am trying to work, but my concentration is continually broken by … a barrage[12] ... from this room at all hours of the day and night. I have not complained before, but it's affecting my work. I'm losing sleep.

Terry: *(with disgust)* Student!

Vic: Losing sleep, eh?

Paul: Yes.

Vic: Well, aren't we all?

Terry: *(his anger flaring up)* Heel[13]!

Paul: *(startled)* What?

Terry: *(viciously)* Heel! *(closing in)* Eh?

Paul: Don't talk to me like that, yobbo!

(Pause. Terry fetches a bicycle chain and crosses to stand over Paul, *the chain dangling from his hand.* Vic *draws in breath through his pursed lips[14] and expels it, shaking his head.)*

Vic: You really go over the top, Mister. Push your luck something rotten[15], don't you?

Terry: Fancies his chance, don't he?

Vic: I mean, I like spirit, yes, but in moderation, please. Where would any of us be without discipline? Goodness me, I mean to say, various gentlemen have been to great pains to convince me of the necessity of discipline, both self-imposed and the other. Were quite insistent, *and* government-backed. So I do speak with some authority.

Terry: Let me have him, Vic.

Paul: You'd better tell your friend to put this toy away.

Terry: Watch it, prat[16]!

Paul: Don't you dare touch me.

Vic: *(pleasantly)* Why not, Doctor[17]?

(Pause.)

Paul: I'm non-violent.

Vic: Pacifist, aren't we?

Paul: Yes. Not that it's any of your business.

Terry: Four-eyed git[18]!

Vic: Ah, now, Terry, easy. The poor Doctor's got his head in the books. Strains[19] his eyes.

Terry: *(showing the chain)* Wants this straining[20] around his head.

(Roy Minton, Bovver. 640 words)

1 short and strong – **2** *Standardhosenträger* – **3** room used for both living and sleeping in – **4** *(formal)* coming from – **5** *Makel, dunkler Fleck* – **6** i.e. Paul's swearing may be a problem because the friends are not ready to accept his rude language – **7** squire = sir (if you address sb. of higher social class) – **8** an expert at – **9** be careful – **10** i.e. for using bad language – **11** *(vulgar) verdammt nochmal* – **12** "gunfire" (of noise) – **13** command given to dogs to sit or walk close to their masters – **14** *gespitzte Lippen* – **15** push your luck something rotten *(slang)* = *seine Karten überreizen:* a reference to his having spent some time in a jail or in a remand home/a borstal *(Jugendstrafanstalt),* which relies on short and sharp "shock treatment" of juvenile offenders – **16** *(slang) Arschloch* – **17** a reference to the fact that Paul is a student at university – **18** wearing glasses; git *(slang)* = *Schwächling* – **19** *überanstrengen* – **20** *„gewickelt bekommen"*

"Thursday... kicked Terry's head in."

6.1.1 Keep Your Language Errors in Check – Prepositions

Handling English prepositions is not always easy. Here are some of the most frequent traps.

Practice 1

Choose the correct preposition from each "three-pack".

1. That's a text **(for/about/on)** ____________ British life in the 1970s.
2. The scene **(from/of/in)** ____________ "Bovver" **(of/from/by)** ____________ British dramatist Roy Minton was published in 1976.
3. It contains **(of/–/about)** ____________ a few references to Nazi emblems.
4. The cast of characters includes two young friends whose behaviour is typical **(for/about/of)** ____________ what in Britain is called "yob culture".
5. It is they, and not Paul, who are responsible **(for/of/–)** ____________ the confrontation in the first place.
6. It is very characteristic **(of/by/from)** ____________ Paul that he tries to settle the conflict peacefully.
7. Paul, for his part, sets a fine example **(for/of/in)** ____________ polite and moderate behaviour.
8. The neighbours discuss **(–/about/over)** ____________ the problem of excessive noise in the house.
9. The scene consists **(in/about/of)** ____________ heated verbal exchanges.
10. Can you prove this **(from/by/through)** ____________ the text by quoting relevant passages?
11. Can you illustrate Terry's thuggishness **(by/through/with)** ____________ quoting relevant lines?
12. What is your first comment **(for/about/on)** ____________ the opening scene?

Practice 2

Sometimes a word or phrase takes different prepositions to express different things. Some false friends are waiting in the wings for you here.

1. Can you **agree (to/with)** ____________ the author's view?
2. And what about you? Do you **agree (to/with)** ____________ him, too?
3. Roy Minton is **concerned (about/with)** ____________ the topic of resentment and aggressive behaviour.
4. I am truly **concerned (about/with)** ____________ the growing tendency of antisocial behaviour in our time.
5. In the play's scene, Vic pretends to **care (for/about)** ____________ good manners (l. 39) while Terry, for one, does not **care (for/about)** ____________ politeness at all.
6. Paul **asks (about/for)** ____________ some quiet so he can work.
7. I would like to **ask** you **(about/for)** ____________ your reaction to what happens in the scene.
8. It is not long before they have made Paul **angry (with/at)** ____________ them.
9. Paul certainly becomes **angry (with/at)** ____________ the way they needle him.
10. **(At/In)** ____________ **the end of** the scene Terry shows him the chain.
11. **(At/In)** ____________ **the end** Paul is willing to use violence, too.

Study

A special case: German **"bei"** and its equivalents in English: the English for "bei" is usually *not* "by".

bei jdm. zu Hause	**at** someone's (house)
bei (in der Nähe von) London	**near** London/**close to** London
das Kind ist bei seinen Eltern	the child is **with** its parents
bei Nacht/bei Sonnenaufgang	**at** night/**at** sunrise
beim Mittagessen/beim Frühstück	**at** lunch/**at** breakfast
bei näherer Betrachtung	**upon** closer examination
bei mir	**with** me/**for** me
arbeiten bei	work **for**
bei z. B. älteren Leuten	**with** e.g. elderly people
bei Filmen, Romanen, Theaterstücken	**in** films, novels, plays

Practice 3

Translate into good English.

1. **Bei** Paul sind gute Manieren kein Problem.

___

2. **Bei** Nacht oder **beim** Frühstück macht er keinen unnötigen Lärm.

___

3. Er verbringt viel Zeit **bei** seinen Freunden vom Studium.

___

4. Er wohnt eigentlich **bei** Leeds.

___

5. Paul hat einen Nebenjob. Er arbeitet **bei** McDonald's.

___

6. **Bei** Vic und Terry ist das etwas anderes. Sie sind arbeitslos.

___

7. Sie sind Parasiten. **Bei** näherem Hinsehen wird das klar.

___

8. **Bei** Filmen sind rebellische Jugendliche im Augenblick populär.

___

Practice 4

The use of the preposition "by" in English. Translate into German.

By [this word] the author means …	______
By this sentence the writer intends to show …	______
What do you mean **by that**?	______
The text **by Roy Minton** is called "Bovver".	______
Do we go **by car** or **by train**?	______
He took her **by the hand/arm**.	______
He contacted her **by phone/e-mail**.	______
You've got to play **by the rules**.	______
I did that all **by myself**.	______
By the end of the day we should be finished./**By the time we got home** we were tired.	______ ______
By the way, this is the last sentence in this practice.	______

6.1.2 Keep Your Language Errors in Check – Relative Clauses

Study

The German **"was"** is a special case:

German		English
Fragepronomen „was?"	→	what?
Relativpronomen „was"	→	which
relativer Anschluss „das, was"	→	that which *or* what
relativer Anschluss „alles, was"	→	everything that *or* what

Practice

Choose the right solution from the box above to fill the gaps.

Paul to Vic and Terry: "____________ are you doing in the middle of the night?"

That was exactly ____________ I had expected.

Terry had the chain in his hand, ____________ seemed to make him feel strong.

Terry asked Vic ____________ he was waiting for.

At the very end of the story the reader is informed of ____________ has happened in the car.

Paul is very polite, ____________ is supported by the way he addresses the two friends.

Terry wants to bully Paul, ____________ proves he is a thug.

Vic did ____________ he could to put the blame on Paul.

____________ initiates the action proper is Paul's first mentioning of the noise.

This is ____________ the two yobs have been waiting for.

This is precisely ____________ Minton succeeds in doing perfectly.

In Britain class has always been ____________ money is to America.

6.1.3 Assignments

A) Comprehension

1

A "neighbourly visit"? Characterize both the friends' and Paul's behaviour: how do they deal with their visitor? Make use of the vocabulary below checking them in your dictionary!

torment sb. · **scare sb.** · **terrify sb.** · **corner sb.** · **humiliate sb.** · **harass sb.** · **lean on sb.** · **intimidate sb.** · **tease sb.** · **taunt sb.** · **needle sb.** · **irritate sb.** · **exasperate sb.** · **annoy sb.** · **infuriate sb.** · **bully sb.**

schikanieren, piesacken
(ständig) belästigen
einschüchtern
„nerven"
Schrecken einjagen
sticheln gegen
verspotten, hochnehmen
reizen
wütend/rasend machen
demütigen
hänseln
in die Enge treiben
unter Druck setzen
ärgerlich machen
quälen, peinigen
ängstigen

2

"Yob" is what you get when you read the word "boy" backwards. Look up the meaning of the word in a dictionary and discuss whether Vic or Terry, or both, are part of the "yob culture" in Britain.

3

Why is the scene you have studied particularly suited as an opening scene to Minton's short play?

B) Analysis/Comment

1
Considering the clues we get as to Vic's background and behaviour, what is striking about the language he employs, and what is rather unsurprising as regards Terry?

2
Who is the more dangerous of the two? Comment.

3
Write Paul's letter of complaint to the Council.

Sirs,

I'm writing to draw your attention to ____________________

____________________ behaviour. They

____

around the clock. This is most ____________________.

The volume of ____________________ peaks between 9 p.m.

and 12 p.m., which, of course, coincides with ____________________.

I must express my own, and other residents', anxiety at ____________________

____________________. To make matters

even worse, ____________________

____________________.

I feel some sort of action is much needed here and long overdue. Otherwise I

would be forced to ____________________

____________________.

The ____________________

____________________ is at stake!

Please, accept my thanks in advance,

Paul Watson

4

"Yes," resumed the younger stranger [...]. "Two nations; between whom there is no intercourse and no sympathy; who are as ignorant of each other's habits, thoughts, and feelings, as if they were dwellers in different zones, or inhabitants of different planets; who are formed by a different breeding, are fed by different food, are ordered by different manners, and are not governed by the same laws."
"You speak of – ," said Egremont, hesitatingly.
"The rich and the poor."

Judging by the text passage from "Bovver", does the above description of 19th century England still hold true? Discuss.

5

At this point of the drama, Paul is certainly in a fix. What would you advise him to do?

C) Translation

Translate the following passage into German.

I'll Buy Houses and a Flash Car, Says Yob Awarded £ 567,000

A teenage criminal who received £ 567,000 in compensation after falling through a roof while trespassing boasted about his wealth yesterday, saying that he was looking forward to buying "a few houses and a flash car".
Carl Murphy, 18, got the payout last week, nine years after being injured in a 40 ft fall at a warehouse in Bootle docks, near Liverpool, prompting angry protests from crime victims and politicians. In his first public interview since receiving the award, Murphy – who has convictions for robbery, burglary and assault – said that he did not care about the response.
"I deserve this money and I don't care what anybody says about me," he said. "I'm going to buy a big house so I have a place to live with me mum when she

gets out of jail. I might buy a few houses – I'll buy whatever I want." He added: "The papers just call me a yob and a thug because I've been done for robbery and assault but those were just silly stupid little things, like. I want to spend my money the way I want without people interfering and I want to have a prosperous future. I want to take my mates to Liverpool games and get a flash car. This money is mine now and I'll do what I want. I don't care about anyone or what they have to say about it."

Murphy received his compensation after suing the company that owned the warehouse. He claimed that if the perimeter fence had not been in disrepair he would not have been able to gain entry and suffer his injuries.

Residents of Bootle, where Murphy lives, said that they were too scared to speak publicly about the case but privately described him as the area "king yob".

(310 words)

6.1.4 Writing Skills – Cause and Effect

Study

The cause and effect-relationship can be expressed in many ways.

How you emphasize **cause:**

The fact that →	drunken youths are causing mayhem in the streets →	cannot be called into question.
One reason for that **One cause of that** →	is that could be that →	drunkenness is now the acceptable sign of a good night out.
A second reason **A second cause** →	is that might be that →	antisocial behaviour and aggression and are fuelled by drink.
Some people also say →	this is because →	there are not enough police officers patrolling the streets.
The most important reason →	is probably that →	there is a total disregard for common decency.

How you emphasize **effect:**

There are those who claim that	there are not enough police officers patrolling our streets.	
As a consequence, Consequently,	there is a notable disregard for common decency in public among the young generation.	
One particular effect of this	is that	drunkenness is now the acceptable sign of a good night out.
Excessive consumption of alcohol among the young	**results in/ leads to/causes/ brings about**	antisocial behaviour and aggression, and this is where the police should step in.

Practice 1

Here is a short dialogue. Paul and Vic are having a debate about "yob culture" (Terry has no view on this): Can you make out what is the cause and what is the effect as regards the problem discussed?

Paul: "To me this rap music is at the bottom of the problem: it tells the young to rebel against anything, do drugs, and abuse women."	→ *Paul's cause*
Vic: "So, you think that getting rid of the rap music would solve the drug and other problems in our society?"	→ ______________
Paul: "Well, I do believe so."	
Vic: "Don't you think that most of the rap singers sing about that stuff because that is what is really going on these days? I mean, people often sing about the conditions of their time, just like the people did in the sixties."	→ ______________
Paul: "Well …"	
Vic: "Well, if there weren't all these problems, the rap singers probably wouldn't be singing about them."	→ ______________

Practice 2

Write a short paragraph in which you state your own view on the issue of rap music. In your argument, use some of these transitional words:

for causes	for effects
because, due to, one cause is, another is, since, for, first, second	consequently, as a result, thus, one result is, another is, therefore

Practice 3

Join these pairs of sentences in two different ways.

1. Have you thought of the upcoming class test? I can't go out tonight.

____

____

2. I haven't had much sleep. I'm in bad shape today.

____

____

3. Taking the class test is a risk. I should think twice before showing up in class.

____

____

4. Our family doctor will certify that I was ill. Perhaps I won't have to take the test then.

____

____

5. Our teacher refuses to accept the doctor's certificate. I'll have to do the test.

____

____

6.2 I Know the Hate That Comes with a Mixed-race Marriage

A few years ago I interviewed an extraordinary woman called Gill Danesh in Manchester. She was a strikingly beautiful former model. Her father owned a retail business[1] and he was devoted to his family. They were happy, they went to church, they lived decent lives.

Then she met Sayeed, an Iranian engineer who had left Iran after the revolution. He was tall, contemplative[2] and, like Gill, very good looking. When they decided to get married, her good girlfriends warned her that Arabs and other Eastern swarthies[3] were very good at captivating white women who were then turned into slaves and mercilessly brutalized. Men she knew at work said she was a slut.

Gill and Sayeed married anyway and had twins – a boy, who was fair with light eyes, and a girl, who had darker skin and looked like her father. When they were out, people treated the children completely differently. Matthew the boy would be admired and Sara, his sister, would be ignored. When they were 18 months old, Gill's father – who had held and kissed her babies – got drunk and accused her of contaminating the family bloodline by having mongrel[4] children. Later at school Sara was called a "Paki" and Matthew would get into fights to protect her. Gill said she simply had to believe that things would get better as time went on and more mixed-race families emerged across the country.

This was back in the Eighties, and in the 20 years since then much has changed. Today this country has one of the highest rates of mixed-race relationships in the western world, and I have written often about how the trend is unstoppable and that this is one of the most remarkable features of modern Britain.

But only the foolishly optimistic would take this to mean that there is now an overwhelming acceptance of these relationships. On the contrary. The increase in numbers only provokes those who, consumed with racial hatred or ideas of cultural and racial purity, feel entitled to use any means necessary to stop this "pollution". It is said that the losers during the last days of a battle often let rip[5] in appallingly brutal ways.

More and more victims of racial violence are of mixed-race or in mixed-race families. *[reference to nine cases of racial harassment, including celebrities, a book based on an authentic case, unknown number of unreported cases]* Mixed relationships face daily insults, comments, lack of respect, accusations which will never grab the headlines[6] but which, like low-level radiation, poison their lives and, in the end, ruin any chance of a half-decent future.

Ten years ago, I interviewed eight couples in what were successful mixed-race relationships. Today only three are together. We know that there is serious over-representation of mixed-race children in our care system[7], and forthcoming research by Dr. Ravinder Barn, of Royal Holloway College, will reveal why this is happening. Her interim findings indicate that low-income, white, lone mothers of mixed-race children are highly likely to put their children into care. And it isn't because these are bad and selfish mothers. Nurturing[8] stable families is hard even when all external conditions are propitious[9]. But if your own family or community expect the worst outcome (even if they smile, attend the wedding and wish you well) an evil spell is already cast.

Everyday problems become racial. You find yourself thinking in hateful ways. A friend who has three mixed-race children says she despises herself but cannot take the darkest one with her when she goes to her posh hairdresser. Another woman I know has resorted to telling people that her child is adopted. As a lone parent, she found the racism directed against her intolerable.

I have been dropped from guest lists by Asian friends I cared about a great deal. Maybe it is because they find me boring and quarrelsome, but I have long suspected that it is because they feel uneasy about my English husband. Like many others who have made the choice to marry out, I have no regrets, but it is exhausting and at times very painful to be in a relationship which is still regarded by society as outside the norm and which makes so many want to kill and maim you and yours.

They should remember, however, that no impediments – not apartheid, not lynchings or burnings – have ever been able to frighten off the passion which drives people to break down social barriers and get together for better or worse[10].

(Yasmin Alibhai-Brown, I Know the Hate That Comes with a Mixed-race Marriage. 750 words)

1 *Einzelhandelsunternehmen* – **2** *nachdenklich, besonnen* – **3** swarthy *(adj.) = dunkelhäutig* – **4** a dog that is a mix of several different breeds – **5** *(coll.) „loslegen"* – **6** *Schlagzeilen machen* – **7** *staatliche Fürsorge* – **8** *ernähren, aufziehen* – **9** *günstig* – **10** part of the marriage vows

6.2.1 The Feature Story

Study

These are component parts of a **feature story:**

- **The anecdotal lead:** it is often the best because it gives readers a character with whom to identify and action to grasp. In directed reporting, an anecdotal lead is a **specific mini-story** that begins teaching the reader about the nature of the overall problem.
- What comes directly after the lead goes by many names – point statement, theme-paragraph, thesis, justifier – but the pungent journalistic expression is **"nut graf".** Generally following an anecdotal or descriptive lead, the "nut graf" gives the **basic news value** and describes the significance of what the reader has just been shown. The "nut graf" is vital because it explains that the story is not about an isolated incident, but that many people are affected. If there are two paragraphs the first serves to lay emphasis on the second.
- **The body of the story:** the goal in a good story is to **convey information** in support of the point made in the "nut graf". Logical transitions contribute to the cause of moving readers from one item of information to the next. Key points of emphasis, i.e. the most emphatic locations, are the beginnings and ends of sentences, paragraphs, and stories.
- **The ending:** endings give readers a **sense of closure** and a sense that the writer knows what he is doing. The summary ending is functional but weak. A metaphorical ending works well to evoke a response by placing the problem reported on in some other cultural context. The nail-it-shut quotation has one of the persons quoted strongly elucidating the story's central theme. The circular ending brings back for a final look a central character of the article to increase reader identification.

6.2.2 Assignments

A) Comprehension

1

Sum up Gill and Sayeed's story (100 words).

2

What is the author's central statement?

B) Analysis/Comment

1

Look at the "Study" above. Can the text be labelled "feature story"? Why or why not?

2

If you contemplated a "mixed" relationship, would you be encouraged by the article or deterred?

C) Translation

Translate the following passage into German.

Mixed-race Children

The census in 2001 was a milestone for people of mixed-race in the UK – for the first time a "mixed" category was included among the racial groups. It followed a long campaign by those opposed to having to tick a box marked "other". But researchers say though the existence of mixed-race people may now be officially acknowledged in statistics, serious concerns remain.
Yasmin Alibhai Brown, author of a recent book "Mixed Feelings" examining the issues facing children of mixed-race, said one major worry was that many organizations and public bodies in Britain had adopted policies from the U.S.
"The movement started there to claim all mixed-race children as black – the argument was if they suffer racism nobody asks them if they're mixed-race. But I think big mistakes were made to drive policy makers and practitioners into accepting this rather ludicrous concept because mixed-race children aren't black and they're not white or brown – they are themselves," she said.
Often mixed-race children lived with white mothers who in many cases were the victims of racism from both whites and blacks, Ms Alibhai-Brown added.
[...] Yasmin Alibhai-Brown believed in spite of the difficulties faced by some couples the trend of mixed-race partnerships was likely to intensify.
She said: "More and more black and Asian and Chinese people will be marrying whites and each other. There is no stopping this, it seems to me. I hope it makes this country become more comfortable with its hybridity as a national characteristic."

(255 words)

6.2.3 Keep Your Language Errors in Check – Word Order

Study

Take another look at the diagramme in chapter 2.1.1 about word order.

Practice 1

Put the words in the right order.

1. In the lead of the feature story / are presented / two characters.

___

2. This / can / you / trace / in ll. 1–16.

___

3. For example / writes / Alibhai-Brown / that / they / two twins / had.

___

4. She / discusses / in her feature story / the current issue / of mixed-race relations.

___

___

5. In the second paragraph / is / the life / described / that Gill Danesh and Sayeed lead.

___

___

6. The relationship / between / Gill's father and the two kids / is / from the grandfahter's side / cool.

___

___

7. Gill's father / sees / in them / "mongrel children".

___

8. This behaviour / can / you / only call / racial discrimination.

___

Practice 2

Translate into English and pay special attention to word order.

1. In Großbritannien sind die meisten gemischten Ehen zu finden. (~~are the highest rates of mixed-race marriages to find~~)
2. Alibhai-Brown löst das Problem für sich, indem sie an die Kraft der Liebe glaubt. (~~solves for herself the problem~~)
3. Sie beschreibt in ihrem Artikel ein Problem von aktuellem Interesse. (~~She describes in her article a problem~~)
4. Jeder assoziiert mit gemischten Ehen Schwierigkeiten für die Kinder aus diesen Ehen.
5. In einer multikulturellen Gesellschaft leben alle ethnischen Gruppen friedlich zusammen. (~~In . . . live all ethnic groups together~~)
6. Im Text wird gesagt, dass die Idee der Rassenreinheit immer noch sehr stark ist. (~~In the text is said that~~)
7. Den Artikel schrieb Alibhai-Brown im Jahre 2000. (~~That article wrote Alibhai-Brown~~)
8. Die Autorin hat die ganzen Jahre gegen Diskrimierung gekämpft. (~~The author has all these years fought~~)

6.2.4 Get a Grip on Your Sentence Building – Reference

Study

Careless sentence building on your part may leave the reader confused (and your teacher not amused). The reference *(logischer Bezug)* must be clear.

reference is unclear or incorrect	reference is clear
Blowing their horns, **the main roads were** congested with cars. *(Do main roads blow their horns?)*	The main roads were congested with cars blowing their horns.
We locked all doors and windows **afraid of burglars**. *(Can you imagine windows afraid of burglars?)*	Afraid of burglars, we locked all doors and windows.
I regret insulting her **deeply**. *(Do you insult sb. deeply or regret sth. deeply?)*	I deeply regret insulting her.
Dressed in the latest fashion, **I** had the impression all the girls were models. *(Who is in fact dressed in the latest fashion?)*	I had the impression all the girls were models dressed in the latest fashion.

Practice 1

The reference is unclear or incorrect. Rewrite the sentences.

1. The Prime Minister tells the BBC correspondent that he (?) will announce the new tax plan soon.

___

___

2. The PM's tax cuts make sense because they (?) think that they (?) are necessary.

___

___

3. He stated that no matter how much they (?) earned would have to pay more taxes.

____

____

4. His spin doctor's advice: if the higher taxes bother the people, cut them (?).

____

____

5. At one time the PM was a student in Oxford which (?) many people still remember.

____

____

6. Having studied (?) the speech must be regarded as poor rhetoric.

____

Practice 2

These sentences sound confusing. Rewrite them.

1. When reading the text for the first time, it seems rather difficult to understand.

____

____

2. The climax of the story comes in the last paragraph. Nevertheless one can find other climaxes, too, but these are not so striking.

____

____

3. The atmosphere is dark and gloomy from the outset and one can compare it to the room in the other story we read.

____

____

4. In contrast to the ten first lines which are marked by a general tone the author then goes into detail.

___

___

5. The example means that, since nobody is perfect, he should be forgiven that he behaved in the wrong way, which is what the author wants to say.

___

___

TIP You should always make sure that the reference in your essay writing is clear, especially when you use personal pronouns!

6.2.5 Writing Skills – How to Organize Your Thoughts

Study

Take another look at the second diagramme in chapter 1.1.2.

Practice

Take three different-coloured text markers to mark each of the three different levels in the following text on the article by Yasmin Alibhai-Brown. Designate (1) text references, (2) verbs of meaning and discourse markers, and (3) the reader's conclusion.

Yasmin Alibhai-Brown constructs a lead of the anecdotal kind in that she tells the mini-story of British-born Gill Danesh and the Iranian engineer Sayeed (ll. 1–16). This is meant to give us a clue as to what she will discuss in her article. The issue itself is a very moving one (social ill).

The following two paragraphs (ll. 17–30) constitute what journalists typically call the nut graf. Alibhai-Brown describes the significance of what we have just read: the personal fate of the couple mentioned in the opening paragraphs is put into the larger perspective of British attitudes towards interracial relationships. Her message is that an increasing number of such relationships over the years have provoked deep misgivings in British public and private life. In the first of theses two paragraphs she alludes to the fact while, in the second, she puts forward her main thesis ("appallingly brutal ways", l. 36). This statement is supported by the body of her story (ll. 31–64). Alibhai-Brown's illustrations (and personal conclusions) include her references to various other cases, the fact that, to her knowledge, a minority of these relationships "survives" (three out of eight interviewed couples, ll. 43–44), an expert's forthcoming research results, and evidence from the author's personal experience and her own situation within the Asian community. Thus her approach is broadened considerably.

Her final paragraph provides an emotional answer to those who are still opposed to interracial marriages: love will prevail over hatred and discrimination. She as an Asian journalist alludes to the Christian marriage vow (ll. 67–68) to demonstrate that she identifies with them.

Answer Key

1 Survival of The Prettiest

1.1.1

Practice

Doreen compares herself unfavourably with "E. M.".
Her father appears to favour an alternative lifestyle and **"gives all our money away" (l. 23).**
The fact that she cannot afford to buy the clothes she craves makes her feel that **she "do[es]n't know how to dress at all" (ll. 14–15).**
And, finally, she apparently does not "sail through" school. **("I'm here because I failed PE", l. 25).**
Unlike the famed Elizabeth, Doreen, for another, feels ugly, she describes herself as fat. **This can be traced in ll. 14–15.**
She worries about her facial skin problems **("my face is all broken out", l. 16).**

1.1.2

Practice 1

	This is what the connecting words used here aim at:
In the story "Elizabeth Montebello Is the Prettiest Girl in School" Doreen **portrays herself** as a hopeless 16-year-old high school student.	← the story is a "self-portrait"
The way she describes her own shortcomings **suggests** that she is not very self-confident.	← reader's conclusion
The school's star, Elizabeth Montebello seems to have it all: she **is said to be** an attractive girl, very popular among her peers	← we see her through Doreen's eyes
and, on top of that, **what we call** an "A" student.	← reader's conclusion
Unlike Elizabeth, Doreen **comes across** as somebody who complains about her looks and her clothes.	← reader's impression
This clearly reveals that she is very unhappy with her personal situation.	← reader's conclusion
As regards her shyness and reserve **we view her as** the type of girl who is commonly known as a wallflower.	← reader's overall impression
It should, however, be mentioned that she will have her chance: will she live up to it?	← reader emphasizes important aspect

Practice 2

Unlike Elizabeth, Doreen **comes across as** somebody who complains about her looks and her clothes.
This clearly reveals that she is very unhappy with her personal situation.
The way her father treats his daughter **borders on** neglect.
The fact that he "gives all our money away" (l. 23) **is indicative of** his out-of-touch attitude.
To put it bluntly, he seems to be a deluded ideologist.
It is hardly surprising, therefore, that Doreen feels left alone.
My explanation is that Doreen's father has never been young.
There is some evidence to suggest that Doreen is not an insensible girl.
The fact that she plans to talk to Elizabeth the following day **suggests** that she has "guts".
It is safe to say that Doreen will come to grips with her life.
It is no coincidence that Doreen admires E. M.
It is true that she is full of self-pity **but** she will grow up one day.
Her present unhappiness **can be put down to** false ideals within our society.
I come to the conclusion that Doreen is very unhappy.
This is due to the fact that she does not feel understood at all.

1.1.3

A)

1

(Compare 1.1.1 Study)

2

There is no denying that Doreen herself compares unfavourably with "E. M.".
She feels she is at a disadvantage because, for one, she has a father who is at odds with her own outlook on life and who, evidently, does not recognize her wishes and needs: he appears to favour an alternative lifestyle and "gives all [their] money away" (l. 23).
What is more, Doreen, unlike the famed Elizabeth, feels ugly. She describes herself as fat, though not obese (ll. 14–15) and worries about her facial skin problems (l. 16). The fact that she cannot afford to buy the clothes she craves makes her feel that she "do[es]n't know how to dress at all" (ll. 16–17). And she apparently does not "sail through" school since she has to make up for a failed PE course in summer school.
So, it can be said that Doreen seems to miss precisely what she finds in her admired peer *(Altersgenossin)*.

3

In summer school, the two girls meet again: Elizabeth as a voluntary to qualify for early college admission and Doreen because she has to make up for a failed PE course. It is here, in a different environment, that Doreen's role model notices her and, eventually, talks to her. Doreen remembers the date with utmost precision (l. 34). And, characteristically, it is a fashion item that arouses the other girl's interest: Doreen's "Hello Kitty" book bag, the "nicest thing" (l. 36) she owns. A girl needs the right outfit to catch somebody's eye, Doreen's point. For once, she feels "as if we were total equals" (l. 37) and she ponders whether she should address Elizabeth the next day. The idea does not strike her as an easy one, though. She feels the need to prepare herself for it.

B)

1

The short story "Elizabeth Montebello Is the Prettiest Girl in School" is told in the first person. The narrative point of view is that of first-person central. The first person narrator lets us in on her most private thoughts and feelings. The personal diary is a very natural text form that allows a person to jot down what he or she feels and thinks.
The only other form suited to the narrator's purpose would be an interior monologue. Choosing that format, the narrator would "record" spontaneous feelings and associations, fragments of thought as they pass through her mind. This would be clearly reflected in her syntactic choices. We might expect to get bits and pieces, sometimes incoherent, sometimes difficult to understand, and incomplete or clipped sentence patterns.
In Doreen's narrative, this is apparently not the case. She tells her story in complete sentences. The sentences are, however, not connected. Take, for example, the story's third paragraph (ll. 8–13). Doreen describes "E. M." and how she herself closely watches what her role model does. She also critically reflects on her (stalker's) role. The predominant sentence pattern is the short main clause, not linked in terms of cause and effect, for example. Two exceptions (coordinated by "and", (l. 8) and by "but" (l. 13)) prove the rule. This, it might be argued, is the way you write diary entries: you put some order into your thoughts, yet you do not organize them like you would do in a piece of writing meant to be read by other people.
A second example can be found when you look at ll. 34–38 where Doreen records the breakthrough moment for her coveted relationship to Elizabeth. Precise dates and word-for-word dialogue plus private assessment of what has happened can be considered as characteristic of "diary style".
Although Doreen does not explicitly mark her narrative as one or several diary

entries (she only mentions once "that I wrote in my diary", l. 2), she clearly tells her story in a style that might pass as a diary entry. It might be added that the way she confesses what is troubling her fits the format very well.

2

(Compare 1.1.5 Practice, model essay)

3

Wondered whether talking to her was such a good idea when I woke up this morning. But then this was the chance of a lifetime.
Over my glass of orange juice I thought about what I would say to her. Gosh, I was nervous. I would ask her where she went to buy her clothes, the sexy skirts she wore all the time and those cool tops. Once she would realize how interested I was in her personal style, she might get interested in me, too, I thought. I kept my fingers crossed.
Guess what! I'm sitting in my room now. It's 11 p.m. E. M. is not only the prettiest girl I know she is also the nicest pal I have ever met. She remembered noticing my Hello Kitty bag and she asked me where I had bought it. Said she would like to have one, too. Picture that. Elizabeth Montebello asking *me* about things like that! And then something happened I'll never forget. Back home again, she said, the two of us might go on a shopping spree together. She would take me to her favourite boutiques. That made my heart jump. I can hardly find words for what I felt. E. M. and myself doing something together. It's a dream!
I am not worried about money right now. There's my Dad after all. I'm sure he will understand. The only thing I worry about is whether E. M. will not be disappointed in me. I must shine like she does.
This is going to be the best summer of my life. Really. Gotta go now. Get my beauty sleep.

C)

Warum Schönheitssalons dem Himmel für kleine Mädchen danken
Mütter, die ihre erst fünfjährigen Töchter zur Gesichtskosmetik und Maniküre bringen, haben einen schnell wachsenden, neuen Markt geschaffen
Laura Lilly klettert am liebsten auf der Welt auf Bäume. Die Siebenjährige ist stolz auf ihre Geschicklichkeit: Sie kann den Apfelbaum in ihrem Garten hinter dem Haus höher hinaufklettern als irgendeine ihrer Freundinnen.
In den nächsten Tagen aber wird sie auf keine Bäume klettern – am Freitag brachte ihre Mutter sie zu einem örtlichen Schönheitssalon für eine Maniküre und Pediküre. „Nachdem ich eine Schönheitsbehandlung bekommen habe, möchte ich mich benehmen wie eine Erwachsene und auf mich aufpassen", sagte sie. „Meine

Mutter sagt, ich sehe aus wie eine kleine Dame, und so möchte ich mich jetzt auch benehmen."
Kleine Mädchen waren schon immer von Make-up-Täschchen fasziniert, aber sie schrauben ihren Ehrgeiz jetzt höher. Mehr Mütter, die das Beste für Klein-Chloë oder Klein-Gemma wollen, bemühen sich um Schönheitsbehandlungen für sie, und ihre Töchter haben angefangen, nach Behandlungen für Schönheitsprobleme zu fragen, die sie vielleicht ehemals nie festgestellt hätten.
Schönheitssalons für Mädchen im Vor-Teenager-Alter schießen in Großbritannien aus dem Boden, da man einen lukrativen neuen Markt wittert, der, wenn er erst einmal erobert ist, für Jahrzehnte verlässlich funktionieren wird. Sogar die konservativen Schönheitssalons führen Behandlungen für erst Fünfjährige ein.
Experten sorgen sich, dass der Trend das zunehmend belastete Verhältnis der Frauen zu ihrem Selbstbild weiter negativ beeinflussen wird: Eine Umfrage durch das „Social Issues Research Centre" in Oxford förderte zutage, dass bei Frauen die Unzufriedenheit mit ihrem Aussehen in sehr frühem Alter beginnt. „Kinder fangen an, sich mit zwei Jahren im Spiegel zu erkennen, und weibliche Wesen fangen nur wenige Jahre später an, das, was sie sehen, nicht mehr zu mögen", stellte der Bericht fest.
Eine von der Zeitschrift „Bliss" durchgeführte Umfrage unter mehr als 2000 weiblichen Teenagern ergab, dass 92 % unglücklich über ihren Körper waren und eins von vier Mädchen Essstörungen gehabt hatte.

1.1.4

Practice

Sixteen-year-old Doreen felt deeply misunderstood by her father. He **made it clear to her** that she could be anything she wanted to be. He **wanted her to wear** recycled clothes and he still **tries** to teach her what counts in life. "We **aren't allowed to** waste our natural resources," he **said**. Doreen did not know what that **meant**. She **had heard** about environmentalists but she did not share her father's alternative views. She **wasn't afraid** of the future. She **thought she was** her mother's daughter.
Like her mother, Doreen has different ideals. Her attention **is caught** by the pretty Elizabeth Montebello. She **hasn't seen** a girl like her before. Elizabeth Montebello is the girl to make her fellow students **feel** envious. Elizabeth **cannot** imagine how shy she makes girls like Doreen when they are face to face.
Doreen **is sent** to summer school where she meets Elizabeth again. Elizabeth compliments Doreen on her Hello Kitty bag. That is the moment Doreen **has been waiting** for. Will this be the beginning of a wonderful friendship?
In this story, the author **has shown** us how important "cool" looks and smart

clothes are for young girls. This text **can be understood** as a warning against the hype that is presently made about people's outward appearance.

1.1.5

Practice

There is no question that the clothes young people choose to wear must be regarded as an important means of self-expression. ← **introduction**

However, is the hype that is presently being made about what to wear a good thing? ← **discourse marker: controversial topic**

To begin with, in an age which values "cool" looks, personal attractiveness and, consequently, expensive clothing styles, the worries about "how do I look" do not come as a surprise, especially among the young – and among those who do not want to grow old. The role models are everywhere: In films, on TV, in the glossy magazines that spill out of the racks. ← **discourse marker** ← **topic sentence: first main idea**

But do I really express myself when I copy or even ape *(nachäffen)* the style dictated by trendsetters and showbiz celebrities? I am not convinced. ← **discourse marker: antithetical**

What is more, there is nothing to be said against "communicating through the clothes I wear" and what statement I want to make about myself. Equally, "feel good" clothes certainly help to boost one's well-being and, therefore, one's self-esteem. ← **discourse marker** ← **topic sentence: second main idea**

Yet can we **really** agree to the idea that a dressing style "makes" the person? Must we not insist that it matters where a person "stands", i.e. a person's mind, views and attitudes, and not how the person is "decorated"? What counts is substance – rather than styling. ← **discourse marker: antithetical**

Last but not least, what do we think about incidents – as reported in the papers – in which the violation of a particular dress code accounts for "freezing out" the person that does not conform? To my mind, it is ← **discourse marker** ← **topic sentence: third main idea**

intolerable that a person is rejected solely for wearing the wrong piece of clothing, or for being unable to pay for the right brand. Here a point is reached where "expressing oneself" and "communicating through clothes" are overdone and where hype turns into harm.	
No doubt, the issue of how to dress up for the occasion and of how "to fit in" matters. It often decides about being "in" or being "out".	← **conclusion**
The point is, though, that the present trend clearly overrates the importance of clothes.	← **discourse marker**

Teacher comment: The "weight" of the main ideas as they follow one after the other suggests an order from less important to more important: (1) "expressing myself" through imitation? – (2) "cool" clothes boost self-esteem – (3) self-expression and communication are overdone.
So do the expressions signalling the author's personal opinion (1) I am not convinced, (2) What counts is …, (3) To my mind it is intolerable; and the discourse markers used in the main body of the text: To begin with – what is more – last but not least. It follows, therefore, a climactic order.

1.2.1

Practice 1

1. answered – 2. speaks – 3. talks – 4. watches – 5. describes – 6. cannot – 7. haven't – 8. divided – 9. reaches – 10. heard

Practice 2

1. really – 2. awful – 3. always – 4. fulfil – 5. character – 6. separate – 7. than – 8. believe – 9. opinion – 10. their

1.2.2

Practice 1

1. A lot of authors **warn of** a development that could be dangerous.
2. Brad Adams, a New York City photographer, **maintains** that a hundred percent of fashion photos are retouched.
3. He **asserts** that usually eyes and teeth are whitened, make-up and skin problems corrected and that the hair is made shiny.

4. He **disapproves of** the fact that models that are already thin are made to look even thinner.
5. He **is convinced of** the idea that despite dieting and the help from personal trainers models still do not look good enough for the industry.
6. Another New York City photographer **assumes** that also movie stars receive a "digital diet".
7. She **underscores** the fact that even celebrity snapshots as they appear in "People" magazine are retouched.
8. She **points out** that "Photoshop", a widely used software programme, can digitally narrow hips, enlarge breasts and make any change look realistic.
9. From that she **concludes** that it is all a fake.

Practice 2

1. She **wants** her readers **to** – 2. She **argues** that – 3. Bordo **presents a good argument** when – 4. young girls **despair** when – 5. **There is no chance** to talk – 6. **provides facts** how – 7. **goes to full lengths about** how – 8. Bordo **takes** this problem very **seriously**. – 9. she **goes into particulars/provides some/a lot of concrete detail.** – 10. she **argues abstractly/remains on an abstract level**.

1.2.3

Practice 1

- … characteristically, … → **discourse marker**
- … fashion item that arouses the other girl's interest → **reader's conclusion**
- … "Hello Kitty" book bag, the "nicest thing" (l. 27) she possesses. → **text reference**

Practice 2

italics: quotes, text references, details
blue: discourse markers, connecting verbs
bold: reader's thoughts and conclusions
There is no denying that *Doreen herself* **compares unfavourably with** *"E. M."* **She feels she is at a disadvantage** because, **for one**, *she has a father* **who is at odds with her own outlook on life** and who, **evidently**, **does not recognize her wishes and needs:** he **appears to favour an alternative lifestyle** and *"gives all our money away" (l. 23)*. **Unlike** the famed Elizabeth, Doreen, for another, **feels ugly**, she **describes herself as** *fat, though not obese (ll. 14–15)* and *worries about her facial skin problems (l. 11)*. **The fact that** she **cannot afford to buy the clothes she craves** *makes her feel that she "do[es]n't know how to dress at all" (l. 16)*. And she **apparently does not "sail through" school** since *she has to make up for a failed PE course in summer school.* **So, it can be said that** *Doreen* **seems to miss precisely what she finds in her admired peer**.

Practice 3

The opening sentence of Bordo's text **contains** the word *why* (in italics), **which indicates that** the author **is concerned with** finding the reason(s) for the interviewees' preoccupation with "getting fat" (l. 7). In the second paragraph, Bordo **fine-tunes the issue** she is going to tackle ("So, too, we need to explore that fact that", l. 17). **By** "exploring" she **understands** finding the causes for the effect that "it is women who are most oppressed by what sometimes **is called** "the tyranny of slenderness" (l. 18). In the following, she **points out** that the wish to gain control over one's body "derives from two sources", l. 22). The word "source" can **be equated** with causes. Having established her pattern of thought, Bordo **proceeds to discuss** the two sources in detail.

1.2.4

A)

1

In the extract from "Unbearable Weight: Feminism, Western Culture and the Body" the author Susan Bordo refers to a survey saying that what a considerable number of people were afraid of most was gaining overweight (ll. 2–3). Furthermore, she points out that the ideal of feminine beauty has undergone a radical change as compared to the post-war period ("femaleness embodied" by Marilyn Monroe, l. 16). Nowadays, especially women are exposed to what she calls "the tyranny of slenderness" (l. 18). These are facts, she argues, that need to be investigated.

2

As Bordo sets out to explain these facts, she provides two different reasons (or "sources", l. 22) that can account for the present body cult. For one, drawing a parallel to bodybuilders and "compulsive runners", (l. 25), she maintains that the slenderness craze can be put down to the people longing to clear all physical obstacles in their way, i.e. to "make it". For another, the motive behind the startling trend is said to be the desire to "control" oneself in a world that allows them so little control over "events outside themselves" (l. 40). Being able to "master" (l. 21) their bodies and to re-invent themselves physically gives them pleasure (l. 38) and dominance over their lives (ll. 41–42).

3

Here is what you can find in the text:

(l. 1) What we need to ask is *why* …

(l. 17) …. So, too, we need to explore that fact that …

(l. 19) Most strikingly, …

(l. 22) … derive from two sources.
(l. 23) First, …
(l. 26) Second, and most dramatic, …
The opening sentence of Bordo's text contains the word *why* (in italics), which indicates that the author is concerned with finding the reason(s) for the interviewees' preoccupation with "getting fat" (l. 7). In the second paragraph, Bordo fine-tunes the issue she is going to tackle ("So, too, we need to explore that fact that", l. 17). By "exploring" she understands finding the causes for the effect that "it is women who are most oppressed by what sometimes is called the "tyranny of slenderness" (l. 18). In the following, she points out that the wish to gain control over one's body "derives from two sources", l. 22). The word "source" can be equated with causes. Having established her pattern of thought, Bordo proceeds to discuss the two sources in detail.
Interestingly, the author chooses to reverse the common pattern of *cause* first and *effect* second in that she starts out with two very striking societal *facts*, or *effects*, which she proposes to "explore", i.e. to explain, or account for. This is meant to involve the reader from the start.

B)

1

This is, of course, another "open-ended" question with the student's answer depending on his or her personal outlook in the matter.
If you tend to subscribe to Bordo's view, you might argue that

- they personally know such body control freaks among their friends and acquaintances,
- they, in a way, find it unfair that outward appearance is overemphasized and that "beautiful" people generally have an easier life in the job market as well as in their partnerships,
- given the progress in genetic engineering, they see the danger of science tinkering with our bodies looming *(dräuen)* on the horizon.

If you are not inclined to follow Bordo's argument, you might argue that

- they feel Bordo exaggerates as she speaks of "fears", "oppression" and "tyranny" in western cultures where still so many children and adults are overweight and where a lot of people are not physically fit,
- they think Bordo's comparison of bodybuilders, runners and anorectics to "sculptors" and therefore "artists" goes too far because people who exercise and who cut back on food want to be and stay healthy,
- they are convinced that especially women who are slim and nice to look at are more self-confident themselves and, therefore, happier.

2

Hi, Charlie's Angel:
It would seem to me that there are other ways of being accepted in school and to make friends than by impressing people with being thin. Can we be sure that making friends by starving ourselves into "perfection" will attract the right people? I think rather not. Let us girls get tough and show those Barbie characters how stupid they are. Let us be ourselves. It's all about girl power! Let *us* decide about what we believe is a nice body and what makes us attractive. Do not let the media industry and the surrounding society dictate to us what we are supposed to look like, i.e. unnaturally boyish waifs *(knabenhafte Gestalten)*. That is degrading.
Charlie's Angel 2

3

There is no question that "cool" looks, personal attractiveness, and (physical) fitness are highly valued by so many who strive to appear and stay young forever. Youthful icons of beauty abound in the media and elsewhere, and the idea of getting a "perfect" body is becoming increasingly popular. The present trend, however, has its advantages as well as its drawbacks.
For one thing, there is nothing to be said against healthy activities such as jogging, working out and exercising in order to lose weight. Excessive overweight not only tends to make people look ugly but may, in the long run, endanger their health. Yet, when the desire to lose weight becomes compulsive *(zwanghaft)*, slimness may turn into skinniness and emaciation *(Abmagerung)*. And what is so beautiful about that?
For another, it cannot be denied that a slender body may make people feel better, i.e. more attractive, and increase their well-being, but "dictating to nature one's own chosen design for the body" (ll. 35–36) is a claim that borders on the insane. Such a wish can hardly be considered healthy.
Most importantly, however, can we regard starving ourselves into "perfection" as control over ourselves and our bodies? Once we have taken the road of cutting back on food, the whole thing may easily become an eating disorder. The name of this disorder is anorexia. It is a recognized illness. What starts as an exercise in self-discipline, often triggered by peer pressure or by the wish to be socially accepted and to be popular, can quickly end in serious harm.
No doubt, the issue of slenderness is an important topic, especially for young women who feel urged to "make themselves attractive" to males. Nevertheless the present obsession with physique and thinness must be seen as a symptom of a society that is on the verge of becoming sick.

C)

Massenmedien und der weibliche Körper

Heranwachsende Mädchen erfahren heutzutage mehr Veränderungen als vor 15 Jahren. Es gibt mehr Möglichkeiten für abweichendes Verhalten, was auch gefährlicher ist als jemals zuvor. Dr. Pipher erklärt, dass junge Mädchen durch ihren Wunsch, sich in die Gesellschaft einzugliedern, verunsichert werden. Dieses Verlangen lässt sie in einen Konflikt mit dem Wunsch, sie selbst zu sein, geraten. Wenn Mädchen in der Pubertät sind, beginnen sie, sich von einen Körper zu distanzieren, von dem sie das Gefühl haben, dass er sie verrät: breiter werdende Hüften und Gewichtszunahme, ohne dass sie dies verhindern können. Dies widerspricht den Bildern, die sie aus den Medien kennen: eine fast vorpubertäre Figur ohne Hüften oder zusätzliches Gewicht. Pipher glaubt auch, dass die Gesellschaft, zu der sie gehören wollen, von den Mädchen verlangt, feminin zu sein, oft auf Kosten ihres menschlichen Wertes. Jeff Morrison hat gesagt, dass er glaubt, dass Mädchen versuchen, sich in die Gesellschaft einzugliedern, indem sie ihre naheliegendsten Autoritäten (Eltern und Lehrer) zurückweisen und sich nach Medienvorbildern ausrichten, die ebenfalls fremde Autorität negiert haben, wie z.B. Madonna.

Gegenwärtige Schönheitsnormen sind sehr schwer zu erfüllen: der bevorzugte Wunsch 11–17-jähriger Mädchen ist es, „dünner zu sein", und eine junge Frau zwischen 18 und 34 hat eine vernichtende Chance von 1 %, so schlank wie ein Supermodel zu sein. Wie Karen Schneider vom Magazin „People" meint, fordern die gegenwärtigen Schönheitsnormen von den meisten Frauen, dass sie fast verhungern. Wer ist also für solche Normen der „Schönheit" verantwortlich zu machen? Als Dr. Pipher's Patientin, die 15-jährige Cayenne, gebeten wurde, sich Fernsehprogramme speziell im Hinblick darauf anzuschauen, wie Frauen dargestellt werden, fand sie heraus, dass das Fernsehen selten ältere, mollige oder unscheinbare Frauen zeigt. Frauen, die Ärztinnen verkörpern, könnten auch im „Playboy" posieren, und weibliche Charaktere werden mit einer höheren Wahrscheinlichkeit Opfer von Gewaltverbrechen als männliche. Nach einer von Mediascope durchgeführten wissenschaftlichen Studie hat eine Frau, bis sie das 17. Lebensjahr erreicht, durchschnittlich über 250 000 Reklamespots in den Medien gesehen. Bei einer Untersuchung von Trickfilmen, die am Samstagvormittag gezeigt wurden, fanden Wissenschaftler heraus, dass 50 % der Reklamespots auf junge Mädchen zielten und davon handelten, wie man attraktiv ist; andere Studien haben herausgefunden, dass 50 % der Werbung in Teenagerzeitschriften das Versprechen von Schönheit als Kaufreiz einsetzen. Mediascope fand auch heraus, dass in der Werbung gezielt unerreichbare Ideale eingesetzt werden, weil dies den Gewinn erhöht. Die Industrie für Schlankheitsprodukte erzielt gegenwärtig $ 33 Milliarden Gewinne pro Jahr, eine Tatsache, die die Wirkung einer solchen Kampagne untersteicht.

2 Two Glimpses of the American Dream

2.1.1

Practice

1. The text says that the hotel looks like a theme park. – 2. Everyone associates casino resorts with Las Vegas. – 3. This world can be called a great illusion. – 4. They solve that problem by positioning a cowboy by the lake to assist the guests. – 5. That statement can be found in l. 45. – 6. The author writes, for example, that the doormen are disguised as U.S. cavalrymen. – 7. Henderson's search for his hotel room is described in the second part./It is in the second part that Henderson's search for his hotel room is described. – 8. In the end, he climbs into the canoe. – 9. He would try anything not to have to spend the night at the hotel. – 10. It was in 1984 that the author William Boyd wrote that text. – 11. As regards American hotels, both the pros and cons are presented in that text. – 12. The entire text is based on facts.

2.1.2

Practice

1. He **finally** decides to park his car and walk up to a side entrance. – 2. What alarms Henderson, **though,** is something else. – 3. **Ironically,** the modern hotel guest can relive the "old American West". – 4. **Strikingly,** there are some Indian maidens running about in mini-skirts and serving drinks. – 5. **Interestingly,** there are rooms which are called "Convention Reservation" or "Swimming Creek". – 6. The whole arrangement is, **undoubtedly,** a total illusion. – 7. **Generally (speaking),** the Monopark 5000 looks like a Las Vegas casino. – 8. The hotel guests have to take risks, **yet** a host of employees make sure that the untrained guests do not come to harm.

2.1.3

A)

1

The narrator intends to spend the night at Atlanta's Monopark 5000 Hotel. He tells that he has considerable difficulties driving up to the hotel since he finds himself stuck in the confusing "system of one-way streets" (ll. 2–3) of downtown Atlanta.

The hotel complex, one of the modern high-rise structures in glass-and-steel, looms large but, although he can see it, he seems incapable of approaching it by car: it strikes him as unreal ("a massive illusion", l. 7). So he finally decides to park his car and walk up to a side entrance.

2

According to the description Henderson gives, the Monopark 5000 Hotel appears to be an enterprise of enormous dimensions (5000 beds?) that boasts all the comforts and conveniences an international hotel can provide: abundant service personnel trained to make the guests feel at ease (ll. 25, 51, 65), a computer-based reception desk to facilitate check-in and check-out procedures (ll. 25–28), modern-day plastic key cards for maximum security (ll. 28–29), state of the art *(auf dem letzten Stand der Technik)* elevators (l. 59) and, indispensable *(unvermeidlich)*, a continual feed *(eine unaufhörliche Berieselung)* of pleasant background music (l. 44). The narrator is truly impressed ("with due reverence and awe", l. 21).
What amazes or, rather, disconcerts him, however, is something else. It is the theme park-like, if artificial, atmosphere the hotel management has chosen to create to make their guests savour their time at the hotel ("Enjoy your stay …", ll. 33, 78). Ironically, the modern hotel guests can "relive" the "olde West" (l. 46) exploring and "opening up" their trail *(Fußweg)* to the hotel rooms. America's "rugged" *(raubeinig)* frontier myth seems to be back: the proud U.S. cavalry in the lobby, the Indian village (bar area), the canoes to cross a lake and the assistance given by good-natured cowboys. Equally important, the scenery is "spiced up" by suggestive, mini-skirted cowgirls and Indian maidens (complimentary [*kostenlos*] drinks)!
The obvious paradox of the environment is best illustrated through some of the special facilities provided: one wonders if a "convention" of doctors or, say, computer scientists is likely to be staged on a barren "reservation" (l. 45), or if the present-day wellness freak prefers a "creek" (l. 46) over a heated indoor pool.

3

The narrator, on entering the "vast" (l. 15) building and approaching the reception desk, confesses that he is struck with awe (l. 21), which gives way to feelings of doubt (l. 35), surprise (l. 61), incredulity and anxiety (l. 82) as he begins to take in the "frontier challenges" he has to face while accessing *(den Weg finden zu)* his room: The humble guest "… felt like an explorer leaving base camp" (ll. 37–38). Plunged into *(eingetaucht in)* what strikes him as a place full of magic ("wands of sunlight", l. 14), he is reminded of a cathedral. He seems so impressed that he has a vision of himself appearing before his Maker to account for his bad and good deeds (l. 22). Confused and, ultimately, unconvinced, he decides to play along.

B)

1

What immediately springs to mind when reading Boyd's text is, of course, the famous casinos and hotel resorts in Las Vegas, Nevada. Out there in the desert, Vegas hoteliers have created countless artificial "paradises" such as the one described by the narrator. Take "Caesar's Palace" and the "MGM Grand", or more recently, "The Venetian". They have all been built to stir people's imagination and to provide them with maximum comfort and entertainment. And the concept seems to work if you consider that Greater Las Vegas is said to grow by about 3,000 to 5,000 new residents per month and that, every year, a double digit number of new hotel resorts are added to the already existing variety on and off the "Strip".

2

William Boyd's episode from "Stars and Bars" is meant to illustrate a modern-day lifestyle that is embraced by many fellow Americans (and aped by so many others in the world at large). It is favoured and sought after by people who appreciate all the indoor comforts and conveniences a sophisticated hotel and holiday industry furnishes while longing for that extra bit of outdoor adventure to make things happen in their otherwise uneventful lives.
Monopark 5000's easy-going and hospitable ambience is clearly Vegas-standard. First-class accommodation in large, luxurious, air-conditioned rooms provided by the management and quality food and drinks at reasonable prices served by friendly and ever present staff leave nothing for the guest to be desired. A good place to relax and spend a quiet evening at the bar: "Enjoy your stay at Monopark 5000" (ll. 33, 78). Everything is centered on the customer's well-being. Let the hotel cater for his every need.
This is of course standard with international hotel chains. And here is where the theme park concept comes in. Your stay at a casino resort, say, in Vegas, is transformed into an "event", into an adventure you will remember. At "Caesar's Palace", for example, you may step into "living history", i.e. meet the Emperor in person, and at "The Venetian" you may stroll along the "Canale Grande" with a "gondoliere" singing away. Monopark 5000, in turn, has recreated the "olde West" and a whiff of life on the frontier from America's pioneering days. Paradoxically, the historical frontier was not noted for its easy-going, risk-free life but, if historians are to be believed, posed great dangers for the individual and required the spirit to survive in an uninviting and cruel wilderness. Individual "challenges" have to be met, too, as the Monopark guests access their rooms. These challenges, however, are merely simulated as is the entire complex, a world of make-believe. The thrills are there, at least for the simple-minded, yet a host of friendly people

make sure that the untrained guests do not get in harm's way.
So, the British author William Boyd can be said to point out an apparent incongruity that characterizes many Americans: while they still hang on to the idea of proud self-reliance and a spirit of "can-do", they are not prepared to do so without enjoying the blessings of civilization and being pampered in every imaginable way.

3

To the foreign visitor the United States may appear as a country where nothing is impossible. He must be prepared to see contradictions that are amazing. The safety-minded Americans' fascination with adventurous "themes" appears to be one of them. It is this paradox that the British author William Boyd pokes fun at.
For one, imagine the hotel's doormen and bellboys decked out in U.S. cavalry uniforms (ll. 17–18) or waitresses in miniskirts, disguised as Indian maidens (ll. 49–50) and you will get the point. This fancy dressing act is ridiculous.
For another, some of the guests, at least, seem to think otherwise ("… a lot of our guests like to make their own way", l. 71). An American couple whom the narrator ironically calls "intrepid" (l. 72) rush headlong into the adventurous crossing of the lake. The good-natured cowboy discreetly watches over our "Westerners" so their daring does not lead them astray. Sympathetic that I am to *(obwohl ich … gut finde)* the friendly open-mindedness of Americans in general, this child-like behaviour makes me laugh.
Finally, the narrator himself seems taken aback by what he stumbles upon. Once he has left "base camp" (ll. 37–38) to "explore" the territory, he admits that he is alarmed (ll. 49–50) and, later, reacts "with a gasp of surprise" (l. 61). Early on, he has a sudden vision of himself "appearing at Heaven's gate" (l. 22) to be judged for his sins! This is, by all means, exaggerated, an incongruity that cannot be taken seriously.
The hotel episode, therefore, carries what I would call a satirical undertone. By pointing out the obvious incongruities of the situation, William Boyd humorously exposes one American idiosyncrasy.

C)

Die vier erfolgreichsten Boomregionen

Die vier laut einer Umfrage des „Inc. Magazine" erfolgreichsten Boomregionen – Atlanta, Georgia, Riverside, Kalifornien; Las Vegas, Nevada; San Antonio, Texas – sind allesamt in republikanischer Hand. Und von den hundert Gemeinden Amerikas, die am schnellsten wachsen, hat Bush nicht weniger als 97 gewonnen. Viele dieser Siedlungen hat es vor fünf Jahren noch gar nicht gegeben. Es sind Instant-Orte, städtebauliche Readymades, die David Brooks, Kolumnist der New York Times, der „Lieblingskonservative der Liberalen", wie er mitunter genannt wird, in

seinem neuen Buch „On Paradise Drive" als „Exurbia" beschrieben hat.
Ohne Bush oder den Irak je zu erwähnen, skizziert Brooks die Bewohner von Exurbia, das wachsende Wählerreservoir der Republikaner. Es sind Menschen, die, wie der Publizist im Untertitel seines Buches schlagwortartig formuliert, „immerfort im Futur leben", den Blick fest auf die Zukunft gerichtet, auf den Weg nach vorn. „Über-Moms", ehrgeizige Mütter, die schon ihre ungeborenen Kinder mit Mozart beschallen, um ihnen einen Vorsprung in der Musikschule zu sichern; College-Studenten, die vor lauter Kursen und außeruniversitären Aktivitäten gar keine Zeit mehr finden, sich zu verlieben; Manager auf der mittleren Ebene, die wie besessen Bonusmeilen sammeln, und ihr Leben der Perfektionierung einer einzigen, winzigen, profitträchtigen Innovation zu widmen bereit sind.

2.2.2

A)

1

On September 11, 2001, beginning at about 8:45 in the morning, a series of terrorist attacks destroyed the twin towers of the World Trade Center and severely damaged the Pentagon. Commercial airliners were hijacked and flown directly into the three buildings. The first crashed into the North Tower at 8:45, and about 18 minutes later the second airliner hit the South Tower. At about 9:40, a third airliner crashed into the Pentagon. At about 9:58, the South Tower collapsed, followed by the North tower at 10:28.

2

In this extract from his Second Inaugural Address delivered on Jan. 20, 2005, George W. Bush focuses on the terrorist attack of Sept. 11, 2001 in New York and Washington D.C. (l. 5) and how this traumatic event has shaped the country's vision of the future.
Bush conjures up the "mortal threat" (l. 10) posed by the (Islamist) "ideologies that feed hatred and excuse murder" (l. 8). Against this enemy he pits *(in Stellung bringen)* the American ideology, i.e. he juxtaposes *(kontrastieren)* tyranny and "the force of human freedom" (l. 12). He considers this as a question of survival for his country as he points out that "the survival of liberty in our land increasingly depends on the success of liberty in other lands" (ll. 13–14). This can be regarded as George W. Bush's (and America's) foreign policy doctrine, namely the right and the duty to export the idea of America (democracy) to the rest of the world. Its ultimate goal is "ending tyranny in our world" (l. 27). He casts America as the friend of burgeoning *(aufblühend)* democratic movements all over the world promising help to the willing but also hinting at America's clout *(Macht)* to pursue her goals with force ("America's influence is considerable, and we will use it confidently in

freedom's cause" (ll. 38–39). This aggressive policy is certainly dictated by the need to protect his country against further attacks by its enemies, but, above all, it is defined as a moral choice – the moral superiority of expanding "human rights" (l. 51) and fighting the forces of "oppression" (l. 44).
In doing so, Bush links up with America's foundation as laid down in the Declaration of Independence and the Bill of Rights.

3

The extract from George W. Bush's Second Inaugural Address is clearly within the tradition of American presidents addressing the American public (and the world). I should like to concentrate on items (1), (5), (7) and (8).
From the very start, the speaker tries to evoke common experiences shared by speaker and audience: he shortly recalls what (most of) his listeners have witnessed during their lifetime: America's glorious role in WWII, the downfall of communism, the years of relative quiet and, finally, Sept. 11, 2001 (ll. 2–5). It is his reference to the terrorist attacks on America (9/11) that serves to strengthen the emotional bonds to his audience ("We have seen our vulnerability", l. 6), whose full support he needs for the mission that America has to fulfil. This mission proclaimed by other presidents before him and reiterated by Bush is dictated by "America's vital interests" (l. 17), i.e. her territorial security, and, even more so, by America's deepest beliefs. These beliefs (freedom, justice, basic human rights and self-government, ll. 17–22) lend to *(verleihen)* the United States a moral superiority to take on *(bekämpfen)* terrorist movements (al-Qaida) and tyrannical regimes all over the world (Iraq, North Korea, Iran) and, ultimately, bring about the triumph of democracy, if needs be, by force of arms (ll. 25–27).
Throughout the speech extract Bush elevates his (and America's) "most solemn duty" (l. 40) and his country's morally justified course of expansion of ideas, and he bluntly devaluates his (and America's) opponents calling them ignoble *(schändlich)* and reprehensible *(moralisch verwerflich)* "tyrants" (l. 11) or "bullies" (l. 47) and "dictators" (l. 51), who deprive their own people of "freedom, which is eternally right" (l. 45).
References to religion (l. 20), the American history (ll. 17–24) and to the will to make sacrifices (ll. 28–29) can easily be traced in the text as well.

B)

1

Two of the most effective devices used by Bush to add emphasis to his words are parallelism and antithesis. An example of syntactic parallelism can be traced in l. 6 ("*We have seen* our … and *we have seen* its …"). The speech contains further examples of semantic parallelism in ll. 25, 30, and 6. Equally, the speaker makes

ample use of antithesis: in ll. 1–2 he states that "our duties are *not* defined *by the words* I use, *but by the history* we have seen together". In ll. 33–35 Bush underscores the idea of American power and influence by antithesis. The most obvious example, however, occurs in ll. 44–45 when Bush elevates America's moral superiority and devaluates her enemies' moral stance ("eternally *right* vs. always *wrong*"). The speech also includes numerous examples of parallelism and antithesis combined. Ll. 13–14 are a case in point: "The survival of *liberty in our land* … depends on the success of *liberty* (parallelism) *in other lands* (antithesis)." Further examples of parallelism + antithesis can be found in ll. 18–19 and in ll. 21–22.
Rhythmic triads are a particularly effective stylistic means to balance spoken sentences. The speaker repeatedly uses this device in the passage under review. His reference to "*years* of relative quiet, *years* of repose, *years* of sabbatical" (ll. 4–5) may be quoted here. While this appears to be rather simple triad, there are more complex triads to be found, too: "… violence will *gather and multiply* … and *cross* … and *raise* …" (ll. 8–9) and "Freedom must be *chosen* … and *defended* … and *sustained* …" (ll. 29–31). A final example echoing the possessive pronoun "their" can be traced in ll. 34–35.
Last but not least, I should like to point out a very moving rhetorical choice on the part of the speaker to create a firm bond between himself and his audience: his use of the "fire" image in l. 5, "and then came *a day of fire*" is the reference point of the whole passage transcribed here (and of the entire address). The speaker alludes to the disastrous events of Sept. 11, 2001. Rhetorically, he prepares the powerful image by antithesis in that he juxtaposes the long period ("years") of relaxation, of peace and of well-being in the 1990s to the "day" on which the terrorists struck America. Technically, this passage is a masterstroke of persuasion, as is the entire passage under discussion.

2

Historically, America, after the Second World War, rose to be one of two world powers. Pitting herself against the other dominant power of the time, the Soviet Union, the country saw this balance of power change dramatically with the downfall of the communist countries in 1991, leaving the United States as the only remaining power to have her say around the globe. In spite of that, the 1990s witnessed the emergence of terrorist movements, in particular the Islamist movement known as al-Qaida. While it seemed that America, owing to her economic strength and her military clout, would enjoy a long period of hegemony disputed by no one and nowhere around the globe, the Islamist movement continued their build-up and – finally – struck America in her homeland. The ensuing traumatic shock led to a permanent feeling of being threatened by further terrorist attacks and, consequently, to the philosophy of pre-emptive strikes to defend America's freedom "in other lands", as Bush says, its purpose

being to impose democracy in regions seen as undemocratic. This is "the calling of our time", as Bush puts it.
While it may be argued that the underlying reasons for the Bush Administration's aggressive policy of bringing freedom and democracy to the oppressed nations (Iraq) may be the concern to bring down terrorism and the determination to control access to oil resources in the Middle East, it should not be overlooked that America's fundamental beliefs are at stake here: "America's vital interests *and our deepest beliefs* are now one" (l. 17).
America's admirable foundations laid down in the Declaration of Independence and the Constitution (democratic principles such as self-government and the consent of the governed, basic human rights such as life, liberty and the pursuit of happiness, the civic freedoms of the Bill of Rights) have always been understood as a mission. They have, from the start, been interpreted as a promise to be shared by mankind and, therefore, to be expanded irrespective of other nations' political persuasions and systems.
America's self-awareness of being the world's only remaining superpower, on the one hand, and her deeply rooted conviction of being in a position to tell others what "is always wrong" and what "is eternally right" (ll. 44–45), on the other, have merged, for the Bush Administration, into one. At this point, America is perceived, by us Europeans, as arrogant and overbearing in its use of power and as inconsiderate in her dealings with her transatlantic friends.

3

As distinguished guests of your high school, we appreciate the honour of being invited to participate in today's debate.
Let me say beforehand that our country – Germany – has been, and still is, deeply grateful for what the American people have done for us in the past. I am talking about your country's tremendous effort in delivering us from the Nazi regime in WWII and about your help in rebuilding Germany in the aftermath. We would especially like to thank former President Bush Senior for his support in reuniting our country in 1990.
We consider ourselves to be America's friends, not only because of the most generous support we have received from you but also because we share basic political and cultural values that both our countries rest upon. The more so after what your country has been through since Sept. 11. We do understand and share your concern about the terrorist threat.
Friends must prove their metal in difficult times. Good friends must understand criticism as it is meant among friends. Close friends must be prepared to listen and to put up with dissenting opinion when it comes from people they trust.
There has been controversy in our country over the course of American foreign policy in recent years. Nobody in our country sympathized with a dictator called

Saddam Hussein. Not everybody in Germany felt that the Iraq mission was an inevitable one. Some believed, and still believe, that other diplomatic roads might have been explored before the *ultima ratio* should have come into play. And we don't blame them.
Sadly, our American friends missed European (especially German) support – except for Britain and Spain – and decided to go it alone. The Iraq crisis does not seem to be resolved.
Consulting her transatlantic friends in this particular situation might have helped America to consider her long-term policy options and the consequences resulting from it.
However, we must look to the future. Are you ready to listen to what good friends may want to tell you?

C)

Amerikas Demokratiedefizit
Sind die Vereinigten Staaten wirklich eine Demokratie? Die Frage diesseits des Atlantiks aufzuwerfen, mag absurd oder fast unverschämt erscheinen. Die amerikanische Verfassung beginnt mit den Worten „Wir, das Volk" und definiert Macht deutlich als etwas, das von unten nach oben fließt, nicht von oben nach unten. Dennoch hat seine eigene Bevölkerung so wenig Interesse an ihrer vermeintlichen Demokratie, dass sie sich selten der Mühe des Wählens unterzieht.
Zudem wird Millionen von Amerikanern das Wahlrecht nicht nur deswegen entzogen, weil sie gegenwärtig aufgrund von Verurteilungen, die weit höher als in jedem europäischen Land sind, im Gefängnis sitzen, sondern auch, weil in manchen Bundesstaaten eine frühere Verurteilung, sogar für ein nichtgewaltsames Drogenvergehen, genügt, um jemandem das Wahlrecht auf Lebenszeit zu entziehen. Es erübrigt sich zu sagen, dass solche Leute überwiegend arm und schwarz sind.
In manch anderer Hinsicht sind die USA weniger demokratisch, als es aussieht. Wenn auch die Pressefreiheit und die Gesetze zum Schutz der Informationsfreiheit mächtiger als in Europa sind, sind andere Freiheiten, wie z.B. die Rechte der Arbeiter, sich in Gewerkschaften zu organisieren, geringer ausgeprägt.
Die gravierendste und grundsätzlichste Schwäche in Amerikas Demokratie besteht in der Tatsache, dass seine Politiker und Parteien nach normalen Maßstäben korrupt sind. Diese Wahrheit wird durch die Offenheit des Systems größtenteils verdunkelt; es gibt kein wirkliches Geheimnis um Wahlkampfspenden oder die Lobby-Arbeit von Interessengruppen, und daher sind Strafverfolgungen selten. Aber ein Politiker wird nicht weniger gekauft, wenn dies öffentlich geschieht.
Jonathan Freedland schärfte den Briten in seinem Buch „Bringt die Revolution wieder nach Hause" ein, die Lektion von Amerikas unverbrüchlicher Treue zu Frei-

heit, Gesetz und Wahlen zu lernen. Aber Lektionen sollten ihren Weg auch in die andere Richtung nehmen. In den USA werden Verfassungsfragen kaum je diskutiert. Die geschriebene US-Verfassung gilt praktisch unverändert seit dem 18. Jahrhundert. Und ihre Mängel für das 21. Jahrhundert werden zunehmend deutlicher: dass nämlich die Gründungsväter als wohlsituierte, sklavenhaltende Grundbesitzer trotz ihrer bewundernswert fortschrittlichen Prinzipien nicht nur der Exekutive, sondern auch der Massendemokratie selbst misstrauten.

2.2.3

Practice 1

1. The speaker wants to make his listeners **understand** that America **cannot** sit back and wait. – 2. His mentioning Sept 11 made us **leave** the grandstand. – 3. The speaker wants his listeners **to approve** of the role he outlines for America in the years to come. – 4. At the end of his address he thought **he had** won his listeners over. – 5. That was the moment the audience had been **waiting** for. They gave him a standing ovation. – 6. "One thing," a listener said, "I don't agree to: that the government **tries** to develop new guidelines on gun control because of homeland security." – 7. Homeland Security's plan is that citizens without a serious reason **aren't allowed** to carry a gun. – 8. "I am used to **carrying** a gun when I feel like it," said another. – 9. His neighbour from the West Coast **told** him to keep quiet.

Practice 2

...is **much greater** than ...	**comparison of adjectives → "great" + "-er"**
... is **extremely difficult** ...	**adverb modifies adjective → "extreme" + "-ly"**
peacefully	**verb accompanied by adverb → "peaceful" + "-ly"**
... to send **a lot more** troops ...	**plural noun "troops" takes "a lot more"**

Practice 3

1. **Generally,** man is a social being. – 2. That is **generally** true. – 3. **General** elections are held every four years in our country. – 4. This fact is **generally** accepted. – 5. **Generally** I go to cast my vote. – 6. What you are saying is **simply** wrong. – 7. She writes in a **clear** and **simple** style. – 8. Put it as **simply** as you can. – 9. The Bush Address met with **extremely** different reactions. – 10. There are **extreme** differences between adversaries and supporters of Bush. – 11. Bush's hint at the expansion of freedom in all the world is not meant **ironically** but **seriously.** – **12.** Bush is **clearly** wrong here. – 13. In his Inaugural Address he does not go into **much detail** as regards the political measures of his administration. – 14. For understandable reasons he remains on a **very general** level.

2.2.4

Practice 1

unlikely: Students **will not** improve their language skills unless they work hard.
very likely: Students who work intelligently rather than hard **will probably** experience the most success.
personal assumption: **It appears that** German students will not improve their language skills unless they work hard.

Practice 2

1. **There is no denying that** America can claim to be the oldest democracy in the world. – 2. **Doubtless** Americans have every reason to be proud of their Declaration of Independence and their Constitution. – 3. **I simply cannot believe that** half of its population has so little interest in their Washington Administration that they do not bother to vote. – 4. Certainly Washington is far, they say. **I can see the point yet I wonder** whether those non-voters understand what democracy is about. – 5. **I have serious/gnawing doubts** when I read that millions of Americans are not allowed to vote, not because they are in prison but because in the past they were convicted of minor offences. – 6. **I am in two minds about** the role money and donations play in American elections. – 7. **Incredibly,** politicians are bought by interest groups. – 8. **It is more than doubtful that** candidates who are not backed by large industries stand no chance in the presidential race. – 9. **It stands to reason that** Americans would be well advised to change their way of electing the president.

2.2.5

Practice 1

tries to evoke = **versucht heraufzubeschwören** – recalls = **ruft in Erinnerung** – It is his reference to = **seine Bezugnahme auf** – that serves to = **dient dazu** – proclaimed = **verkündet**, reiterated = **wiederholt**

Practice 2

Two of the most effective devices used by Bush **to add emphasis to** his words are parallelism and antithesis. An example of syntactic parallelism **can be traced** in l. 6 ("We have seen our … and we have seen its …"). The speech transcript **provides further examples of** semantic parallelism in ll. 25, 30, and 46. Equally, the speaker makes **ample use of** antithesis: in ll. 1–2 he **states** that "our duties are not defined by the words I use, but by the history we have seen together". In ll. 33–35 Bush **underscores** the idea of American power and influence by antithesis. The most obvious example, however, **occurs** in ll. 44–45 when Bush elevates America's moral superiority and devaluates her enemies' moral stance ("eternally right vs. always wrong"). The speech extract also **abounds in examples of** parallelism and antithesis combined. Ll. 13–14 are **a case in point:** "The survival of liberty in our land ... depends on the success of liberty (parallelism) in other lands" (antithesis). Further examples of parallelism + antithesis **may be quoted here** ll. 18–19 and in ll. 21–22.

Rhythmic triads are **a particularly effective stylistic means** to balance spoken sentences. The speaker repeatedly uses this device in the passage under review. His reference to "years of relative quiet, years of repose, years of sabbatical" **can be found** in ll. 4–5. While this appears to be a rather simple triad, there are more complex triads to be found, too: "... violence will gather and multiply ...and cross ... and raise ..." (ll. 8–9) and "Freedom must be chosen ... and defended ... and sustained ..." (ll. 29–31).

2.2.6

Practice 1

1. America the beautiful.
2. Will the world ever recover from it?
3. And what about beauty in the eye of the beholder if they all look alike?
4. It is time somebody told them to behave. / When will they ever learn?
5. He is a real slave-driver. / Does he think the sky is the limit?

Practice 2

1. old – 2. will be worse – 3. their parents – 4. I make too many spelling mistakes – 5. contents – 6. accommodation – 7. freedoms ... rights – 8. be respected ... meets them in their own country – 9. heroic ... cynical – 10. different ... at worst

Practice 3

1. ... **life,** liberty, and **the pursuit of happiness**."
2. ... everyone belongs ... **deserves** ... **injustice and inequality**
3. ... easier, **more exciting** and **more rewarding**
4. ... it's men's fault ... **men are blamed for it** ... **men are held responsible for that**
5. ... lying, to **cheating** and to **getting their advantage at any cost**
6. ... some take their jobs rather easy ... **others are plainly indifferent** ... **there are a few who couldn't care less.**

3 Future Images of Man

3.1.1

A)

1

Generally speaking, Ray Kurzweil foresees that intelligent machines will surpass the capacities of the human brain in a variety of fields, including not only skills but also emotions. The skills mastered by intelligent computers will comprise movements and creative powers (ll. 1–9).
In particular, he expects that, by 2019, the average computer will have caught up with the power of human brains (ll. 10–11). He also claims that, ten years later, the software for artificial intelligence will have become so sophisticated that a personal computer will equal 1,000 brains (l. 13). At that point it will be difficult to distinguish between human and machine intelligence. He imagines a scenario in which we will be able to enjoy simulated and real communication of all kinds no matter where we are physically for ten years later (ll. 20–23). To top it all, we will be able to scan and upload complete human brain patterns on to advanced virtual bodies (robots, ll. 24–30).
This technology will, if we are to believe Kurzweil, eventually result in a merging of humans and machines.

2

In the second part of his article, Ray Kurzweil deals with the implications that this awe-inspiring scenario has. First and foremost, the question poses itself whether an intelligent machine, which possesses a human-like individual memory, history and personality, can be said to have consciousness. This is a very controversial topic. Kurzweil quotes a physicist, who admits that the computers of the future may "become conscious in a new way" (l. 38).
Secondly, it has to be debated if such nonbiological "entities" (l. 39), which are equipped with a human "mind file" (l. 32), can be considered to have a free will of their own. Kurzweil does not arrive at a conclusion here. He argues that the complete database will induce such a new "person" to act and speak as the old "self" and, therefore, will *believe* he/she has consciousness and a free will.
Will the new entity, Kurzweil asks finally, be able to have emotional and spiritual experiences since its brain processes are the same and its behaviour resembles that of the "donor" (ll. 48–49)? Again, the author is not certain. He goes as far as saying that the machine will at least maintain it has those experiences (ll. 61–62).

3

(1) Artificial intelligence: Artificial intelligence (AI) is defined as intelligence exhibited by an artificial entity. Such a system is generally assumed to be a computer. Although AI has a strong science fiction connotation, it forms a vital branch of computer science, dealing with intelligent behavior, learning and adaptation in machines. Research in AI is concerned with producing machines to automate tasks requiring intelligent behavior. Examples include control, planning and scheduling, the ability to answer diagnostic and consumer questions, handwriting, speech, and facial recognition. As such, it has become a scientific discipline, focused on providing solutions to real life problems. AI systems are now in routine use in economics, medicine, engineering and the military, as well as being built into many common home computer software applications, traditional strategy games like computer chess and other video games.

(2) Turing test: The Turing test is a proposal for a test of a machine's capability to perform human-like conversation. Described by Alan Turing in the 1950 paper "Computing Machinery and Intelligence", it proceeds as follows: a human judge engages in a natural language conversation with two other parties, one a human and the other a machine; if the judge cannot reliably tell which is which, then the machine is said to pass the test. It is assumed that both the human and the machine try to appear human. In order to keep the test setting simple and universal (to explicitly test the linguistic capability of the machine instead of its ability to render words into audio), the conversation is usually limited to a text-only channel such as a teletype machine as Turing suggested or, more recently IRC or instant messaging.

(3) Nanobots: see Nanorobotics: the technology of creating machines or robots at or close to the scale of a nanometre (10^{-9} metres). More specifically, nanorobotics refers to the still largely theoretical nanotechnology engineering discipline of designing and building nanorobots. Nanorobots are typically devices ranging in size from 0.1–10 micrometres and constructed of nanoscale or molecular components. As no nanorobots have so far been created, they remain a hypothetical concept at this time.
Another definition sometimes used is a robot which allows precision interactions with nanoscale objects, or can manipulate with nanoscale resolution. Following this definition even a large apparatus such as an atomic force microscope can be considered a nanorobotic instrument when configured to perform nanomanipulation. Also, macroscale robots or microrobots which can move with nanoscale precision can also be considered nanorobots.

B)

1

The text under discussion clearly breaks into two distinct parts. In the first part comprising ll. 1–30 the author Ray Kurzweil focuses on predicting a future scenario as regards artificial or machine intelligence. After putting forward his general thesis in the first paragraph ("the intelligence of machines will exceed that of humans", ll. 2–3), the author delineates his vision devoting a separate paragraph to each of the coming decades (2019 through 2030). Summarizing the developments he foresees for "the third decade of the 21st century" (l. 24) Kurzweil is convinced that we will live to see the emergence of virtual "entities" that are capable of knowing, acting and feeling like human beings.
From l. 31 onward, he addresses three fundamental questions arising from what he considers as given future facts. Again, he devotes a separate (in one case two) paragraph(s) to each of the questions that must be raised about the developments he outlines in the first part. Addressing and debating those questions, he proceeds from what we may call a mainly factual to a decidedly argumentative approach.
In his final paragraph, Kurzweil confirms his main thesis ("Earth's technology-creating species – us – will merge with our own technology", ll. 63–64).
It may, therefore, be inferred that the author makes use of a cause-to-effect pattern in that he lays out his cause, i.e. the coming accomplishments in AI research first, in order to deal with some of the implications or "effects" that must be considered in terms of a new relationship, or even competition, between man and machine.

2

The author's cause-to-effect approach to his topic is reflected in his tone. As he outlines his future scenario in a field in which he is regarded as one of the leading scientists, he appears very straightforward. He leaves little or no doubt that the predictions he makes *will* come true. In part, this impression is owing to the systematic time scale he suggests. So convinced does he seem of his topic that he does not hesitate to break down *(konkret verteilen auf)* future developments in AI to single decades. To define his predictions in detail, he repeatedly uses the will-future, which generally denotes *(bezeichnen)* giving information about the future, or talking about possible events which are not already decided or obviously on the way (he uses will-future 13 times).The preferred sentence pattern is very significant as well: Kurzweil uses straightforward main clauses to state what will happen in the future. No question allowed *(das ist unbestreitbar)*.
In the second part of his text the author's tone changes completely. While being more than sure about the future scientific developments concerning AI, he

appears a lot more cautious when assessing the implications on a philosophical scale *(wenn er die Folgen philosophisch bewertet)*. His fast-paced *(rasant)* enumeration of coming events gives way to a more argumentative style: "Suppose we can … Will the entity … be …?" (ll. 33–34). While the "facts" seem clear to him, their meaning is to be debated. It does not come as a surprise that the straightforward main clause is replaced by numerous conditional clauses (ll. 43, 44, etc.) and contrastive discourse markers ("For some … For others …", ll. 35–36) that render this part a lot more complex. An occasional clause of concessive contrast ("although", l. 37) serves the same purpose. What sets the second part of the text off *(was den zweiten vom ersten Teil des Textes absetzt)*, however, is the fact that the author uses the argumentative pattern of raising questions and attempting to answer them in the following (ll. 31–38, 38–42). This pattern is repeated three to four times.

3

This is another stimulus to elicit a personal comment on the part of the reader. A possible answer might consider the following points:

- At first glance, the 43-year-old might appear to be short-tempered or incompetent using his personal computer; he seems to have suffered a breakdown.
- The news item's reference to his frustrations seems to indicate that there could a story behind the man's outbreak of violence.
- The outbreak itself and the attempt at "killing" the machine might tell another story; he might have considered his personal computer as a (non)biological entity, as something like a "person", with whom he seems to have developed a troubled relationship.
- Who is ultimately to be blamed for the incident remains unclear. The irony is, however, that the incident might be indicative of a future "relationship" between man and machine that is becoming more complex.
- For the time being, the incident sounds more like science fiction.

4

In the past we have tended to see ourselves as the pink of perfection *(Krone der Schöpfung)*, priding ourselves on being the intelligent race. Recent developments in computer science and robotics, however, are beginning to cast a shadow over this arrogant notion. Ray Kurzweil's article, discussing the possibility of AI (machine consciousness), is a case in point. Although meant to strike a positive note, his view is by no means reassuring. On the contrary, I believe that, if Kurzweil is right, there will be cause for concern.

First of all, Kurzweil's scenario sounds like a foregone conclusion *(beschlossene Sache)*. What he predicts as technological progress (he uses the factual "will

be, will at least …", not the more cautious auxiliaries "may/might") is indeed impressive.
I wonder what communicating intellectually or emotionally with smart machines will be like. Will these robots "understand" us, will they be prepared to empathize *(mitfühlen)* with real humans, or will they just take stock *(zur Kenntnis nehmen)*, check their options *(Handlungsmöglichkeiten „abchecken")* and act as they "think" fit? There is more to a human being than just memory space and enhanced neurons. I do not see any type of robot achieve a degree of consciousness that will enable him (her? it?) to meet a human face-to-face.
Assuming that tomorrow's machines will soon surpass the intelligence of its creators (ll. 2–3), I can well imagine that, in a world driven by greed and power, this is a very tempting vision for some people – the movers and shakers of our time whether in the industry, in the military or in the political sector. They will certainly use the advances in robotics for their own (commercial, military or political) purposes. We may be travelling the road to another Brave New World. This is a frightening prospect.
Last but not least, we cannot rule out the vague possibility that, once the new "species" of humanoid robots has outwitted the human race, it will attempt to be in charge. While this may belong to the realm of *(ins Reich von … gehören)* science fiction for some people, others seem fascinated by the sheer idea. To me, however, the very thought is repugnant and disgusting.
On balance *(bei Abwägung aller Punkte)*, there is still no clear evidence that things may not turn out the way they seem to now. If we know one thing, it is that technological progress itself is unpredictable!

C)

Werden Computer jemals einen Zustand von Bewusstsein erreichen?
Sicher, Computer werden zunehmend intelligenter werden, wie die Niederlage des Schachweltmeisters Gary Kasparow gegen den IBM Deep Blue uns gezeigt hat. Heutige Computer können sich auf Englisch über begrenzte Themen unterhalten, sie kontrollieren mechanische Arme, die schweißen und Farbe sprühen können, und sie können menschliche Fachkompetenz in Dutzenden von Bereichen um das Doppelte übertreffen, vom Verschreiben von Medikamenten bis zur Diagnose von Maschinenausfall. Dennoch kommen heutige Computer nicht auch nur in die Nähe eines vierjährigen Menschen und seine Fähigkeit, zu sehen, zu sprechen, sich zu bewegen oder seine Vernunft zu gebrauchen. Ein Grund dafür ist die bloße Rechnerkapazität. Es wird geschätzt, dass die Fähigkeit zur Informationsverarbeitung sogar des stärksten Supercomputers dem Nervensystem einer Schnecke gleicht – ein winziger Bruchteil der Kapazität, über die der „Supercomputer" in einem angewachsenen menschlichen Schädel verfügt.
Computern fällt es leicht, eine 25-stellige Zahl zu memorieren, aber sie finden es

schwer, den Kern des Märchens vom Rotkäppchen zusammenfassen; Menschen finden es schwer, die Zahl zu behalten, aber leicht, das Märchen zusammenzufassen. Ein Grund für den Unterschied ist, dass Computer einen einzigen, zuverlässigen Prozessor (oder eine kleine Anzahl) besitzen, der sehr, sehr schnell arbeitet; die Gehirnprozessoren sind langsamer und lauter, aber von ihnen gibt es Hunderte von Millionen, von denen jeder mit tausenden anderen verbunden ist. Das erlaubt dem menschlichen Gehirn, komplizierte Muster in einem Augenblick zu erkennen, wohingegen Computer Schritt für Schritt jedes vertrackte Detail abarbeiten müssen.
Menschliche Gehirne haben auch den Vorteil, dass sie in den Menschen integriert sind und im Laufe der Jahre 10^{12} Bytes an Informationen aufnehmen können, da Menschen mit anderen Menschen und ihrer Umgebung interagieren. Gehirne profitieren auch von dem Nutzen von millionenjahrelangem Ausprobieren und Weiterentwickeln, einem Prozess, in dem die Evolution sie mit Täuschungsstrategien ausgestattet hat, die dem Austricksen von Gegenständen, Pflanzen, Tieren und anderen menschlichen Wesen dienen.
Wie gut werden die zukünftigen Maschinen also sein? Der technische Fortschritt ist nicht voraussagbar. Was das Ersetzen von Körperteilen angeht, wer konnte ahnen, dass künstliche Hüften Standard werden würden, künstliche Herzen aber ein Irrweg? Was die Leistung von künstlichen Gehirnen anbetrifft, so ist die überzeugendste Antwort, dass Computer für einige Denkdisziplinen wahrscheinlich sehr viel leistungsfähiger als heute werden, und dass sie in anderen Denkbereichen wahrscheinlich mit einem Menschen nicht werden konkurrieren können.

3.1.2

Practice 1

1. will be … will have – 2. are going to find … is claiming – 3. is/will be busy … will be giving … is leaving/will be leaving … is about to leave/is leaving – 4. Are you getting up/Are you going to get up … are you staying/are you going to stay – 5. get up … will be … will be aware of … step – 6. will be travelling … go … will meet – 7. are you going to book … leaves

Practice 2

… that artificial machines **will be capable of** intelligent thought … computers **will match** the power … intelligence **is going to be** more powerful … we **will be** in a position …
… intelligence **will be limited**. … **Are we going to regard** … How **are we going to assess** the problem … We **will be discussing** these questions …
… that God **is going to interfere** … and **will always be** so.

Practice 3

1. … just acts as if it is conscious?
2. … does that settle the issue?
3. …, it will strenuously claim to be the original person.
4. If we scan, let's say, me and reinstate that information into a neural computer, …

Practice 4

1. What would you do if you **were** asked – 2. If your parents **didn't allow** you – 3. If you **tell** me – 4. It would be much better if scientists **could** research – 5. …, we **would have been** better informed. – 6. Your household robot **would have come** – 7. It **would have done** the job

3.1.3

Practice 1

1. One **ought to** tell the truth. – 2. He **is said to** have been a famous man. – 3. **Shall we** arrive a little later today? – 4. The text **is meant to** express what I think. – 5. What **is** that **supposed to** mean? – 6. The article **is intended to** stir up the reader. – 7. The doctor **is expected to** come at once. – 8. She **is said to** have worked as a model for "Vogue". – 9. I **ought to** have given my parents a ring./I **was supposed to** have given my parents a ring.

Practice 2

1. mustn't – 2. needn't – 3. must – 4. didn't have to – 5. needn't – 6. had to – 7. 'll have to – 8. won't have to – 9. won't be allowed to

Practice 3

1. **Let** us talk about it. – 2. He **had** the students **learn** a lot of vocabulary. – 3. The hit-and-run driver **left** the injured **lying** in the street. – 4. My parents **let** me **watch** as much TV as I want. – 5. The customs officer **made us open** all our suitcases. – 6. **Leave** us in peace. – 7. He **left** his car **standing** where it was. – 8. What **made you change** your opinion so quickly? – 9. She **left** the engine running. She just wanted to post a letter. – 10. **Take** (!) your time. – 11. The doctor **had** the patient **taken** to hospital. – 12. He **let** us go home earlier.

3.1.4

Practice 1

1. done – 2. make – 3. made – 4. do – 5. do – 6. done – 7. made – 8. do – 9. do – 10. make

Practice 2

We were all very **excited** when we discussed the **exciting** class trip to London. – When the teacher asked the class, all **except** one **accepted** his idea of a class trip to London. – We had to **realize**, though, that his idea was quite difficult for us to **put into practice**. – When we **eventually** put the idea to the vote, our teacher said we could **possibly** plan for a five-day trip. – I was **lying** in bed when our family doctor **laid** the prescription on the bedside table where it **lay** until my mother got the medication. – Our doctor was quite old. He worked **fewer** hours, for which he got **less** pay, a fact he liked **less** and **less**. – She was a **sensitive** girl who had **sensible** views on family planning. – She is rather **self-conscious**, but she might learn to become more **self-confident**. – I am **sympathetic** to her situation because she is a **likeable** girl. – Why are you not setting your dog **loose**? Are you afraid of **losing** him? – How do you feel about our **economic** system? Should our politicians not be more **economical** when spending the taxpayer's money? – The **critic** was very harsh in his **criticism** of government policy. His **critique** was very harsh.

Practice 3

1. He has no opinion **of his own**. – 2. **In contrast to** me, you have a job. – 3. Nevertheless I'd like to give you **some good advice**. – 4. We received a lot of useful **information**. – 5. I'd like to explain the reason for it **in detail**. – 6. That is a **sensible** decision. – 7. **There is/remains** a lot to be discussed. – 8. You will **receive** a beautiful present. – 9. In his article the author **provides** a lot of facts. – 10. He argues **consistently**. – 11. That is **typical of** you: never admit anything. – 12. Her/Their life circumstances are simply **inhuman**.

3.1.5

Practice 1

1. **Although** *(concession)* – 2. **because** *(reason)* – 3. **whereas** *(contrast)* – 4. **soon after** *(time)* – 5. **since** *(reason)* – 6. **so that** *(purpose)* – 7. **when** *(time)* – 8. **that** *(result)* – 9. **Once** *(time)* – 10. **because** *(reason)* – 11. **unless** *(condition)*

Practice 2

1. **If** you/we think positive, the merging of man and machine predicted by Kurzweil will be a breakthrough. – 2. **Unless** Ray Kurzweil delivers on his promise, he will make a fool of himself. – 3. **Despite the fact that** we may believe in the possibility of an intelligent computer, it is hard to imagine the possibility of a conscious computer or a computer with a free will. – 4. **Although** a smart robot can be like us one day, it will not be accepted by humans as one of us, i.e. as a person. –

5. It will be possible to call the new neural computers intelligent **if** we redefine our idea of intelligence. – 6. **Unless** we stop AI research now, it might be too late. – 7. **Although** I read all of Kurzweil's articles on machine intelligence, I remain unconvinced. – 8. **If** you ask the machine, it will vehemently claim to be a person with consciousness.

Practice 3

1. I didn't ask her to leave. **On the contrary/Instead** I tried to make her stay for another hour. – 2. He has been here for two weeks only. **Nevertheless** he has achieved more than we expected. – 3. The hotel caught fire. **Yet/However** no hotel guest was killed. – 4. Don't be so aggressive. **At the same time/ Nevertheless** you shouldn't be too timid. – 5. He doesn't listen. **Instead/On the contrary/But** he just sits and day-dreams. – 6. She hadn't slept for days. **Still/All the same/Yet** she managed to look as fresh as a daisy. – 7. So far the weather has been bad indeed. **Nevertheless/At the same time/Yet** we are enjoying our stay.

3.1.6

Practice 1

The scrambled paragraph from the student's essay might be re-arranged as follows:

1. (C) topic sentence states the main idea of the paragraph
2. (E) supporting argument 1: "being socially accepted"
3. (A) supporting argument 2: "clothes impress friends"
4. (D) supporting argument 3: "social competition"
5. (B) summarizing sentence: "if you cannot compete, you'll have a problem"

Practice 2

Good Looks:

supporting statement 1: A model we see in a TV advert for 15 seconds remains a stranger. Television has thus created a demand for memorable contours: it needs "telegenic" people.
supporting statement 2: At the same time, we see more beautiful faces and bodies than ever before, and people can't help comparing themselves to those considered "perfect". We feel that we, too, have to live up to it.

Car Crazy:

supporting statement 1: For one thing, cars are all about individual freedom while public transport is seen as "un-American" in that it inhibits the "right" of an individual to go exactly wherever he wants whenever he wants.
supporting statement 2: For another, the automobile can be seen as a medium

of personal self-expression since we can observe so many Americans modify and customize their cars so that they are individual creations.

Technological Change:
supporting statement 1: Until some hundreds of years ago, the only machines were those moved by natural forces or the muscles of men and animals: windmills, ploughs.
supporting statement 2: Look at the 20th century: there you had primitive motor cars and telephones at the beginning, and just 80 years later nuclear power, space shuttles and computers. The world has indeed been transformed.

Practice 3

There is no denying that computers will become more and more complex and that their abilities will grow massively.	← **general undebatable statement**
They can support us in lots of daily things. You can say that, today, nobody can live without computers.	← **"supported" by two general claims**
When I read Pinker's article, I'm not much afraid of the future.	← **topical sentence "I'm not afraid ..."**
But there are other people who see the development of robots in another way.	← **antithetical second topic sentence: not supported in any way**
Maybe in a few years AI will surpass human intelligence. It is my view that mankind should begin to worry then. Because, if robots are in charge, humans are capable of controlling them.	← **concluding passage: rather a concluding paragraph. Too long to wind up the paragraph!**

Teacher Comment: This paragraph clearly lacks unity. We find its topical sentence in the middle of the paragraph. It is followed by a second topical sentence. Both are not supported by examples or arguments. The opening statement talks about computer "abilities" but fails to mention the key point of AI, which emerges only at the end. What then is the paragraph's topic?

3.2.1

A)

1

At first glance, the events narrated in the short story "The Satisfied Customer" may seem to take place in our day. Lonely Melvin indulges in nightly TV sessions that are broadcast on a 24/7 basis. Consumer's paradise seems just around the corner. Soon, however, we begin to suspect a different tale. Infomercials (l. 3) are, obviously, omnipresent since no other TV format is mentioned. Services such as a "free, five-minute psychic reading" (l. 4) – compare Domian! – and hair growth devices sound true enough. Things take a different turn when we read about a complicated surgical procedure such as lobotomy (l. 41) being administered to patients via telephone in just "two minutes" (l. 50) reducing them to helpless idiots (ll. 50–51). The swift (and painless?) procedure appears to upset nobody but, instead, is taken for granted. This is pure science fiction.

2

The fact that the protagonist, and possibly a considerable number of other people in Melvin's world, too, spend the night watching TV suggests that they cannot sleep. Their real lives, which they have to put up with, seem to fall short of their dreams and are an utter disappointment. These are the circumstances that a variety of consumer-oriented TV services cater to. They promise, each in their particular field and some for a small or larger fee, help and a better, if not perfect, life.

Melvin Duncan, the story's main character, is presented as an infomercial addict. He has, in the past, repeatedly requested the services of channel eleven's "agony aunt", who tried, unsuccessfully, to comfort him by giving him "psychic readings" (l. 4). He seems dissatisfied with his job and is very likely single (l. 9), in short he leads a life that can be described as dull. To make himself physically more attractive and to compensate for his growing bald, he has sought scientific advice, again via TV, and bought a hair growing stimulator (l. 12). Its painful application has proved a disaster and left Melvin with a lasting physical defect (ll. 16–18). So, apparently, Melvin is unhappy. He experiences his life as deeply unsatisfying and burdensome and the false professional promises as a letdown.

This changes when he happens to switch to channel "00". In the name of Hypnotic Lobotomy INC., a trustworthy "man in a white lab coat" (l. 24) addresses his very problems (l. 26) and promises a comprehensive solution: "continuous, internal bliss" (l. 33). After Melvin has accepted the necessary payment formalities, Hypnotic Lobotomy INC. instantly delivers *(prompt liefern; ein Versprechen erfüllen)*. Seconds later Melvin, "his mouth agape" and "his eyes vacant" (l. 51), has left his worries behind and he has escaped "the hassle life brings" (ll. 29–30). He is a satisfied customer now, reduced to the state of an unfeeling vegetable.

3

To be relieved of his troubles, the miserable customer Melvin seeks help from three different medical services. The first two treatments – repeated psychic readings via TV and the fake gadget bought to stimulate hair growth – are rather

standard. Both fail and, what is more, leave the patient psychically ("Madam Ursula was a liar", l. 9) respectively physically impaired ("the twitch in his left eye that never went away", ll. 17–18). The third, the most damaging of the three, turns out to be a total success. No hard feelings left and no need to get a refund on Melvin's part this time, but complete satisfaction as promised! The hitch, however, is that Melvin from now on is beyond repair. Having been rid of his mental capacities, he is a different man now: a dummy.
Unlike the regular channels, Hypnotic Lobotomy INC. offers its services through channel "00". The curious double zero suggests that the company is involved in some highly suspect business. For its services the customer's phone bill is charged, and the promised "cure" is effected via telephone, too. Unlike Madam Ursula's famed readings, for example, which can be listened in on by the viewer community, or Mr Sponk's miraculous hair electronic stimulator, which can be passed around, Hypnotic Lobotomy INC.'s discreet policy guarantees that any unnecessary attention is being avoided, for the benefit of the customer. This is a clear hint at the dubiousness of the company's dealings.

4

The satire has been defined as a format that exposes the absurdity or incongruity of a situation or a person and makes it appear laughable and ridiculous. It does so by exaggerating the points or traits in question. The present story clearly contains both verbal irony and exaggeration.
Let us begin by looking at some examples of verbal irony on the narrator's part. Sleepless though exhausted, Melvin is glued to the "mighty tube" (l. 3). Powerful and invasive *(in die heimische Sphäre eindringend)* as the electronic medium may be, the term "mighty" is a reference to fairy tales or cartoons. Channel two advertises a service based on "vigorous research" (ll. 10–11) done by a "renowned scientist" (l. 11) to restore hair growth. A gadget that causes pain and lasting bodily harm can hardly claim to be really helpful. Madam Ursula, for her part, "guarantees ... accuracy and authenticity" (l. 5) yet feels obliged to add "for entertainment purposes only" (ll. 5–6) in fine print. This is an amazing contradiction.
The final part of the story involving Hypnotic Lobotomy INC. is a more serious case in point. The effect of "hypnotic brain alteration" (ll. 33–34) is a wildly funny exaggeration of a complaint often raised by critics of the medium, i.e. that too much TV time affects our brains. The mention of the easy processing of the "small fee of only $ 199.99 (!)" is a reference to infomercial TV's practice to urge the viewers to "Call now ...". More importantly, the customer's worries about the costliness of the treatment will go unnoticed once the hypnotic has been applied. The fee will be charged "by direct deposit" (l. 36) anyway. This is not only ironic but highly sarcastic. The crowning irony is that a "vegetable" is booked *(statistisch verbucht)* by Hypnotic Lobotomy INC. as "another satisfied customer" (l. 54).

So, there can be hardly any doubt that the story is rich in satirical overtones. Its author, Nathan Carter, is poking fun at two remarkable phenomena. For one, TV viewers fall for a romanticized, more beautiful, more exciting version of reality, for another, the modern viewer is highly susceptible *(empfänglich)* to infomercial sales talk and consumer-friendly net commerce. Consequently TV producers serve up a menu that is supposed to "satisfy their customers".

B)

1

Notice how the e-mail-format is a lot more informal and personal in structure as well as in its use of language. This does not mean that it is without any logical structure. As a whole, it is much closer to spoken language than a comment proper (compare answer to question 3.2.1 B) 2).
Letters A and B take a different stand each on the question of the fictitious Hypnotic Lobotomy INC. service. You are entirely right when you work out your own version.

Letter A:
From: …
To: hypnolobotomy@aol.us
Re: Your offer as advertised on channel 00
Dear sirs,
Allow me to congratulate you and your doctors on your ← **main purpose**
sensational breakthrough in medical science. I can't wait ← **colloquial**
to benefit from your wonderful treatment myself. I'm
standing in line.
I cannot but agree that we are surrounded by cheats and
LIARS! Take that Madam Ursula, for instance, and her
stupid psychic readings. Mental striptease if you ask me.
All she and the likes of her do is ripping us off. She ought
to consult your doctors.
It is true that, like so many other people's, my life hasn't ← **discourse marker**
turned out as I had reason to expect. My job is a drag, my
career is a shambles, and my wife is a pain in the … neck.
I can't seem to get through to her. She is, by the way, an
ardent supporter of Madam Ursula's.
My future right now: NONE! ← **emotional**
And there's where you come in. I need to get away from it ← **colloquial**
all. I need my sleep. I need my freedom. I want a way out. ← **derogatory**
I am confident that, with your help, I'll be able to start a
new life, leave my nightly worries behind and enjoy the

simple things in life again. Eat, drink …
You are rendering the world a big service. You really are. ← **emotional outcry**
You're helping people to shape up and you're giving them ← **colloquial**
the chance to cope with their lives. What more can we
ask?
One little question before I close my letter: You charge ← **spoken syntax**
$ 199,99 for one telephone session if I'm not mistaken. ← **colloquial**
Don't you think your fee is a bit high for our average
earner? Do you give discounts for people like me who are
very desperate? Or if I get some of my acquaintances
interested in your programme? Let me know if you do, ← **formal query**
please. I'm asking now because, as you are saying, later
I won't remember the price you charged.
Yours electronically,
…

Letter B:
From: …
To: hypnolobotomy@aol.us
Re: Your offer as advertised on channel 00
Dear sirs,
I happened to watch your channel double zero the other ← **main purpose**
day and I must say I was scandalized.
Do you really believe that those quacks of yours are doing ← **informal insult**
the world a service?
You claim that you help people to "leave behind the
pressure of real life and live on in a state of continuous,
internal bliss" when in reality what you do is depriving
them of what should be an essential part of their lives:
their memories and the chance of being UNHAPPY when a
situation calls for that. We can only be happy if we have a ← **serious argument**
notion of what unhappiness is. Instead you put people in
a state of "happiness" that I would call obliviousness.
And your customers, do they realize what is going to
happen to them? I bet they don't. And once they are ← **colloquial**
"cured", they won't care anyway. How can human beings
care who have been reduced to the state of VEGETABLES?
And vegetables they are: helpless … dependent on the ← **emotional argument**
charity and aid of others. This is an outrage.
I am not a human rights fanatic but I feel I must protest
against your criminal practices. Has it ever occurred to you

that you exhibit a deep contempt of humankind?
YOU MUST BE STOPPED!

...

P.S. I am sending copies of this letter to friends and acquaintances of mine so the news will get around. It is time for us to take a stand now. ← **personal threat**

2

You will notice that, leaving the introduction and the conclusion aside, the "middle" or main part shows a listing structure. You may also note how the three aspects mentioned in the introduction are "picked up" in the main part and developed in that order.

In Nathan Carter's story, Melvin Duncan comes across as a mindless consumer, who desperately longs for a better, or rather, for a carefree and untroubled life. He believes in the false promises of a wellness industry and their "quick-fix" remedies to cope with the inconveniences of real life. In more than one respect we may recognize ourselves in Carter's protagonist.

We only need to remind ourselves to what extent we have become bargain hunters, always on the lookout for the best price, which, when obtained, seems to make us "happy". Or, think of the steadily growing community of ebayers and internet traders on the prowl. Our world is a market place. On the other hand, we believe we are entitled to have all our troubles and worries taken care of by somebody else, preferably, free of charge. We expect a lot from life but we are seldom prepared to assume responsibility for our lives. We are victims, in some way or other.

And then, are we ready to face up to the realities of life? Are we in a position to deal with facts of life, or do we not tend to cover up what we believe is "unpleasant", such as our illnesses and the fact that we are mortal? Instead, we are easy prey to what the media, especially TV, dish out to us – in the daily soaps, the endless game shows, and the incessant commercials showering down on us and spoiling us by parading beautiful, successful, and happy young people.

Finally, we may consider the up and coming wellness industry. We certainly live in the age of the culture of the body. Workout and fitness studios abound, quick-fix remedies for our physical deficiencies are just around the corner, and anti-ageing recipes are sought after. And if nothing helps, there is always cosmetic surgery to turn to. In America there were nine million plastic surgery operations in 2003 and in Britain the number of procedures is currently rising around 65 % a year, now that breast surgery costs little more than a decent family holiday. And, at the same time, we are growing older and older.

So, taking everything into account, we may wonder if we are not indeed travelling down the road that Melvin Duncan has agreed to take. The question is if we still need the services of companies such as the fictional Hypnotic Lobotomy INC. or if we are not hypnotizing ourselves already. There is no easy answer to this one.

C)

Ein Riesenspaß

Im Fernsehzimmer unterbrach seine Frau die Lektüre ihres Manuskripts lange genug, um aufzublicken.

„Was gibt's heute Nachmittag?" fragte er müde.

„Nun, dies ist ein Stück, das in zehn Minuten auf dem Wand-zu-Wand-Kanal kommt. Sie haben mir meine Rolle heute Morgen zugeschickt. Sie schreiben das Drehbuch so, dass eine Rolle ausgespart ist. Es ist eine neue Idee. Die Hausfrau, das bin ich, ist die ausgesparte Rolle. Wenn der Moment für meinen Text kommt, schauen sie mich von den drei Wänden her an und ich sage meinen Text. Hier, zum Beispiel, sagt der Mann, ‚Was hältst Du von dieser ganzen Idee, Helen?', und dann schaut er auf mich, die ich hier in der Mitte sitze, verstehst Du? Und ich sage, ich sage –" Sie hielt inne und fuhr mit ihrem Finger eine Zeile im Drehbuch entlang. „‚Ich finde sie prima!' Und dann spielen sie im Stück weiter, bis er sagt, ‚Stimmst Du dem zu, Helen?', und ich sage, ‚Auf jeden Fall!' Ist das nicht lustig, Guy?"

Er stand im Flur und sah sie an.

„Das macht Superspaß", sagte sie.

„Worum geht es in dem Stück?"

„Ich hab's Dir gerade gesagt. Da sind diese Leute. Sie heißen Bob und Ruth und Helen."

„Oh."

„Es ist ein Riesenspaß. Es wird noch mehr Spaß machen, wenn wir es uns leisten können, eine vierte Wand installieren zu lassen. Wie lange, glaubst Du, wird es dauern, bis wir genug gespart haben und die vierte Wand herausreißen und dafür die vierte TV-Wand installieren lassen können? Sie kostet nur zweitausend Dollar."

3.2.2

Practice 1

1. Do you often **watch** infomercials on TV? – 2. Can you **see** what is wrong with Melvin? – 3. No matter how you **look** at it, Melvin himself is to blame. – 4. If I **see** that correctly, Melvin should have **looked** for help elsewhere. – 5. **Look** over there, what can you **see**? – 6. Have you **seen** the film in which Truman Burbank (Jim Carrey) is being **watched** by the whole world? – 7. I wanted to **look** away but I could not but **watch** the accident.

Practice 2

The man in the white lab coat **raised** his voice when he addressed the viewers. Melvin didn't **rise** from his chair, he leaned forward. – Madam Ursula, **whose** readings had proved fruitless, was a liar! **Who's** the one to blame in Melvin's case? – The **actual** state Melvin is in resembles that of a vegetable. His case is of **topical** interest to us. – He is a satisfied customer **at last**. **At least** we can say that he is not very smart. – Melvin has to face a **hard** life. It is **hardly** surprising therefore that he seeks help. – Is this an **interesting** story? Are you **interested** in discussing its implications? – What in your **opinion** is the **meaning** of the short story? Does it possibly have more than one **meaning**? – Sorry, I haven't **finished** my essay but I'll be **ready** to listen in a minute. – He **lets** himself be talked into undergoing the treatment. Hypnotic Lobotomy INC. **leaves** nothing to chance. Let's **leave** it at that for the moment.

3.2.3

Practice 1

1. … if somebody **gave** you … – 2. … he **would** perhaps **have said** yes. – 3. … your father **would have allowed** you to fly to China. – 4. If you **tell** me … – 5. She **would have come** if …

Practice 2

a)

1. … I **would certainly make it**. – 2. … if I **had been more fortunate**. – 3. … I **would let you know** at once. – 4. … I'**ll be most fortunate**. – 5. … some people **turn** to religion.

b)

1. If he had not stumbled across channel "00", he would not have got interested in Hypnotic Lobotomy INC.'s brain treatment. – 2. If he had not got interested in Hypnotic Lobotomy INC.'s brain treatment, he would not have rung up their number. – 3. If he had not rung up their number, he would not have accepted their charges to his local phone bill. – 4. If he had not accepted their charges to his local phone bill, he would not have been lobotomized a few minutes later.

Practice 3

1. If we **want to face up to** the facts of life, we'**ll have to change** our way of life. – 2. We **would act** more sensibly if we **didn't run** after the ideal of eternal youth. – 3. We **would be** a lot happier, too, if we **did not always want to possess** what we do not have. – 4. If we **were not afraid** of ageing, we **would grow old** in dignity. – 5. If we **did not delude ourselves** so much, we **would not believe**

the promises of the wellness industry. – 6. If we **believe** we simply **need to book** a weekend in a wellness hotel, we **are definitely** wrong. – 7. If we **knew** that cosmetic surgery is not without risk, we **would be** more reluctant in this respect. – 8. If we **concentrated** on the important things in life, our lives **would not be** such a hassle.

3.2.4

Practice 1

A. Huxley's "Brave New World" can be called welfare tyranny **in contrast to/differing greatly from/compared to/as against** G. Orwell's "1984", which is based on sheer violence and terror. In "Brave New World" **however/by comparison** drugs play an important part.
The rulers of "1984" are not reluctant to use intimidation and torture, **whereas/while** the system in "Brave New World" …
The two novels are very **different indeed/are very dissimilar/very much opposed to each other. Unlike/In comparison with** "Brave New World"-citizens, …
On might say that life in "Brave New World" **is the very antithesis of/contrasts sharply with/has nothing in common with** that in "1984". **On the one hand/It is true that** "Brave New World's" world controllers …

Practice 2

Some people say that German television can easily **be compared to** American TV. They **both** put advertising and entertainment …
In the first place, there can be no doubt that advertising time on German **as well as** on American TV is excessive, **the only difference being** that over here…
Similarly, in both countries entertainment is the order of the day. Even the news shows, sometimes poorly disguised, are expected to have a high entertainment value. Hence the term "infotainment". **Unlike** German anchors, however, their American counterparts are more professional and entertaining.
However, German and American TV **aren't similar in every respect**. In a few key ways, they are **more different** than they are the same. **Whereas** the major German channels run at least some informative programmes, in the U.S. TV the human interest angle is central. Finally, **the biggest difference between** the two countries is that, in America, TV is generally free of charge, while in our country there is a competition between commercial TV and fee-paying TV stations.
Given that TV in both countries can appear to be **quite similar**, it makes sense to draw attention to one or two significant differences between them that cannot be denied.

4 Genetic Engineering

4.1.1

Practice 1

1.	Children are given to us, they are not our property.	C
2.	Cloning is the answer to many medical questions, and to a better quality of life.	P
3.	The catch is …	C
4.	Should we travel the road to the brave new world that science and technology are taking us towards?	C
5.	It is clear that cloning has enormous potential.	P
6.	We are not playing God, we are merely using technology to improve our lives.	P
7.	It is a wonderful additional reproductive option.	P
8.	We will push the boundaries of science.	P
9.	It will be possible to make clones of exceptional people in hope that their gifts and talents can be passed on.	P
10.	A world driven by greed and power will abuse the technology.	C
11.	The very thought is repellent and disgusting.	C
12.	It is the beginning of a slippery slope.	C
13.	Being able to clone humans is a tantalizing idea.	P
14.	The technology will bring along life-saving treatments.	P
15.	I believe such a practice unethical.	C
16.	The impact will be profound, pervasive, and largely unpredictable.	C
17.	Every aspect of human culture will be affected.	C
18.	Nature has created the proper way to make babies and we shouldn't do it in a different way.	C

Practice 2

a)

supporting argument 1: In her outstanding novel (1818) Mary Shelley describes how a mad scientist creates a "monster" but does not take responsibility for it.
supporting argument 2: Our wonderful geneticists are not prepared to assume responsibility either for the consequences that may result from genetic research.

b)

supporting argument 1: They claim the right of every child to be born with a sound physical and mental constitution.
supporting argument 2: Humanity, they say, has the right to be protected from suffering and disease.

c)
supporting argument 1: He will feel that he or she is a less unique individual than other people.
supporting argument 2: Because he or she is genetically identical, they will have almost everything in common with their genetic parent.
d)
supporting argument 1: A child conceived in the normal way is a unique product of the union of its mother and father, and is not a genetic replica of either parent.
supporting argument 2: In normal procreation *(Fortpflanzung)*, the genes of a child are determined by chance through the union of two people.

Practice 3
… **To begin with,** I have to admit … cannot be dismissed. **Yet**, the time …
Moreover, it is often said that … **Admittedly,** these cells are …
More importantly, bearing in mind that …
However, that kind of cell research …
Therefore, if the genetic research …

4.1.2

A)

1

In his personal column for "Better Humans" the author James Hughes pleads for the right of every human individual to clonal reproduction. He is opposed to any law that forbids making genetic replicas of living individuals.
On the condition that the technology of reproductive cloning is "safe" (l. 3), Hughes claims that "our reproductive freedoms" (l. 2) such as having children are crucial and that these personal decisions should not be interfered with.
To support his view Hughes refers to the history of in-vitro-fertilization (IVF), which, at the time of the first "test-tube babies" (l. 6), was a very controversial issue, too. Hughes blames science fiction movies and religious dogmas (l. 5) for the controversy surrounding IVF, a technology that has been accepted and widely used since then.
After discussing some of the main arguments raised against the prospect of human cloning, Hughes winds up by confirming his standpoint once again in the name of personal freedom and choice (ll. 38–40), both of which would be impaired *(beschädigt)* if this option were banned.

2

In the main part of his column, James Hughes debates some of the main arguments in the ongoing controversy surrounding human cloning. He begins with a reference to the widely known Francis Fukuyama who foresees the danger of illicit *(gesetzlich verboten)* relationships within families if, for example, parents decide to have a daughter cloned from the mother. The father might feel urged to consider his daughter as a younger "copy" of her mother, a mother whom the father once fell in love with.
Hughes continues with what can be seen as a more serious argument than the first: It is the "Brave New World" or totalitarian argument. In Aldous Huxley's dystopian novel babies are not born naturally to be raised and cared for by families anymore but "produced" on a large scale *(in großem Stil)* in factories, prepared and educated for their future roles in children's homes. Cloning, the argument goes, could be used by unscrupulous dictators to create armies or work slaves.
The author then picks up the reproach that cloned offspring *(Nachwuchs)* might have to face unrealistic expectations from their parents. A clone of a successful Formula One racing driver would be expected to become a Formula One champion one day, and a super model might expect her cloned daughter to become her equal in beauty. Everyone would suffer if clones did not live up to their expectations.
The next to last argument the author deals with is the socially divisive *(spaltend)* cost argument. Wealthy people would be able to afford cloning themselves to have organ banks in case they might need "spare parts". These clones could be made without heads, so they could be used for transplants. Less well-off people would be barred from such a treatment since they would not be able to pay for it.
Finally, Hughes is concerned with one of the most frequently raised ethical arguments of all: since clones are not biologically unique, they will necessarily be regarded as second-rate, as carbon copies of the original. Their inferior value would increase with the rate of copies made and it would deprive them of their human dignity. This is the photocopy machine argument.

B)

1

The author of the column "Cloning as a Valid Reproductive Choice", James Hughes, defends what he calls people's "right to control their own reproduction" (l. 10). In arguing his case he dismisses *(herabwürdigen)* any counterarguments as "makeshift … [and not] … weighty enough" (ll. 9–10) and the concerns shared by many as "irrational fears" (l. 39). He is, therefore, not prepared to seriously consider any opposition to his view.

To endorse *(untermauern)* his point, he debates five of the more common arguments raised against human cloning. Each of the five paragraphs dedicated to a different argument is built in the same way: He generally introduces the opposing view using a negative verb ("warns", l. 11; "worry", l. 15; "fret", l. 22; "oppose", l. 26) in order to dismantle *(entkräften)* it with a few careless remarks. The basic structure of all of these paragraphs is antithetical.
While, superficially, this may be a persuasive strategy, his choice of words when dealing with the counterarguments clearly gives him away. In the past, "*bad* science fiction movies … were *arrayed against*" IVF (ll. 5–6) while "today in-vitro fertilization is an *accepted, mundane, widely used* tool" (ll. 6–7). On the one hand, Hughes uses derogatory *(abwertend)* terms to characterize opponents, on the other, he elevates his own position by using positively charged words. Further instances of the author's biased *(tendenziös)* vocabulary can be traced in each of the ensuing paragraphs: "There is no *slippery slope* [to totalitarianism] from parents *freely choosing* to use cloning", ll. 18–19). Equally, the phrase "*lust* after their daughters" (l. 12) contrasts with "this *is really an argument for* adoption" (l. 13), as is "will only be available to the *wealthy* and is a *waste* of resources" (l. 27) vs. "to give more people *access to quality health care*" (ll. 28–29).
There can be no doubt that James Hughes does not mince his words *(kein Blatt vor den Mund nehmen)*. He uses the internet platform to contribute to the ongoing debate in a very personal – and coarse *(derb, grob)* – way.

2

Since this is another open-ended task providing the frame for students to take a stand in the heated debate surrounding human cloning, opinions will be divided.

Letter A:
From: …
To: j.hughes@changesurfer.us
Re: Your column on reproductive cloning
Dear James Hughes,
You really seem to think it is as easy as that. "Let freedom ring" – the freedom to do anything! You call the fears that many people have "irrational" and you compare the "right to have a cloned child to the right to wear a red hat". Have you no shame?
I feel that children are given to us, they are not our property, and we should treat them as gifts, not as products. Yes, we would be travelling the road to the brave new world that science and technology are taking us toward if you and your bunch of irresponsible scientists had your way. We can't have that.
I'm NOT talking about the enormous risks that the donor and the mother are put

at. I'm NOT talking about the fact that, for every animal cloned so far, hundreds fail, either.

No, I'm talking about the abuse of human life. Nature has created the proper way to make babies and we shouldn't do it in a different way. Period.

That way each child is genetically unique, a cloned child is not genetically unique. Since it is genetically identical with another person, it will feel it is an individual of another kind.

The other point I'd like to make is that cloning involves throwing away some fertilized embryos, and many of the embryos selected to live fail to develop and eventually die before birth. To me, that is murder!

It is true that we humans have the choice. Let's hope we will not try to play God.

Yours (un-)truly,

…

Letter B:

From: …

To: j.hughes@changesurfer.us

Re: Your column on reproductive cloning

Dear James Hughes,

Cloning is the answer to many medical questions, and to a better quality of life. Very soon, we will see medical breakthroughs based on stem cell research, and scientists will develop new cures for the sick. The technology of cloning has the potential to save millions of lives. Let's do all we can to save all the people who suffer, right?

Besides, I couldn't agree more that reproductive cloning is a wonderful additional reproductive option, like you say. We are not playing God, we are merely using a technology to perfect ourselves and our children. I have a vision that we will be able to make clones of exceptional people in hope that their gifts and talents can be passed on. For the first time in our history, we stand a chance of being able to really IMPROVE our genetic material and become "better humans". Isn't that what your column is called?

I have read a lot of far-fetched horror stories about human cloning these days. They are utter nonsense. To imagine that we'll enrich life, prolong life … this new technology has enormous potential benefits and few real negative consequences. True, in the beginning, there might be some accidents. But handicapped clones can be sure to receive all the care and help they need. And who knows, one day they might be cured with a new therapy. We should be optimists, shouldn't we?

Yours electronically,

…

C)

Klon- und Stammzellenforschung

Die Klon- und Stammzellenforschung erlebte im Jahre 1997 die Geburt des Schafes Dolly, des ersten Tieres, das aus einer adulten Zelle geklont wurde. Dies war eine bemerkenswerte Leistung, die eine weltweite Debatte über die mit dem Klonen verbundenen ethischen Probleme anstieß. Internationale Institutionen wie das Europäische Parlament, die UNESCO und die WHO erklärten übereinstimmend, dass das Klonen von Menschen sowohl moralisch wie gesetzlich falsch sei. Wir müssen jedoch zwischen dem reproduktiven und dem therapeutischen Klonen unterscheiden. Heute ist die Vorstellung vom Klonen eines ganzen Menschen – die Kopie eines anderen Menschen herzustellen – für Wissenschaftler nicht länger interessant. Stattdessen löst das therapeutische Klonen in der Welt der Biotechnik gespannte Erwartung aus. Der Schlüssel zu dieser Technologie sind Stammzellen, welches die Kernzellen sind, die das Potential haben, im Körper zu irgendeiner anderen Zelle zu werden, so z.B. zu Nervenzellen, zu Blut-, Herz-, Muskel- oder sogar Gehirnzellen.
Stammzellen selbst haben zu einer weit verbreiteten Kontroverse geführt, da man glaubte, dass nur menschliche Embryonen diese liefern könnten. Es scheint jedoch jetzt so zu sein, dass adulte Stammzellen die gleiche Möglichkeit bieten. Dies würde bedeuten, dass ein Patient, der eine Herzattacke erlitten hat, den Ärzten eigene adulte Stammzellen liefern könnte, die dann wiederum in sein Herz zurückverpflanzt werden könnten, um neues Muskelgewebe wachsen zu lassen, das den geschädigten Muskel ersetzen könnte. Da der genetische Code identisch ist, würde es für das Implantat keine Abstoßungsreaktion geben, wie es leider bei Organtransplantationen vorkommt. Für die Zukunft hoffen die Biotechnologen, dass Stammzellen dazu genutzt werden können, ganze Organe zu züchten.
So bietet die Biotechnologie die Hoffnung, die medizinische Behandlung zu revolutionieren.

4.2.1

Practice 1

1. **The desire** to **preserve** one's youth or event to become younger again is strong in many. – 2. Many people lead a **perfectly normal** life. – 3. Old age **draws** near, as senses **dull** and organs begin **to fail**. – 4. The body clock **runs down**. – 5. Old age makes life no longer **worth living**. – 6. We experience years of **decline**. – 7. We enjoy the years of **health** and **productivity.** – 8. We must learn to grow old **with dignity**. – 9. We are **ravaged** by age and, finally, **pass** away. – 10. We should think twice before we **tinker with** the God-given human condition. – 11. Many scientists say we should **grasp** the opportunity. – 12. Cracking the DNA code

has **paved** the way for a bright future. – 13. The **cure** may turn out to be a **curse.** – 14. We are **in a position** to eventually decide about our lives. – 15. Genetic treatment may be **helpful** in some fields but **harmful** in others. – 16. We are **well-advised** to pause and think again. – 17. Biotechnology **inspires** hope in some but **raises** fears in others. – 18. Progress **opens up** enormous possibilities for treatment of age-related illnesses. – 19. What we know so far **proves,** at least for the time being, regenerative medicine to be an illusion. – 20. I **reject** any dehumanizing treatment. – 21. A genetic **modification** of your genetic make-up is dangerous. – 22. We will be able to **control** and even **reverse** the ageing of human cells.

Practice 2

1. one of the most far-reaching developments – 2. slow down the ageing process dramatically – 3. fixing the faulty gene – 4. have a complete understanding of what every gene does – 5. repair individual genomes by replacing defective genes – 6. it's human nature to give your kids any advantage you can – 7. is currently viewed with horror

4.2.2

A)

1

The numbers in the illustration placed in the story proper appear to be arranged at random. The story's title however provides a clue for understanding its composition: the top number 10 correlates with the uppermost part of the body, i.e. the head. It sits in a commanding position above the other numbers, which form a human body with its arms slightly extended and its feet spread and planted firmly on the ground. The various numbers downward from its head, as we may guess, represent the parts of a (female) body. The number 10 appears in larger font size *(Schriftgröße)* than the other figures, which suggests that, within the abstract female form, the head (and what goes on in it) is the crucial *(entscheidend)* element of the entire body structure.

2

As we begin to read, we learn that Julie "died at seventy, but [that] her head was only ten", l. 1). Are we to take that seriously? As we read on, we begin to understand that the story's protagonist has not lived with one but with several different "body clocks" inside her, some, such as her heart for example, running down but others, strangely, running in reverse order, i.e. making some parts of her body grow younger with the years.
A closer look at the story reveals that there seems to be an obvious logic behind

the various ageing, resp. rejuvenating processes competing against each other in Julie's body. When she dies at 70, her central organ, the heart, her neck, and her upper and lower extremities (arms, hands, and feet) have aged naturally. Certain other parts of her body appear to have continuously grown younger, at different speeds though. While her buttocks had begun their "back-to-youth" trip more recently than her breasts (53 years of age vs. 39), her waist is said to have been down to the age of 30 already. Interestingly, it is her head (face, hair but also Julie's mind, l. 30) that must have started the journey towards the "Fountain of Youth" *(Jungbrunnen)* since "by the time of Julie's death, her head of ten was half its way to nine" (ll. 32–33). Imagining her head (mind!) continuously growing younger, one wonders about the wisdom of her struggle.
The areas of Julie's body that had been revitalized as they grew younger are what can be called her female properties that, while still young and not subjected to the ravages of old age yet, made her attractive to men. Apparently, Julie, while she was alive, had been trying to preserve her attractiveness as a woman.

3

When her husband died, he must have made provisions for Julie's future: he left her "a home with no mortgage and a reliable monthly pension" (ll. 18–19). At the time of her own death at 70, both the mortgage-free *(hypothekenfrei)* house and the pension fund have been squandered *(verschwendet)*. Since Julie's sole focus in her latter years seems to have been her desire to become younger again, it can be inferred that her financial means appear to have gone into the care for her body. One can hardly imagine that cosmetics and toiletries have eaten up her money. Considering the vital changes having occurred in certain parts of her body, we have good reason to believe that she may have subjected herself to experimental genetic "morphing" *(Verwandlung)* (l. 22), using practically all the money available to her to pay for it.

4

Julie's funeral is attended by four anonymous men (l. 34), who seem very worried about Julie's passing away. The text mentions that all four of them had formed a strong attachment to her and that her death must have been a serious blow to them (ll. 34–36), and it also hints at the fact that they have "worked on her", each of them regarding Julie as his "life's finest work" (l. 42). As she lies in state *(aufgebahrt liegen)*, dressed in pink like a darling little girl with her young and immaculate *(makellos)* face, her four admirers (l. 42) are dismayed that their wonderful patient is to be cremated *(verbrennen)* and, thus, ruined forever.
The "long starched white coats" (ll. 34–35) they are wearing at the funeral instead of the conventional colour black, finally give them away as what they are: the four gentlemen are in fact doctors, or human geneticists, working to control, or

more precisely, reverse the ageing of human cells by interfering genetically with their growth and ageing process. Julie, whose heart is seventy when she dies and whose head is as young as ten again, "half its way to nine" (ll. 32–33), has been their controversial *(fragwürdig)* masterpiece.

B)

1

Julie's "bizarre" head had not only triggered *(auslösen)* her wish to become young again but had also travelled the longest way back on its journey into youth gaining in child-like perfection and innocence. Mercifully, her heart stopped beating when she turned seventy. It is therefore her head that the narrator focuses on as he follows the stages of her growing old respectively young in his story.
He begins in a seemingly matter-of-fact tone when he states the barely credible difference between Julie's biological age (70 when she dies) and her head (only 10). At first glance this discrepancy might be attributed to *(zurückführen)* the still immature state of her mind while her heart has failed due to age. This, however, is misleading. The fact of her head "being by far the youngest" (l. 4) is to be taken literally *(wörtlich nehmen)*. The narrator, for a moment, imagines a scenario such as the American futurologist Ray Kurzweil likes to predict for example, when he imagines (the contents of) Julie's head to be transferred onto a computer enabling her mind to live forever.
As he lists the successive stages that Julie's head goes through, his tone becomes imperceptibly *(unmerklich)* more ironic: "When Julie's heart went down at seventy, her head got pulled along", (ll. 8–9). The two verbs "go down" and "get pulled along", which he employs, are clearly familiar *(umgangssprachlich)* and jar with *(nicht passen zu)* the seriousness of her moment of death. Further examples of his playful and ironic tone can be traced in ll. 23–24 and l. 24 ("passed over the big six-0", "nose-dived", "on the course to zero, a point from which it could only go negative"). Later, her head "of ten" is described to be "half of its way to nine" (ll. 32–33).
The effect of irony is not only achieved through the narrator's use of inappropriately *(unangemessen)* familiar terms. At times, his style becomes unexpectedly formal, or even pompous, to keep his narrative tone ironic: until Julie's flirt with genetic treatment, her "head and body had co-existed in perfect concordance" (l. 13). A few lines earlier he states that Julie experiences her inner conflict as "a tragedy" (l. 11). The pain she feels seems to give, some years later, way to a more peaceful mind "in concert with her head … [which] grew blissfully unaware …" (l. 30). Finally, learning about Julie's "impending cremation" (l. 40) the four funeral guests, blunt caricatures of overzealous *(übereifrig)* scientists, are overcome with grief.
All things considered, the narrator's tone is clearly ironic. There can be no doubt

that he is out to criticize the prospect of genetic rejuvenation believed, by some, to be just around the corner.

2

As old age draws near, as senses dull *(nachlassen)* and organs begin to fail, the wish to preserve or to regain what once was taken for granted – youth, health and beauty – is not only a tantalizing *(verlockend)* idea but, for some people, an obsession. The story's protagonist Julie is possessed by the wish to grow young again.

Until the age of forty, she appears to have led a perfectly normal life (l. 16). Sensing the first signs of age and deterioration *(körperlicher Verfall)*, she turns to regenerative medicine with its promises of genetic cell treatment still in its early stages. When her head responds positively to its brain cells' telomeres *(Telomere; sie verursachen das Altern der Zellen)* being fully extended to their original youth, the quick success must have satisfied her deeply and whetted her appetite for more. Four scientists cooperate to fulfil Julie's wish for more. She becomes, as her daughter Anne sees it, a biological perversion (ll. 22–27). Julie's part-rejuvenation not only transforms her into a "monster", it also affects her family life deeply. Her compulsive vanity *(zwanghafte Eitelkeit)* wastes her financial means and alienates *(vertreiben)* her daughter.

Sadly, the fate that Julie suffers proves regenerative medicine to be an illusion. She falls prey to four "sorcerer's apprentices" *(Zauberlehrlinge)*, who are dismayed at their wonderful toy being taken away from them. Technology-based genetic treatment may bring forth human beings who do not deserve that name: the cure may turn out to be a curse.

Worse still, once the technology is perfected, there will be an economic angle to it. After her husband's death, Julie is a woman of means. She can afford to pay for her obsession. Generally, we will face the prospect of young and old, of mortals and "immortals" existing alongside one another since privileged western societies and its wealthy citizens only will be able to meet the expense of treatment. If it is reserved for the wealthy, this will increase the gap between rich and poor. If it is spread widely, perhaps even globally, the outcome will be a demographic disaster.

Most worryingly, what Julie, assisted by her willing doctors, does is tinker with *(herumbasteln an)* the God-given human condition. Her child-like mind has deprived her of *(rauben)* a sound judgement and maturity that come with age.

Yet it is growing old and dying that Julie and so many of us we want to run away from. Our horror of age stems from our obsession with youth; if we can outgrow the obsession with youth, men and women can move into age and become more themselves. What we rather need is not a "Fountain of Youth" but a "fountain of age", i.e. for ethical reasons we need to reject dehumanizing treatment that makes life no longer worth living even if we are kept technically young.

If we are to believe the narrator of the story, Julie herself considered it a tragedy that her "slack" waist was not keeping the pace set by her speedy head. Real tragedies occur on a different plane, though; they require a moral dilemma and often involve death. Julie's personal conflict, however, is not tragic – it is pathetic *(jämmerlich)*.

3

There will be general agreement that "we live in interesting times" (Fossel). Whether our "biotech" future inspires hope or raises fears in us is a matter of our personal outlook on life.

Those who feel that the biotechnology's benefits outweigh its risks may consider the following aspects:

- The dream of the "Fountain of Youth" has always been with us.
- A breakthrough will open up enormous possibilities for treatment of illnesses associated with old age and will help to control the process of the human "to wear out", so the years we add will be years of health and productivity, not years of decline.
- Advances in biotechnology could significantly reduce the astronomical medical costs caused by people who live in sickly, frail old age and trigger developments in other fields that can be marketed successfully, thus stimulating economic growth and prosperity for all.
- Being in a position to eventually decide about what we look like is a wonderful privilege. Man should grasp the opportunity. That's how culture evolves *(sich entwickeln)* and how science works. We should let the process of progressing continue.

Those, however, to whom the prospect seems frightening may want to argue as follows:

- Treatment may be helpful in some fields but harmful in others (negative side-effects). Age-related phenomena and illnesses are part of the human condition: eradicating *(ausmerzen)* them will lead to an absurd fitness race. It will bring sharp rivalry between the generations for living space and jobs, and the young will resent having to support the old.
- Advances in genetics will demand a massive amount of money to pave the way for extremely expensive research.
- Growing old and decrepit *(hinfällig)* is a fact of life. Life ends with death. So let us live meaningful lives and not play God by tinkering with our genes.
- We rather need to relearn coming to grips with age, i.e. we are well-advised to reject treatment that dehumanizes us even if we remain technically young. If we can get rid of our obsession with youth, we can grow old in dignity.

C)

Glückwunsch zum 150. Geburtstag? Neue Epoche des Alterns zeichnet sich ab
Die High-Tech-Medizin wird die Lebenserwartung steigern, sagen Fachleute voraus
Oxford, England, 16. März 2006 – Die moderne Medizin ist dabei, die Grenzen des Alters neu zu definieren und wird Menschen vielleicht bald ermöglichen, auf einer regelmäßigen Basis über die gegenwärtige Höchstgrenze von 120 Jahren hinaus zu leben, sagten Fachleute am Mittwoch.
Bisher hat man geglaubt, dass es eine eingebaute Begrenzung der Lebensspanne für Menschen gebe, aber diese Idee wurde bei einer Konferenz zum Thema eines längeren und besseren Lebens von einer Gruppe von Wissenschaftlern als unhaltbar erklärt.
Paul Hodge, Direktor des Harvard Programms für Generationenpolitik, sagte, dass Regierungen weltweit – die mit krisenhaften Rentensystemen, vergreisenden Werktätigen und steigenden Gesundheitskosten kämpfen – jetzt mit dieser Herausforderung konfrontiert seien.
„Die Lebenserwartung wird mit Sicherheit deutlich steigen, und die gegenwärtigen politischen Maßnahmen werden sich als völlig unzureichend erweisen", prophezeite er.
Nur wie hoch und wie schnell die Lebenserwartung steigen wird, ist eine offene Frage, aber die Zielrichtung und der sich beschleunigende Trend sind unumstritten. Richard Miller von der Michigan University Medical School sagte, Tests mit Mäusen und Ratten – genetisch den Menschen sehr ähnlich – hätten gezeigt, dass allein durch die Begrenzung des Kalorienverbrauchs die Lebenspanne um 40 Prozent ausgedehnt werden könnte.
Übertragen auf Menschen würde das bedeuten, dass die durchschnittliche Lebenserwartung in reichen Ländern von annähernd 80 auf 112 Jahre steigen könnte, wobei Einzelne noch viel länger leben könnten.
Aubrey de Grey, ein biomedizinischer Altersforscher von der Cambridge University, geht viel weiter. Er ist überzeugt, dass der erste Mensch, der 1000 Jahre alt werden wird, bereits geboren ist. Er sagte den Konferenzteilnehmern, dass regelmäßige körperliche Reparaturen durch Nutzung von Stammzellen, Gentherapie und andere Technologien den Alterungsprozess schließlich ganz anhalten könnten.

4.2.3

Practice

1. Lack of money **seems** to be the main problem. – 2. You **look as if** you haven't slept all night. – 3. In interviews she **comes across as** naive, but she's very good at her job. – 4. **It is undeniable that** she is an intelligent girl. – 5. It **looks** all very easy but **the truth is that** I work very hard. – 6. He **gives the appearance of**

being shy and modest but **underneath** he is a bully. – 7. She **didn't strike me as** the type who would want to become a teacher. But **deep down** she has always wanted just that. – 8. The situation at our school **is not what it seems: There is some solid evidence that** most students lack a proper attitude. – 9. Many people say teachers have to be strict, but **the reality is that** some overdo it. – 10. My form teacher **gives the impression of** being in control but **there is more to it than meets the eye**: **In reality** he is quite helpless.

4.2.4

Practice 1

1. That's **certainly/definitely** wrong. I can assure you. – 2. I **simply/completely/ entirely** forgot about her birthday. – 3. I **certainly/frankly** enjoyed the show. It was exciting. – 4. I **barely** enjoyed the show. Most of it was **simply/absolutely** boring. – 5. In the grammar test he failed **completely/entirely**. No correct answer. – 6. In the grammar test he failed **partly/to some extent**. Half his answers were wrong. – 7. I **simply/entirely/definitely** agree. What you are saying convinces me. – 8. I **partly/more or less** agree. I would perhaps add another point. – 9. **Frankly** I can't follow you there. That's rubbish. / I cannot follow you there **at all/in the least**. That's rubbish. – 10. I can **certainly/indeed** follow you there. You're right, that's rubbish.

Practice 2

a)

1. World War II **was won by the Allied Forces.**
2. Cancer **is caused, among other things, by smoking.**
3. America **was discovered first by the Norsemen in the 11th or 12th century.**

b)

1. white wine – 2. in the north – 3. a human brain – 4. being lazy

Practice 3

1. **It is the new free TV sports channel** I want to watch.
2. **It is because the class test raised so many difficult questions** that it took a long time to write.
3. **It was after Peter and his friends had left** that the party got going.
4. a) **It was the class speaker who** reported this incident to the headmaster.
   b) **It was this incident** that the class speaker reported to the headmaster.
   c) **It was to the headmaster** that the class speaker reported this incident.

5 A Taste of William Shakespeare

5.1.1

Practice 1

1. constituted – 2. could entail – 3. provides the clues for – 4. makes use of – 5. was thus regarded as – 6. goes to full lengths – 7. his focus changes. – 8. is concerned with – 9. serves to underscore – 10. revolve around – 11. take … as an example. – 12. can hardly be called

Practice 2

1. come true/materialize – 2. is based on/is dependent upon/results from – 3. examine/consider/deal with – 4. learns/discovers/knows from experience – 5. keeps to/limits himself to – 6. represents the reality of/is accurate as regards – 7. contrasts with/is very much opposed to – 8. asserts/claims/states – 9. criticize about – 10. contributes to/reinforces/supports – 11. produces/creates/brings about – 12. strikes me as – 13. can be attributed to – 14. becomes apparent – 15. suggests/implies – 16. is rich in/abounds in – 17. forms/can be considered as – 18. has its advantages/has its good side to it

5.1.2

A)

1

Criteria for subdivision: The introductory first sentence of the entire paragraph provides the clues for our subdivision: the author of the exhortation addressed to the "rulers" and "magistrates" of the time systematically describes the hierarchy of "all things" (l. 2). He logically begins with the sphere above earth, namely heaven, and proceeds to the sphere of earth before he deals with "man himself" (l. 17) and natural hierarchy among men.

Almighty God hath created and appointed **all things** in heaven, earth and waters, in a most excellent and perfect order.
In heaven he hath appointed distinct and several orders and states of archangels and angels.
On earth he hath assigned and appointed kings, princes, with other governors under them, in all good and necessary order. The water above is kept, and raineth down in due time and season. The sun, moon, stars, rainbow, thunder, lightning, clouds and all birds of the air, do keep their order. The earth, trees, seeds, plants, herbs, corn, grass, and all manner of beasts, keep themselves in order: all the parts

of the whole year, as winter, summer, months, nights and days, continue in their order. All kinds of fishes in the sea, rivers, and waters, with all fountains, springs, yea the seas themselves keep their comely course and order.
And **man himself** also hath all his parts both within and without, as soul, heart, mind, memory, understanding, reason, speech, with all and singular corporal members of his body, in a profitable, necessary, and pleasant order: every degree of people in their vocation, calling, and office, hath appointed to them their duty and order. Some are in high degree, some in low, some kings and princes, some inferiors and subjects, priests and laymen, masters and servants, fathers and children, husbands and wives, rich and poor; and everyone hath need of the other; so that in all things is to be lauded and praised the goodly order of God, without which no house, no city, no commonwealth can continue and endure or last.
For where there is **no** right order, there reigneth **all** abuse, carnal liberty, enormity, sin and babylonical confusion. Take away kings, princes, rulers, magistrates, judges and such states of God's order, no man shall ride or go by the highway unrobbed, no man shall sleep in his own house or bed unkilled, no man shall keep his wife, children, and possessions in quietness, all things shall be common; and there must needs follow all mischief and utter destruction both of souls, bodies, goods, and commonwealths.

2

People in Shakespeare's time believed that the universe (God's creation) constituted a harmonious pattern that was based on a strict hierarchy. For harmony to be kept in the universe, "all things" must occupy their "appointed" (l. 1) place within the system. This was called "The Great Chain of Being". It was imagined that "in heaven" (l. 2) archangels presided over ordinary angels; in the same way "on earth" (l. 5) man ruled over "beasts" (l. 13), who occupied a higher place on the ladder than plants or inanimate matter. Among men, too, God-given hierarchies had to be respected so that kings and princes had a higher degree than their subjects, masters ruled over their servants and fathers over their wives and children. The principle of a harmonious order was pervasive. As the sun enjoys prime status among the planets (cosmos), so does the noble king among his subjects (body politic), the courageous lion among the other animals, the proud eagle among the birds, and the sturdy oak among the trees.
The generally accepted doctrine was that of non-resistance. Disobedience or rebellion against the place or position one was assigned inevitably *(unausweichlich)* led to cosmic disorder among the stars or among the elements in the macrocosm (e.g. a thunderstorm), or political unrest to civil war and chaos. The unlawful attempt to overthrow a ruler was sparked *(ausgelöst)* by disorder within the soul of a man in the microcosm (e.g. ambition), or resistance against the father in the family was interpreted as a son's unauthorized behaviour

(e.g. disobedience). Moreover, rebellion against the established order in one place could entail disturbances in other places. The evil consequences of any rebellion were considered greater than any evil that was meant to be redressed *(beseitigen)* by any step of insurrection *(Aufstand)*.
Nature placed below the angels and above man in the hierarchy, acted according to her own rules, carrying out God's will without being conscious of doing so. Nature was thus regarded as a visible expression of God's intentions. On the highest rung of the ladder God watched over his creation from heaven situated outside the universe he had created. Degree established the different positions of created beings, binding them together: Degree helped nature to order the variety of God's creatures, preventing them from falling back into chaos; degree established harmony, mutual assistance and dependence among creatures.

3

The title of the "Exhortation" as well as its introductory sentence set the tone for what will follow in the body of the text. In ll. 1–27 its author goes to full lengths about the order-disorder antithesis. He describes the various elements of the interlocked pattern in positive terms: order, state, degree, duty.
In ll. 27–33, however, his focus changes. The last part of his text can be read as a warning (hence: exhortation). Here the author is concerned with possible consequences that have to be faced if the general order is disturbed or upset: disorder affects the cosmos (danger of universal chaos); it also disrupts the law within the state (danger of a revolution); finally it threatens or destroys man's physical and mental health (danger of insanity, loss of humanity and morality, danger of death).

B)

1

The "Exhortation Concerning Good Order and Obedience to Rulers and Magistrates" is a rhetorically well crafted text. It follows a clear line of thought, illustrating the concept of order from the "prime mover" (God) down the ladder of being, and, finally, gives a warning of what would happen when that divine order is disturbed.
A closer look at the author's choice of words reveals his moral stance *(moralische Position)*. Whenever he refers to the idea of order or its synonym ("degree"), he does not hesitate to describe it in the most positive terms: "a most excellent and perfect order" (ll. 2–3). Throughout the text, a large variety of "elevating" terms can be noted to accompany the headword. The God-given order is "good and necessary" (ll. 7–8), "the seas themselves keep their comely course and order" (l. 17), "so that in all things is to be lauded and praised the goodly order of God"

(l. 25). For emphasis the author makes use of an adjectival triad: "in a profitable, necessary, and pleasant order" (l. 20). The reigning order has been "appointed" (l. 1), "assigned" (l. 6) and "created" (l. 1) by God, and it has to be kept (ll. 8, 11, 13). By contrast, the author's choice of words changes dramatically when he issues his deeply-felt warning against the loss of "the right order" (l. 27): the scenario that he conjures up to deter potential rebels and insurgents *(Aufständische)* have a decidedly negative denotation. The author feels very strongly about "abuse" (wrongful use), and he condemns sex outside marriage ("carnal liberty"). It is interesting to note that the term "liberty" understood positively by modern governments and activists carries a negative connotation here as in phrase of "taking liberties with someone" and, what is more, that the author denounces "enormity" (the opposite of moderation and measure *(Mäßigung)*) as a criminal act. Acts of political and personal disobedience will result in "babylonical confusion" (l. 28). These activities will not only lead to a state of general lawlessness and chaos (robbery, murder, betrayal and dispossession, ll. 30–32) but, equally important, corrupt and destroy man's health and well-being (ll. 32–33). The author's interesting choice of words serves to underscore his religiously-tinged commitment *(religiös gefärbtes Engagement)*: by elevating the "holy" order that God has "appointed" and "assigned" to be respected and kept by man and the entire creation, and by devaluating the forces of "sin" and "evil", he clearly reveals himself to be a "King's man".

2

In fact *all* of Shakespeare's plays revolve around the order-disorder antithesis, be it on the macrocosmic (cosmos, earth, or body politic and family) or on the microcosmic level (man, body and soul, reason and passion). It is safe to say that the struggle between reason and immoderate passion in his heroes' souls with its subsequent break of civil law and the laws of nature, is a key motif in his plays. It is usually the breach of *(Verstoß gegen)* the doctrine of non-resistance that sets the dramatic action in motion.
Let us take the tragedy of "Macbeth" as an example. The play is set in a society in which the honour of keeping one's word and loyalty to one's superiors are of prime importance. The king presides over this consistent and closely-knit hierarchy; he is God's representative on earth. All other relationships also depend on loyalty: comradeship in warfare, hospitality of host towards guest, and the bonds between husband and wife. In this play, all these basic relationships are disrespected or even broken. Lady Macbeth's influence on her husband, Macbeth's bold act of regicide, and his destruction of natural ties, all go against the natural order of things. Thus, when Lennox and the Old Man discuss the terrifying alteration in the natural order of the universe – tempests, earthquakes, darkness at noon, etc. –, these are all reflections of the upheaval of the natural order that Macbeth has

brought about in his own microcosmic world.
It is, therefore, his ambition to become king that violates the natural order and that, ultimately, precipitates his downfall. In the play, Duncan is always referred to as a "king," while Macbeth soon becomes known as the "tyrant." The difference between the two types of rulers seems to be expressed in a conversation that occurs in Act IV, Scene 3, when Macduff meets Malcolm in England. In order to test Macduff's loyalty to Scotland, Malcolm pretends that he would make an even worse king than Macbeth. He tells Macduff of his reproachable qualities – among them a thirst for personal power and a violent temperament, both of which seem to characterize Macbeth perfectly. On the other hand, Malcolm says, "The king-becoming graces/[are] justice, verity, temp'rance, stableness,/Bounty, perseverance, mercy, [and] lowliness" (IV, 3, 92–93).
The model king, then, offers the kingdom an embodiment of order and justice, but also comfort and affection. Under him, subjects are rewarded according to their merits, as when Duncan makes Macbeth thane of Cawdor after Macbeth's victory over the invaders. Most important, the king must be loyal to Scotland above his own interests. Macbeth, by contrast, brings only chaos to his realm – symbolized in the bad weather and bizarre supernatural events – and offers no real justice, only a habit of murdering those he sees as a threat. As the embodiment of tyranny, he must be overcome by Malcolm so that Scotland can have a true king once more.

3

Throughout the 20th century, we have seen dictatorships evolve, peak, and fall. Those dictatorial regimes were based on absolute obedience and thrived on the oppression of their citizens. Stepping into the 21st century, we have witnessed the rise of world wide terrorist threats. Terrorist cells demand of their activists absolute obedience and the will to sacrifice their lives. Against such barbarous beliefs we pit *(in Stellung bringen)* ourselves and our idea of democracy.
The doctrine of non-resistance and political thought at the time of the Elizabethans can hardly be called democratic. Perhaps the most striking aspect of England in the 16th century was the general refusal to admit that any case can be made for a right of rebellion. It derived from the sense of the need of order, from the sense that the welfare and very existence of the commonwealth was bound up with obedience to authority, from the sense of danger from foreign enemies. We do indeed see things differently. The best expression of what we believe in can, perhaps, be found in the ideas that have been laid down in the Declaration of Independence and the American Constitution. The former declares that "all men are created equal, that they are endowed by their creator with certain unalienable rights, that among these are life, liberty and the pursuit of happiness". These human rights have been accepted since by democracies around the

world. Furthermore, "The Bill of Rights" demands protection of the citizens' civic freedoms, such as the freedom of the press and others. Most importantly, perhaps, we are indebted to the idea that "governments are instituted among men, deriving their just powers from the consent of the governed, that whenever any form of government becomes destructive of these ends, it is the right of the people to alter or to abolish it, and to institute new government" (Declaration of Independence). We do believe in the right to resist - against a government or regime that we feel is unjust and unlawful. This is part of the German *Grundgesetz*, too.
Recent German history can provide a legitimate example of a peaceful revolution where the governed did not consent to their government anymore but took to the streets to protest against oppression and government harassment of its citizens. The Berlin Wall came down in 1989, the GDR regime had to step down, and the reunification of the two Germanys was achieved soon after.

C)

Ein Zeitalter der Erfindungen, Entdeckungen und Erkundungen
Die Renaissance war ein Zeitalter der Erfindungen, Entdeckungen und Erkundungen, und vielleicht spiegelt sich der Geist der Epoche am besten in den Entdeckerreisen. Christoph Columbus erreichte Amerika im Jahre 1492, Vasco da Gama umsegelte auf dem Weg nach Indien das Kap der Guten Hoffnung im Jahre 1498, und während des nächsten Jahrhunderts brachen unzählige spanische, portugiesische und englische Seeleute auf, um überseeische Gebiete zu erforschen.
Die Gründe für diese Reisen und die Umstände, unter denen sie unternommen wurden, können viel zur Erklärung dessen beitragen, was die Renaissance war. Zunächst war die Renaissance ein Zeitalter, in dem die Menschen begannen, die Horizonte ihres Universums zu erweitern; die Entdeckerreisen waren dafür der geographische Ausdruck. Sodann war die Renaissance ein Zeitalter wissenschaftlicher Erfindungen, und eine der wichtigsten Erfindungen - wenngleich den Chinesen schon seit Jahrhunderten bekannt - war der Seemannskompass, der es den Seeleuten erlaubte, sich auf die offene See hinauszuwagen, anstatt der Küstenlinie zu folgen, wie sie es bis dahin getan hatten. Schließlich war die Renaissance ein Zeitalter des wachsenden Handels zwischen souveränen Staaten; bis dahin in Europa unbekannte Reichtümer wurden aus dem Nahen und Fernen Osten und aus der Neuen Welt, als die Amerika zuerst bekannt war, mitgebracht. Die Stadtstaaten Norditaliens waren die ersten, die den neuen Reichtum (und damit verbunden die Macht) erfuhren, einen Reichtum, der dem Handel mit den Nahen Osten entsprang. Kapital wurde angesammelt, Banken wurden gegründet, und ein Handel in großem Stil blühte; dies war der Anbruch des kapitalistischen Zeitalters. Der Kreis schließt sich an dieser Stelle. Da die Erträge aus dem Handel mit dem

Nahen Osten so groß waren, dass sie nicht alle für die Re-Investition in den Handel benötigt wurden, war Geld auch für die Künste und die Wissenschaften verfügbar. Die Renaissance war damit der Beginn einer neuen Epoche der Geschichte; sie war der Anfang unseres Zeitalters der Moderne. Tiefgreifende Veränderungen im System der Wirtschaft fanden statt, die wiederum zu neuen Entwicklungen nicht nur in Politik und Diplomatie, sondern auch in der Kultur und den Künsten führten. Im frühen 16. Jahrhundert hatte die Renaissance ihren Höhepunkt erreicht und bewegte sich in Italien, dem Land ihres Ursprungs, auf ihr Ende zu. In England hatte sie jedoch gerade begonnen und sollte ihren größten Einfluss dort in der Zeit Shakespeares haben.

5.1.3

Practice 1

1. Mein Freund ist ein **mitfühlender** Mensch. – 2. Wenn er zu sehr unter Druck ist, kann er **schließlich** zusammenbrechen. – 3. Ich habe noch einen Freund: er ist der **normalste** Mensch, den ich kenne. – 4. Gleichzeitig ist er sehr zurückhaltend und **schüchtern**. – 5. Seine Freundin soll ein **vernünftiges** Mädchen sein.

Practice 2

1. take a seat. – 2. take place – 3. not … either – 4. reasonable.

Practice 3

1. We believe that this day will make you **happy**. – 2. He has no opinion **of his own**. – 3. The text **can be divided into/divides into** five main sections. – 4. In the **introductory** part the author presents his topic. – 5. In the main part he **provides** a lot of facts. – 6. The text **is meant to** shape the reader's responses. – 7. The author argues **one-sidedly/with a bias**. – 8. The author argues **consistently**.

5.1.4

Practice 1

a)

1. taking/looking at – 2. make up – 3. achieve/pursue his aims. – 4. Could you come to/speak to – 5. cope with – 6. assumed/adopted – 7. follows/appears – 8. arises/must be posed – 9. reveals

b)

1. put forth/advance – 2. find/hit upon – 3. give/provide – 4. practice/exert – 5. draw – 6. make – 7. give/provide

Practice 2

zusammenfassend	in **sum/brief**
um es kurz zu machen	to cut a long story **short**
mit einem Wort	**in** a word
im Ganzen	on the **whole**
alles in allem	(all) in **all**
kurz gesagt	to put it in a **nutshell**
wenn man alles zusammen betrachtet	all things **considered**

Practice 3

a)

1. deeply/profoundly impressed – 2. vividly imagine – 3. vaguely hints – 4. bitterly/grimly comments – 5. flatly refuse – 6. accurately explains – 7. increasingly difficult – 8. completely/utterly wrong – 9. strongly/highly/ fully – 10. strongly/violently ... extremely

b)

1. great/prime/vital/utmost – 2. little/minor/secondary – 3. reasonable/ sensible – 4. vivid/colourful – 5. close/intimate – 6. strained/tense – 7. have in common/share – 8. decently/with respect/with dignity.

5.1.5

Practice 1

Your examination of the paragraph should roughly look like this:

The main reason that seems to drive people to watch daring and breathtaking events is their desire for sensations. ← **short, straightforward (topic-giving) main clause**

Sensational events in general prove to be good material for conversations and chats. ← **short developing sentence, which expands the topic**

If, on a given day, **one TV channel presents the pictures of someone** jumping off a 150-feet cliff and diving into the water safely, ← **conditional clause with added double participle phrase**

this jump certainly will be the topic of conversations and chats on the other. ← **precedes main clause (complex developing sentence)**

Consequently **people can brag about having** seen it in the evening news, **having** watched the TV broadcast immediately after the jump or even **having** been at the scene of attraction itself, the cliff. ← **longer compound sentence (three successive objects)**

By talking about a sensational event, **one automatically draws attention to oneself.** ← **gerund phrase, precedes short main clause**

And this is something that few people can resist, of course.	← **short (sweeping) concluding main clause**

Teacher comment: Excellent job by the 12-grader: She definitely knows how to handle her paragraph. Both her introductory and her concluding sentences are short and to the point. In between the student develops her initial statement by choosing not only longer but also more complex sentence structures. The variations in sentence lengths make the above paragraph very readable.

Practice 2

Why are so many people drawn to events that are out of the ordinary?	← **short (topic-giving) question: OK!**
It is their longing to escape the dull and uneventful routine of their lives.	← **short main clause (MC) (premise): OK!**
The endless repetitiveness of their daily lives makes them hunger for a change now and then.	← **short MC (developing): parallel but unconnected!**
This change should be sensational. It should also not be dangerous for themselves.	← **ultra-short MC;** ← **ultra-short MC: parallel developing sentence: unconnected**
They like excitement but it must not involve any personal risk for them.	← **compound sentence = two main clauses: repetition of idea!**
They like watching from the sidelines even better.	← **ultra-short MC: repetition of idea!**
They also do not mind watching catastrophes.	← **ultra-short MC: second idea!**
Take the scene of an accident on the Autobahn, for example.	← **short command: OK! (introduces example)**
You can see that car drivers in the opposite direction stop to get a good view of the damage done.	← **complex sentence: unconnected MC + nominal clause ("that") + infinitive phrase**
They block the traffic because they are curious.	← **complex sentence: unconnected MC/ adverbial clause of reason**
These are my reasons why I believe that ordinary people are highly interested in sensations.	← **complex concluding sentence: MC + indirect question + nominal clause ("that"): no clincher!**

Teacher comment: There is surprisingly little variation in sentence length and even less variety of sentence patterns. There is an overemphasis on short, even ultra-short, main clauses throughout, except for the passage that provides an example (= two comparatively simple "complex" sentences). More importantly, the endless piling of one short main clause on the other has been done without connecting or contrasting them in any way: a major flaw! The author of this paragraph certainly has a long way to go yet.

Practice 3

Why are so many people fond of sensations whether they read them in the gutter press, watch them on TV or witness them with their own eyes?
For one, it might be argued that, considering their, perhaps, uneventful and, sometimes, dull lives, a lot of people appreciate a little distraction from their daily routine. The circus or road show sensation in town has been replaced by worldwide TV broadcasts and sensational media events: it is the excitement that comes with events out of the ordinary. For another, there is no denying that some people love courting danger – from a safe vantage point. You may call it the thrills of spectator sport. If you take the example of car crashes on the Autobahn, you will see car drivers in other lanes stop to get a good view of what has happened, oblivious of the danger they themselves might create. They have been there and have a story to tell!

5.2.1

Practice 1

1. The playwright has his character **portray** a bee colony. – 2. By **comparing the working of a bee colony to Henry's kingdom he encourages** King Henry. – 3. I **believe/feel** that Canterbury's analogy is false. – 4. **In ll.9–25 Canterbury compares** a bee colony and Henry's kingdom. – 5. In these lines Canterbury **unfolds** the topic of order and obedience. – 6. Later in the play, **Canterbury's advice** is proved right. – 7. **It ought to be mentioned that** Shakespeare uses a rich metaphorical language. **The original character of his imagery makes his text sound very fresh**.

Practice 2

a)

1. He **meets** his King **with deference**. – 2. **A beehive and Henry's kingdom differ in that an animal society works by instinct whereas a state is based on political thought**. – 3. The relationship between England and France is **strained.** – 4. Canterbury describes England **as a haven of peace and tranquillity**.

b)

1. He begins by describing the working of a beehive and **ends by drawing his conclusion.** – 2. The **final** conclusion can be found in l. 34. – 3. Throughout his speech he **uses a variety of images**. – 4. The **dialogue can be read as a discussion** between the king and his advisors. – 5. The **political concept laid out by Canterbury** makes me think of constitutional monarchy. – 6. **The speaker is concerned with** the question of whether to stay in England or to leave the country and go to war. – 7. **According to him/In his opinion** Henry's throne is safe.

Practice 3

1. The image in l. 12 not only suggests the bees' degree of organization but also **their ability to defend their hive**. – 2. The message Canterbury would like to impress on the King is the **fact that his throne is safe** and that he need not worry about leaving his country. – 3. What he says and **what he means** are two different things. – 4. He praises **both** England and its political stability. – 5. By examining Shakespeare's imagery and **by studying** his language in general you will understand the way he writes. – 6. Canterbury explains the present situation and **his conviction that** Henry should go to war. – 7. He expresses himself through vivid images but, sometimes, **uses abstract terms,** too.

Practice 4

1. We **learn** that Henry is about to leave England. – 2. He tries to **obtain** some advice as to the wisdom of his mission. – 3. As he speaks, Canterbury **becomes** more and more involved. – 4. Canterbury **makes the King understand his** message. – 5. This **becomes** clearer as we read on. – 6. Where can you **purchase** tickets for the Shakespeare play?

5.2.2

A)

1

Henry's main interest for going to war in France is in gaining control of lands in France – lands that he believes to be his right. Determined to regain the lands in France held by his ancestors, he prepares to attack France, thus reopening the Hundred Years War between England and France. Both Exeter and Canterbury as his advisors reassure him as regards his military mission. Henry expresses concern that the Scottish rebels on his northern border will invade the country and dethrone him while he is away. Nevertheless he resolves to proceed with the invasion.

2

Fearing unrest and rebellion from other pretenders *(Thronanwärter)* to his throne in England while he is away in France to reconquer parts of the country he believes to be rightfully his, Henry turns to his uncle and the Archbishop of Canterbury for advice. Especially Canterbury encourages him to set off for France and pursue his interests there ("Therefore to France, my liege", l. 34). In the passage under scrutiny *(besagter Abschnitt)*, the Archbishop addresses Henry's fears concerning a possible inner feud *(innenpolitische Auseinandersetzung)* and his status as king of England. He reassures Henry by saying that his kingdom is in perfect order and his position as ruler will be uncontested *(unbestritten)*. Henry's absence from home and the fact that he will take an army with him, leaving only part of his military forces to guard the country at home, will not jeopardize *(gefährden)* his throne ("I this infer,/That many things, having full reference/To one consent", ll. 25–27). While he will be waging war in his country's interest in France, his position back in England will be safe.

B)

1

In their attempt to reassure and encourage the King in his enterprise, both of his advisors emphasize the natural harmony in a body politic (Henry's England) that is based on strict hierarchy and the division of labour. Clearly defined rank and degree are a safeguard against rebellion and chaos, the citizen's awareness of degree establishes harmony, mutual assistance and interdependence for the welfare of the whole.
While the King's uncle, Exeter, compares the work of a government to that of a well-trained orchestra (ll. 1–4), in which the various musical instruments contribute to create a harmonious piece of music, Canterbury draws an analogy between the King's realm and the perfect order that reigns inside a beehive. Speaking at length to the King, he expands his comparison into an extended simile: all members of the community occupy their place and fulfil the "divers function[s]" (l. 6) they are given, "obedience" (l. 9) being the prime virtue *(hervorstechendste Tugend)* among men as well as among the honeybees. The bees, Canterbury argues, "by a rule in nature teach/The act of order to a peopled kingdom", ll. 10–11). Their colony is peopled with a "king" (the queen "who, busied in [her] majesty, surveys the singing masons building roofs of gold", ll. 18–19), officers and "sad-ey'd" (l. 23) magistrates, merchants, soldiers, porters (worker bees), and "lazy yawning drones" (l. 25), who pursue their course each. As Canterbury warms to his subject *(engagierter werden)*, his manner of speaking becomes more and more metaphorical blending the two spheres into one *(die beiden Ebenen miteinander verschmelzend)*: "soldiers, armed with their stings,/Make boot upon the summer's velvet buds" (ll. 15–16) carrying their prey back to the "tent-royal" (l. 17), where masons busy themselves with "building roofs of gold" (combs, l. 19) and where you can observe citizens "kneading up the honey" (l. 20) (manufacture goods from raw materials). However, he seems to get carried away by his enthusiasm when he imagines bee "judges" at work to mete out the death penalty to workshy drones, who refuse to contribute their share to the common good (ll. 23–25). We know that, within the bee colony, drones serve to fertilize the queen and, having done their duty, die. Having said that, Canterbury can now press his point: the "one purpose" (l. 33) warrants a division of forces in the country's interest. To his mind, Henry may rest

assured about the home front *and* deploy troops abroad to reclaim parts of France that the English Crown believes it is entitled to. To support his view, Canterbury makes use of a different set of similes. Four different comparisons drawn from nature (rivers, sea), man's technical achievements (ways, town; partitions, sundial), and warfare (arrows, mark, ll. 28–31) illustrate what the speaker wants to prove: if, in a kingdom that is in good care, many *different* single forces work towards the one common goal, the prospect of winning the day is good ("That many things, having full reference/To one consent, may work contrariously ... [but]/End in one purpose, and be all well borne/Without defeat" (ll.26–34)). Pointing out a striking correspondence *(Entsprechung)* to the perfect organization of bee colonies, Canterbury has convinced his King that his realm is in good order and that he need not fear to leave it. Henry decides to go to France and wage war.

2

Though its seemingly perfect organization and the dedicated social behaviour of its members may be marvellous to watch, a beehive may well be compared to a prospering kingdom as the Elizabethans believed it should be, but it can hardly be taken as a model for our modern western societies.
A bee colony appears to resemble a stable and well-functioning monarchy at the time of the Elizabethans in more than one way. The *raison d'être ("Staatsräson")* that dominates in a beehive and that protects the rightful ruler of a monarchy is the law of "non-resistance". Bees instinctively cling to collective patterns of genetically programmed dutiful behaviour. Birth determines their place, and they cannot escape their fate whether as a queen, as workers, or as drones. While the king's subjects may not have been programmed to pull their weight *(ihre Last tragen)*, it was still believed that they, too, were born as future kings, soldiers, merchants, or work slaves and educated to accept the place they were assigned *(zugewiesen)*. Respecting rank and degree, every citizen had to work for the benefit of the whole. This applies to *(gelten für)* the humble worker as well as to the ruler. A bee queen can only claim to rule as long as she is capable of strengthening the colony through reproduction. If not, she is replaced by a younger queen. Equally, the legitimate monarch in Elizabethan times had to reign vigorously *(kraftvoll)* and wisely. When he neglected his duty through misrule and mismanagement, his position then – but only then – was jeopardized *(gefährdet)*.
We moderns, however, have learnt to believe in the ideal of democracy. Democracy invests its leaders with power for a limited span of time – not for a lifetime. When an elected government's term of office *(Amtsperiode)* runs out, it has to hand its power back to the people, who then may, or may not, decide to re-elect it. We, the governed, also claim the right to withdraw our consent expressed in general elections every four or five years when we feel the power we have invested our political leaders with is not used to the best of our country. We then

seek legitimate ways to overthrow the government as we are convinced it fails in its duties. As citizens "endowed with ... unalienable rights" (Declaration of Independence) we finally trust in the idea of personal advancement in life based on individual achievement *(Leistung)* and merit *(Verdienst)* – not on privilege or disadvantage by birth. Strict adherence to rank and degree, an unquestioned social position once established and never to be changed, would deny us the opportunities to shape our lives as we please.
The belief in absolute obedience and loyalty to appointed rulers shared by Shakespeare's contemporaries lends itself to *(sich eignen für)* a comparison to the behaviour pattern ruling a beehive. It cannot be considered as a solid basis for a modern democracy that relies on the free consent and loyalty, not the complete obedience, of its citizens.

C)

Honigbienen

Honigbienen sind gesellige Insekten, die in perfekt organisierten Kolonien zusammenleben. Jedes Mitglied dieser Gemeinschaft hat eine besondere Aufgabe zu erfüllen. Eine einzelne Honigbiene kann nicht aus sich selbst wachsen oder überleben. Die drei unterschiedlichen Arten der Honigbiene in der Kolonie sind die Königin, die Arbeitsbiene und die Drohne.
Die Königin ist die längste Biene im Bienenstock, hat aber die kürzesten Flügel. Sie ist die Mutter aller anderen Bienen. Ihre wichtigste Aufgabe ist das Eierlegen. Ihre Produktivität hängt ab von der Menge an Nahrung, die ihr die Arbeitsbienen bringen, und von dem verfügbaren Platz in der Kolonie zum Brüten. Sie kann pro Tag mehr als 1500 Eier legen.
Arbeiterinnen sind kleiner als die Königin und die Drohnen, dafür gibt es viele von ihnen. Es können über Winter und im Vorfrühling nur einige hundert sein, aber gewöhnlich sind es im Sommer bei reichlich verfügbarem Blütenstaub und Nektar viele tausende. Eine große Kolonie kann in voller Stärke bis zu 100 000 Arbeiterinnen haben. Diese Bienen erhalten die Kolonie am Leben. Ihre Aufgaben ändern sich mit ihrem Alter. Junge Exemplare, Hausbienen genannt, tun die Hausarbeit im Stock. Sie produzieren Wachs und formen es zu Waben (Zellstrukturen, die Honig und die Brut enthalten) und verwenden Propolis (eine gummiartige Substanz, die von Pflanzen gesammelt wird), um im Stock Spalten zu versiegeln oder raue Ecken zu glätten. Hausbienen können auch ihre Flügel bewegen, um den Stock im Sommer zu durchlüften und damit die Temperatur und die Feuchtigkeit zu kontrollieren, und sie sorgen im Winter für Wärme. Einige bewachen den Stock gegen fremde Räuber. Viele produzieren Honig und Gelee Royale. Viel Zeit wird darauf verwendet, die Brut zu füttern und die Zellen zu säubern und auszubessern. Hausbienen füttern auch die Königin, die Drohnen und einander. Ältere Arbeits- oder Feldbienen sammeln Nektar, Blütenstaub und Wasser.

Drohnen sind größer als Arbeiterinnen, aber nicht so lang wie Königinnen. Eine Drohne hat große Augen, die einander an der Spitze Kopfes berühren. Drohnen haben keinen Stachel, keine Blütenstaubkörbe an ihren Beinen oder wachsproduzierende Drüsen, und ihre Mundwerkzeuge sind zu kurz, um Nektar zu sammeln. Darüber hinaus erfüllen sie nicht einmal Aufgaben, die ihnen möglich wären, wie z.B. das Durchlüften des Stocks. Ihre einzige Funktion ist es, die Königin zu befruchten, und sie sterben dabei.
In vielerlei Hinsicht gleicht eine Honigbienenkolonie einem einzigen Tier. Individuelle Bienen und Kasten sind wie die Zellen und das Gewebe. Wenn ein Teil bedroht ist, reagiert die gesamte Kolonie. Wenn ein wichtiges Segment einer Kolonie krank oder zerstört wird, kann die Kolonie als Ganzes sich häufig selbst heilen. Sie kann sich in zwei oder mehr getrennte Kolonien aufspalten.

5.2.3

Practice 1

a)

The article can be **understood** as a warning against warmongers. – Our attention is **caught** by the long list of gruesome facts about war reality. – As always the author **chooses** his words carefully. – That war was a great risk; it has not **paid** off. – The author has **shown** us which way to take in the years to come.

b)

The text under discussion is about the problems our educational system **is faced** with right now. – **Taking** everything into consideration we'll have to make a complete U-turn. – Nobody **needs** to feel left behind if the financial stakes are raised. – Success at school **does not depend** on one's intelligence alone. – The unexpected PISA results have made the school administrations' heads **work**. – They did not understand what the results **meant**. – They had **heard** about the Scandinavian countries top ranks.

Practice 2

In contrast to the members of her Indian family, Jess loves football and worships David Beckham. – According to her family clan **there is** no chance for her to play for a local girls' team. – The **proof** can be seen in the way her mother reacts when she learns that Jess plays football. – Jess **argues** with her mother but she has to quit playing. – Jess gets to know her coach and she is fascinated by his **good looks**. – When her team mate Jules finds out about Jess and her coach, Jess has the **worst** time of her life. – Her sister's Indian wedding **reminds** her of traditional Indian customs. – She feels she is old enough now and thinks she is **able** to stand on her own feet. – At one time in the movie there is **hardly any** chance for her to continue playing on her local team. – She is **desperate** until her father, who is more understanding than the rest of her family, lets her slip away to join her team and score the winning goal with a Beckham-style free kick.

Practice 3

1. settled/resolved – 2. complex/intricate – 3. make us see/make us understand – 4. can be explained by/can be attributed to – 5. derogatory – 6. speech/use of English – 7. In brief/To sum it up – 8. Frankly/To cut a long story short – 9. beside the point/out of place. – 10. I'm uncertain/I wonder/I can't make up my mind

5.2.4

Practice 1

1. to – 2. with – 3. to – 4. on – 5. on – 6. to – 7. of – 8. with – 9. of – 10. about, at – 11. to

Practice 2

1. A king is not **chosen** but appointed. – 2. He **chose** the right life; he may **choose** whether to keep the law or not. – 3. My **belief** is that man is independent; the **beliefs** that were held at Shakespeare's time are outdated. – 4. I **believe** he is definitely wrong; **believing** is matter of faith; in my **belief** that sounds odd. – 5. He was afraid he might **lose** his throne; and indeed he **lost** it; winning is better than **losing**, right? – 6. You **fulfil** expectations; the text is **full** of images; I remember **full** well what it was like; a **faithful** friend; an **awful** experience; she has **fulfilled** all my hopes.

Practice 3

a)

1. asserts/affirms – 2. understood/read – 3. destroyed; destruction – 4. lists/enumerates – 5. encourages

b)

1. The doctrine of non-resistance was not called into question. – 2. Man was assigned a firm place within the hierarchy. – 3. Man is too complex to fit into a hierarchy obediently. – 4. Henry's fears of going abroad are deep-rooted/profound.

Practice 4

1. Clearly – 2. Admittedly – 3. Undoubtedly – 4. Frankly speaking – 5. Unfortunately – 6. Apparently – 7. Certainly – 8. Unsurprisingly

Practice 5

There are some **advantages that speak for** the Elizabethan world picture. – The "Exhortation" **is meant to/is supposed to** warn rulers and magistrates in Shakespeare's time of neglecting their duties. – As everything and everybody was assigned their firm place in the hierarchy, it was almost impossible for people to **advance personally/climb on the social ladder**. – The doctrine was formulated to **prevent/avoid conflicts** within the body politic. – Chaos and destruction might **arise/crop up** if the laws were not respected. – A good king and ruler must **deal with/cope with** rebellion and unlawful behaviour in his realm.

6 The Changing Face of Britain

6.1.1

Practice 1

1. about – 2. from … by – 3. (-) – 4. of – 5. for – 6. of – 7. of – 8. (-) – 9. of – 10. from – 11. by – 12. on

Practice 2

1. **agree to** ← *you agree to a thing!* – 2. **agree with** ← *you agree with a person!* – 3. **concerned with** ← **to be concerned with** = *befasst sein mit, behandeln* – 4. **concerned about** ← **to be concerned about** = *besorgt sein über* – 5. **care about** … **not care for** ← **care about** = *Wert legen auf*, **not care for** = *verzichten auf* – 6. **asks for** ← **ask for sth.** = *um etw. bitten* – 7. **ask** … **about** ← **ask about sth.** = *Informationen über etw. einholen* – 8. **angry with** ← **angry with sb.** = *auf jdn. wütend sein* – 9. **angry at** ← **angry at sth.** = *wütend sein/werden wegen einer Sache* – 10. **At the end of** ← **at the end of sth.** = *zeitliche oder örtliche Position* – 11. **In the end** ← **in the end** = *schließlich (Ende eines Prozesses)*

Practice 3

1. **With** Paul good manners are no problem. – 2. **At** night or **at** breakfast he avoids unnecessary noise. – 3. He spends a lot of time **with** his student friends. – 4. He actually lives **near** Leeds. – 5. Paul has a part-time job. He works **for** MacDonald's. – 6. **With** Vic and Terry this is different. They are unemployed. – 7. They are parasites. **Upon** closer examination this becomes clear. – 8. **In** films rebellious adolescents are popular at the moment.

Practice 4

By [this word] = *mit [diesem Wort]* – **By this sentence** = *mit diesem Satz* – **by that** = *damit* – **by Roy Minton** = *von Roy Minton* – **by car** or **by train** = *mit dem Wagen/mit dem Zug* – **by the hand/arm** = *an der Hand/am Arm* – **by phone/ e-mail** = *telefonisch/per E-Mail* – **by the rules** = *nach den Regeln* – **by myself** = *ganz allein* – **By the end of the day** = *bis heute Abend* – **By the time we got home** = *als wir (erst einmal/endlich) zu Hause waren* – **By the way** = *übrigens*

6.1.2

Practice

Paul to Vic and Terry: "**What** are you doing in the middle of the night?" – That was exactly **what** I had expected. – Terry had the chain in his hand, **which** seemed to make him feel strong. – Terry asked Vic **what** he was waiting for. – At the very end of the story the reader is informed of **what** has happened in the car. – Paul is very polite, **which** is supported by the way he addresses the two friends. – Terry wants to bully Paul, **which** proves he is a thug. – Vic did **what** he could to put the blame on Paul. – **What** initiates the action proper is Paul's first mentioning of the noise. – This is **what** the two yobs have been waiting for. – This is precisely **what** Minton succeeds in doing perfectly. – In Britain class has always been **what** money is to America.

6.1.3

A)

1

The way that visit unfolds can by no means be called neighbourly. From the moment Paul enters the two friends' room there is trouble in the air.
In the introductory note, the two friends are described as skinheads and collectors of German Nazi emblems, which can be taken as a hint at their nationalist and violence-prone *(gewaltbereit)* attitude. These two right wing extremists display a special kind of "hospitality". Terry, who is the younger of the two and seems to be a dumb thug *(primitiver Schläger),* is plainly hostile and barely hides his aggressiveness. Vic, his fatherly mentor, affects *(sich zulegen)* a formal politeness and correctness in manners and speech towards Paul while determined to humiliate his "guest", whom they have lured *(locken)* into their territory.
They seem to spot the shy and soft-spoken visitor with longish hair and spectacles as their natural enemy. It is especially Vic who needles him by addressing him formally and who insists on a formal introduction. Basking in *(„sich aalen")* a socially inferior position of class-proud underdogs as compared to Paul's status as a student, Vic boasts of his and Terry's close friendship (ll. 38–44), which alone provides them with strength and conviction.
Gradually Vic establishes his dominance and the diffident *(schüchtern)* Paul begins to feel more and more uneasy. When Paul eventually brings up his cause (excessive noise), Vic's seemingly playful taunting gives way to downright intimidation and bullying (ll. 59–82). The trap for Paul has been set, the (noise) provocation has done the job, the game of cornering and humiliating can begin. Against all evidence the existence of a radio is vehemently denied (l. 21), Paul's decent complaint is turned into an aggressive act and intolerable insult on Paul's part, his irritation that begins to show is interpreted as disrespect for the hospitality their guest has kindly been offered. They – as victims of Paul's trespassing *(Übertretung)* – feel entitled to block Paul's way to the door and threaten him by denying him the right to leave the room. The blunt command to

behave like an obedient dog (ll. 55–57) is aimed at infuriating Paul further, who – so far – has kept his nerve, and is meant to make Paul blow his lid *(ausrasten)* so that the two bullies can get going and "have it out on" *(verprügeln)* the frightened and helpless Paul.
Their aggressive anger, their rude behaviour, and their blatant *(unverhohlen)* disrespect of other people's rights mark the two "blood brothers" as yobs, who are bent on trouble. There is no question that they must be called antisocial.

2

Dictionaries define a "yob" or "yobbo" as a rowdy, aggressive, or violent young man, who displays a disregard for orderly behaviour, and disrespect for his fellow citizens.
The "blood brothers" Terry and Vic both can be said to fall into that category. Terry, the younger of the two, likes to openly demonstrate his physical superiority by threatening the student and yelling abuse *(beschimpfen)* at him. His older friend Vic, however, is by no means less aggressive. He is the one who sets the trap into which the well-meaning Paul walks and which gives Vic the opportunity to embark on his collision course *(Kollisionskurs einschlagen)*. Both are, certainly, troublemakers.
At that point, early in the play, their motive remains still unclear. It might be a vague resentment *(Groll)* that two lower-class people, possibly unemployed – they are at home during the day –, feel against a student with a different background. The provocations aimed at Paul might also be seen as forms of recreation: carried out not as expressive acts of disaffection *(Hass)*, alienation, or marginalization *(Ausgegrenztsein)*, but played out for the fun of it, to let off steam, wind down, and escape from the rationalization and regulation of the ordered weekday routines of work or school. To them the "good" life is the life of ceaseless entertainment, effortless joys. From this perspective, for some people, delinquency *(Gesetzesübertretung)*, antisocial behaviour, and violence are means of amusement.

3

A short play such as Roy Minton's "Bovver" (= "Bother"), even more than a full-length drama, has not much time to waste. The play's setting must be telling, the limited number of characters must be introduced, the situation established beyond doubt, and the conflict must get under way. The audience has to be involved.
This is precisely what Minton succeeds in doing perfectly. The play's exposition is swift, and the play's action gets off the ground at once. The basic situation is that of a neighbourly visit, which is headed for confrontation from the start, since the cast of characters has been chosen so as to provide rich verbal action *(verbaler*

Schlagabtausch) and the prospect of physical violence. That is the stuff that a good drama is made of.
Any dramatist – particularly when writing a short play – must see to it that the audience is acquainted with the time and place of the action and the main characters as quickly as possible. While Roy Minton obviously neglects the time of the play's action – it can be assumed to be the present – he leaves no doubt about its setting: few stage directions serve to establish the place and its atmosphere (the room, the scarce furniture, the Nazi emblems) thus characterizing its occupants – the two bullies. The playwright sketches the situation they are in and thus initiates the conflict. That is the exposition. Until then the prevailing topic has been the "blood brothers'" – ironic – claim to impeccable manners *(untadelige Manieren)* and their incomparable "hospitality". At that point the spectator has been introduced to all the necessary information.
Now the action is set in motion. What initiates the action proper is Paul's first mentioning of the noise. This is what the two yobs have been waiting for. Paul's mention of the cause and the ensuing request *(folgende höfliche Bitte)* to turn down the radio starts off the movement of the plot. The fact that the unsuspecting Paul has walked into their trap, i.e. is ready to lodge his complaint, can be considered as the inciting moment *(auslösendes Moment).* It gives them the coveted *(ersehnt)* chance to play their cat-and-mouse game with their visitor. The transition of the action from needling and taunting to intimidation and open menace marks the beginning of the rising action or dramatic complication. From here the play will proceed to its climax (degrading violence?) and – finally – to its solution of the conflict (triumph or check for the tormentors?) if there is one.

B)

1

Both Vic's background and his behaviour towards the friendly and cautious Paul characterize him as an antisocial extremist. His haircut and his outfit give him away as a skinhead, and the fact that he is at home during daytime is a clue that he is unemployed and lives on social welfare. He has, apparently, had a brush with the law *(Konflikt mit dem Gesetz)* and served some time in prison (l. 62). So, he must be seen as a man who lives on the fringes *(Rand)* of society.
Nevertheless, he claims to attach great importance to "decent" language ("Oh, language, please, please", l. 24) and "polite" manners (l. 34), and he skilfully switches register *(Sprachebene)* when he feels like it even if he does so only to mock the "educated" student Paul. At the same time, Vic is capable of talking bluntly when he wants to press his point home. His command of language and verbal versatility *(Geschicklichkeit)* are razor-sharp. This fact indicates that the older of the two "blood brothers" has an educational background.

Terry, for his part, is a different type: he is a simple-minded brute, who constantly needs to let off steam. He is used to asserting himself by threats and physical violence. He seems to hate everyone who is different from himself and likes to insult them by calling them names. His frame of mind and his verbal as well as physical actions are very consistent *(stimmig).*

2

Vic's and Terry's resentment and hatred of anything civil *(zivilisiert)* and, by extension, of a civil society, have persuaded them to join forces and become friends.
Their repertoire of routine incivilities *(Unhöflichkeiten)* and antisocial behaviour appears to be considerable and, generally, they are up to no good.
At first glance, simple-minded, tight-lipped and violence-prone Terry might seem to be the more dangerous of the two. He cannot be trusted to behave decently and not to "let fly" at anyone who crosses his way, he needs guidance to direct and restrain *(zügeln)* him. Otherwise he would probably get into mischief *(Ärger bekommen)* ten times a day.
Vic, his older friend and mentor, is willing to guide the hot-blooded Terry and channel his aggressions, if only for his purposes. It is Vic who is not only more intelligent and more educated than his friend but who also has the smarter strategies at his disposal. Vic's disaffection and resentment go far deeper than Terry's. He has the far greater talent to bring his hatred to bear *(ausleben).* The way he first needles, then provokes his victim Paul and, finally breathes down his neck give proof that Vic is, indeed, the more dangerous of the two: he is what may be called the mastermind.

3

Sirs,
I'm writing to draw your attention to **two of my neighbours' rude and unacceptable behaviour.** They **play loud music and create disturbances** around the clock. This is most **upsetting**.
The volume of **the noise they make** peaks between 9 p.m. and 12 p.m., which, of course, coincides with **the time when I need to do my studies at home.**
I must express my own, and other residents', anxiety at **my two neighbours' antisocial and criminal behaviour.** To make matters even worse, **they even deny it is they who are making that noise in the first place.** I feel some sort of action is much needed here and long overdue. Otherwise I would be forced to **move into another area of our town.** The **peace among the residents of our council estate** is at stake!
…

4

The angry clash *(Zusammenstoß)* over the complaint lodged by Paul against his neighbours suggests that there is something amiss *(im Argen)* between them, which reaches far deeper than the harmless incident would allow for. There is a gulf that separates them. Are they "dwellers in different zones, or inhabitants of different planets"?
In Britain class has always been what money is to America, and class disparities have always influenced the way the British see the world. In modern Britain the ways of living, the range of lifestyles have become a lot more varied. While class is no longer the overriding organizing principle of British society, the American sociologist Charles Murray (in a series of articles in The Sunday Times, in 1994) found that, in the 1990s, the old "them" vs. "us" antagonism has resurfaced – and gave it a new name.
The new middle classes, dubbed the "New Victorians" (!) by Murray, are particularly keen on education and professional occupations, strive for high incomes, and flock to London or England's southwest (north-south divide). They show a revived interest in spiritual life and a renewed concern for decency in manners and partnerships. Paul is a student; he takes his studies seriously (ll. 47–48); in the introductory note he is described as "gentle". So, he may well be the type of person that Murray has in mind.
On the other hand, the term "us" defined the solidarity of the traditional (19th and 20th century) working classes. In recent decades many of them have worked their way up into the large middle classes, and Murray, interestingly, found a new underclass – the "New Rabble". Poorly educated and largely dependent on welfare and the black economy *(Scharzmarkt)*, they do not enter the labour force when times are good. Instead their ranks are growing steadily, spreading what we may call the "yob culture", and they constitute an interesting market for violent and pornographic films, for television and music. Whereas Vic cannot be pronounced poorly educated, Terry certainly can. In the play, they can be suspected of living on social benefit, and their loutish *(rüpelhaft)* and aggressive behaviour leaves little doubt that they fall into the category of the "New Rabble".
Broadly speaking, Paul respectively Vic/Terry are people "between whom there is […] no sympathy; who are ignorant of each other's habits, thoughts, and feelings, […] who are formed by a different breeding, are fed by different food, are ordered by different manners, and are not governed by the same laws."

5

This is, of course, an open-ended question. The possible answers are manifold. The answers given here can show you how to argue your case.
In this situation, the peace-loving, gentle student is confronted with rough bullying and blunt thuggery. He has, basically, three different options.

For one, he might decide to steel himself *(Zähne zusammenbeißen)* to face up to the insulting provocations that are coming his way, and, if the need arises, to fight back risking a bloody nose and losing the punch-up. Responding that way would certainly pose something of a challenge to Paul, who would probably not come out of it unhurt.
For another, Paul might wait for the right moment to run for it *(entkommen)* and call in the police to let them deal with the two thugs. Provided that the occasion presented itself, this would save his hide for the time being. He might find, however, that the police would dismiss the incident as immaterial *(nicht wichtig)* advising the complaining Paul to be more careful next time since no serious harm was done.
Finally, Paul might pretend to comply *(sich fügen)*, to pander to their whims *(auf ihre Launen eingehen)* and bow out while avoiding direct bodily confrontation and tiring them out, thus giving the two friends the feeling that they have taken him for a ride *(sich auf seine Kosten amüsieren)* and seeing their antisocial behaviour and violence for what they are, perhaps are their way of amusing and entertaining themselves at the expense of others. In a way, this strategy might prove most successful especially if he considered moving out as soon as possible.
A final note: If you're interested in how the play ends, you may get a copy and read it.

C)

Ich werde mir Häuser und einen schnellen Schlitten anschaffen, sagt ein „Yob", der mit £ 567000 belohnt wurde

Ein jugendlicher Krimineller, der £ 567 000 als Schmerzensgeld bekommen hat, nachdem er bei einem Einbruch durch ein Dach gefallen war, brüstete sich gestern mit seinem Reichtum. Er erklärte, dass er sich darauf freue, „ein paar Häuser und einen schnellen Schlitten" zu kaufen.
Carl Murphy, 18, bekam die Auszahlung in der letzten Woche, neun Jahre, nachdem er sich in einem Warenlager in den Bootle Docks in der Nähe von Liverpool bei einem Fall aus 40 Fuß Höhe verletzt hatte. Diese Nachricht rief wütende Proteste von Verbrechensopfern und Politikern hervor. In seinem ersten öffentlichen Interview seit dem Empfang der Geldsumme sagte der wegen Raub, Einbruchdiebstahls und Überfällen verurteilte Murphy, dass ihm die Reaktion völlig egal sei. „Ich habe einen Anspruch auf dieses Geld, und es kümmert mich nicht, was irgend jemand über mich sagt", meinte er. „Ich habe vor, ein großes Haus zu kaufen, so dass ich einen Platz zum Leben für mich und meine Mutter habe, wenn sie aus dem Gefängnis kommt. Ich werde möglicherweise mehrere Häuser kaufen – ich werden kaufen, was immer ich will." Er fügte hinzu: „Die Zeitungen nennen mich einen Rowdy und Schläger, weil ich für Raub und Tätlichkeiten im Gefängnis gesessen habe, aber das waren nur vergleichsweise dumme Kleinigkeiten. Ich

möchte mein Geld ausgeben, wie ich es will, ohne dass andere Leute sich einmischen, und ich möchte eine Zukunft mit genug Geld haben. Ich möchte meine Kumpels zu Liverpool-Spielen einladen und einen schnellen Schlitten kaufen. Das Geld gehört jetzt mir, und ich werde damit anfangen, was ich will. Ich höre auf niemanden, auch nicht darauf, was andere Leute dazu zu sagen haben."
Murphy erhielt sein Schmerzensgeld, nachdem er die Firma, der das Warenlager gehörte, verklagt hatte. Er behauptete, dass er sich, wenn der umgebende Zaun nicht baufällig gewesen wäre, keinen Zugang hätte verschaffen und sich nicht hätte verletzen können.
Einwohner von Bootle, dem Ort, wo Murphy lebt, sagten, dass sie aus Furcht nicht öffentlich über den Fall sprächen, aber privat beschrieben sie Murphy als den „König der Rowdys" in der Gegend.

6.1.4

Practice 1

Paul: "To me this rap music is at the bottom of the problem: it tells the young to rebel against anything, do drugs, and abuse women." → **Paul's cause**

Vic: "So, you think that getting rid of the rap music would solve the drug and other problems in our society?" → **Paul's effect**

Paul: "Well, I do believe so."

Vic: "Don't you think that most of the rap singers sing about that stuff because that is what is really going on these days? I mean, people often sing about the conditions of their time, just like the people did in the sixties." → **Vic's cause**

Paul: "Well..."

Vic: "Well, if there weren't all these problems, the rap singers probably wouldn't be singing about them." → **Vic's effect**

Practice 2

As this is an open-ended question, it is up to you to express your view on the effect of rap music on your peers. The point is that you have made sure of your transition words!

Practice 3

Your cause-and-effect-sentences might look like this:

1. Have you thought of the upcoming class test? **That is why** I can't go out tonight. / I can't go out tonight **because of** the upcoming class test.
2. I haven't had much sleep. **As a result** I'm in bad shape today. / **Since** I haven't had much sleep, I'm in bad shape today.
3. I should think twice before showing up in class. **The reason is that** taking the class test is a risk. / Taking the class test is a risk. **Therefore,** I should think twice before showing up in class.
4. Our family doctor will certify that I was ill. **So that**, perhaps, I won't have to take the test then. / Perhaps I won't have to take the test **because** our family doctor will certify that I was ill.
5. Our teacher refuses to accept the doctor's certificate. That **implies that** I'll have to do the test. / **The reason** that I'll have to do the test **is that** our teacher refuses to accept the doctor's certificate.

6.2.2

A)

1

According to Yasmin Alibhai-Brown the Caucasian Gill Danesh, who has a respectable middle-class background and looks back on a model career herself, marries, against the advice of her friends and colleagues, Sayeed, an Iranian engineer who has left his country after the Khomeini revolution. The couple have two children – twins, a fair-haired boy and a girl with darker skin. Gill and Sayeed have to learn that the boy is fully accepted while the foreign-looking girl is discriminated against at school and even at home by her own grandfather. Their mother Gill hopes that she will live to see more tolerance as the number of mixed-race marriages grows in Britain.

2

Starting out from a case of mixed-race marriage in Britain, the author states that despite the country's continually growing rates of mixed-race relationships Britain (l. 29) has not adopted a more liberal view on interracial marriage (ll. 32–35). She points out the paradox that one of the highest rates of mixed-race marriage in the western world has been accompanied be growing prejudice, hatred, and violence. She is, however, confident that the present discriminatory practice cannot stop people from breaking down social barriers and getting married across the colour bar (ll. 67–68).

B)

1

The newspaper article by Yasmin Alibhai-Brown, who is from Ugandan-Asian extraction and who herself lives in a mixed-race relationship, attempts to see her own situation from a broader perspective. Her text can be regarded as a classic example of the feature story.
She constructs a lead of the anecdotal kind in that she tells the mini-story of British-born Gill Danesh and the Iranian engineer Sayeed (ll. 1–16). This is meant to give us a clue as to what she will discuss in her article. The issue itself is a very moving one (social ill) *(gesellschaftliches Übel).*
The following two paragraphs (ll. 17–30) constitute what journalists typically call the nut graf. Alibhai-Brown describes the significance of what we have just read: the personal fate of the couple mentioned in the opening paragraphs is put into the larger perspective of British attitudes towards interracial relationships. Her message is that an increasing number of such relationships over the years have provoked deep misgivings *(Unbehagen)* in British public and private life. In the first of these two paragraphs she alludes to *(anspielen auf)* the fact while, in the second, she puts forward her main thesis ("appallingly brutal ways", l. 36).
This statement is supported by the body of her story (ll.37–64). Alibhai-Brown's illustrations (and personal conclusions) include her references to various other cases, the fact that, to her knowledge, a minority of these relationships "survives" (three out of eight interviewed couples, ll. 43–44), an expert's forthcoming research results, and evidence from the author's personal experience and her own situation within the Asian community. Thus her approach is broadened considerably.
Her final paragraph provides an emotional answer to those who are still opposed to interracial marriages: love will prevail over hatred and discrimination. She as an Asian journalist alludes to the Christian marriage vow (ll. 67–68) to demonstrate that she identifies with them.
There can be no denying that the author follows the conventions of a feature story.

2

This is another open-ended comment question that, as it should be, leaves the issue to your private systems of thought. Possible answers might consider the following points:

encouraged:

- The current situation as regards mixed-race relationships in Britain, and probably in Germany as well, does not look too promising.
- However, western Europe has been, is and will be a magnet for people who

cannot make a decent living in their home countries; there will be a continual influx *(Zufluss)* of economic refugees both legal and illegal, who follow the jobs.
- The European Union with its agenda of admitting more and more countries with different ethnic backgrounds and cultures and opening its borders, will bring about more, not fewer, multi-ethnic and cross-cultural relationships and, ultimately, marriages quite naturally.
- Trading and commercial ties will strengthen personal bonding *(Bindungen)* across the colour bar.
- Time will be a crucial factor: in twenty or thirty years' time we may be looking at a different ethnic and social picture in western Europe than we are now.
- So, there is reason to be optimistic as is the British journalist Yasmin Alibhai-Brown.

deterred:
- Given the fact that Britain's (and, by implication, Germany's) "face will change", this may not mean that a different ethnic make-up of our countries will make peaceful intermingling and mutual acceptance easier.
- The statement of the article is cause for concern *(Grund zur Besorgnis)*; the author's hope expressed in the last paragraph is not convincing.
- With many people, emotions involved run deep when intercultural relationships come into play and are, generally, not subject to reason; so, when figures multiply, hatred, drawing the line and – violence – might increase instead of decreasing.
- It might be males with a different racial background who might have to bear the brunt of *(die Hauptlast tragen)* growing resentment: "They take our jobs; they take our girls – why have they come here in the first place?"
- A clear-cut, restrictive immigration policy defining the qualifications for those seeking admission to our countries might easily win support (and votes).
- At best, the scenario hinted at by Alibhai-Brown may take a very long time to come to fruition *(Wirklichkeit werden)*.

C)

Kinder gemischter ethnischer Herkunft

Die Volkszählung im Jahre 2001 war ein Meilenstein für gemischtrassische Bürger des Vereinigten Königreichs – zum ersten Mal fand sich für die verschiedenen ethnischen Gruppen eine Kategorie „gemischt" auf dem Fragebogen. Aber Forscher führen an, dass, obwohl die Existenz gemischtrassiger Bürger jetzt statistisch offiziell anerkannt sein mag, ernste Sorgen nicht zu verhehlen sind.

Yasmin Albhai-Brown, Autorin des kürzlich erschienenen Buches „Gemischte Gefühle", in dem sie die Probleme untersucht, denen sich Kinder gemischter Herkunft ausgesetzt sehen, sagte, dass eine größere Sorge darin bestehe, dass

viele Organisationen und öffentliche Körperschaften in Großbritannien ihre Politik aus den USA übernommen hätten.
„Die Bewegung dort begann, für alle Kinder gemischter ethnischer Herkunft zu fordern, dass sie als schwarz zu bezeichnen seien – das Argument lautete, wenn sie unter Rassismus leiden, fragt sie niemand, ob sie von gemischter Herkunft seien. Aber ich glaube, die schweren Fehler bestanden darin, dass man die Politiker und Praktiker in dieses absurde Konzept getrieben hat, weil Kinder von gemischtrassiger Herkunft weder schwarz noch weiß noch braun sind – sie sind sie selbst", sagte sie.
Häufig lebten Kinder gemischtrassiger Herkunft bei weißen Müttern, die selbst wiederum Opfer einer Diskriminierung sowohl durch Weiße wie Schwarze wurden, fügte Ms Alibhai-Brown hinzu. [...] Yasmin Alibhai-Brown war überzeugt, dass trotz der Schwierigkeiten für eine Reihe von Paaren der Trend zu gemischten Partnerschaften wahrscheinlich zunehmen werde.
Sie sagte: „Mehr und mehr schwarze und asiatische und chinesische Bürger werden Weiße und untereinander heiraten. Diese Entwicklung, so scheint mir, wird nicht aufzuhalten sein. Ich hoffe, das wird dieses Land mit seiner ethnischen Vielfalt als nationalem Charakteristikum versöhnen."

6.2.3

Practice 1

1. In the lead of the feature story two characters are presented. – 2. You can trace this in ll. 1–16. – 3. Alibhai-Brown writes, for example, that they had two twins. – 4. In her feature story she discusses the current issue of mixed-race relations. – 5. The life that Gill Danesh and Sayeed lead is described in the second paragraph. – 6. From the grandfather's side, the relationship between Gill's father and the two kids is cool. – 7. Gill's father sees "mongrel children" in them. – 8. This behaviour you can only call discrimination.

Practice 2

1. In Britain the highest rates of mixed-race marriages are to be found. – 2. For herself Alibhai-Brown solves the problem through believing in the power of love. – 3. In her article she describes a problem of topical interest. – 4. With mixed-marriage marriages everybody associates difficulties for the children from these marriages. – 5. In a multi-cultural society all ethnic groups live peacefully together. – 6. The text says that the idea of racial purity is still very strong. – 7. Alibhai-Brown wrote this article in the year 2000. – 8. All these years the author has fought against discrimination.

6.2.4

Practice 1

Your sentences might look like this now:

1. The Prime Minister tells the BBC correspondent that the new tax plan will be announced soon. – 2. The PM's tax cuts make sense because everybody thinks that they are necessary. – 3. He stated that everyone no matter how much they earned would have to pay more taxes. – 4. His spin doctor's advice: if the higher taxes bother the people, the PM should cut them. – 5. At one time the PM was a student in Oxford, a fact that many people still remember. – 6. Having studied the speech I regard it as poor rhetoric.

Practice 2

The sentences sound much better like this:

1. If you read the text for the first time, it will seem rather difficult to understand. **(vorher: unklarer Bezug!)** – 2. The climax of the story comes in the last paragraph. Besides you can find less striking highpoints of action. **("nevertheless" und "but" nicht in einem Satz!)** – 3. The atmosphere is dark and gloomy from the outset and one can compare it with that in the room in the other story we read. **(vorher: unlogische Parallele!)** – 4. In contrast to the ten first lines which are marked by a general tone, the following lines contain a detailed description. **(vorher: unklare Parallele "lines" und "author"!)** – 5. The example implies that nobody is perfect, so he should be forgiven for behaving wrongly. This, I believe, is what the author wants to say. **(vorher: Satzungetüm!)**

6.2.5

Practice

italics: text reference
blue: verbs of meaning/discourse marker
bold: the reader's conclusion

Yasmin Alibhai-Brown **constructs a lead of the anecdotal kind in that she tells the mini-story of** *British-born Gill Danesh and the Iranian engineer Sayeed (ll. 1–17).* **This is meant to give us a clue as to** **what she will discuss in her article**. The issue itself is a very moving one (social ill).

The following two paragraphs *(ll. 18–30)* **constitute** what journalists typically call **the nut graf. Alibhai-Brown describes the significance of what we have just read:** *the personal fate of the couple* **mentioned in the opening paragraphs is** put into **the larger perspective of British attitudes towards interracial relationships**. **Her message is that** *an increasing number of such relationships over the years have provoked deep misgivings in British public and private life.* **In the first of theses**

two paragraphs she alludes to the fact while, in the second, she puts forward her main thesis *("appallingly brutal ways", l. 36).*
This statement is supported by the body of her story (ll. 37–64). Alibhai-Brown's **illustrations (and personal conclusions)** include **her references to various other cases**, the fact that, *to her knowledge, a minority of these relationships "survives" (three out of eight interviewed couples, ll. 43–44), an expert's forthcoming research results, and evidence from the author's personal experience and her own situation within the Asian community.* Thus her approach is broadened considerably.
Her final paragraph provides an emotional answer to those who are still opposed to interracial marriages: love will prevail over hatred and discrimination. She as an Asian journalist **alludes to** the Christian marriage vow (ll. 67–68) to **demonstrate that she identifies with them**.

Glossary

A) Words and phrases

A

etw. entschieden **ablehnen**	to feel strongly about sth.
etw. **abtun** als	to dismiss sth. as / to be dismissive of
absurd	senseless/pointless
beim Leser darauf **abzielen,** dass	to aim for the reader to
ganz **ähnlich**	similarly
alles in allem	all things considered
allgemein gesagt	broadly speaking
zum **Anfang** zurückkehren, indem	to return to the beginning by
es wird allgemein **angenommen,** dass	it is generally understood that
gut **ankommen** bei	to go down well with
lasst uns **annehmen,** dass	let us assume that
man kann **annehmen,** dass	a commonly held view/sentiment is that
wenn man einmal **annimmt**	given the fact that
sich **anpassen** an	to adjust to / to be in agreement with
einen falschen **Anschein** von … erwecken	to give a false appearance of
auf etw. **anspielen**	to allude to sth.
eine **Antwort** liefern für	to provide an answer to
es gibt **Anzeichen,** dass	there are indications that
ein **Argument** wirkt überzeugend	an argument carries conviction
das **Argument** bringen, dass	to put forward the argument that
argumentieren für/gegen	to argue for/against/in favour of
jd. **argumentiert** dahingehend, dass	sb. argues from this that
was hier in der Tat **auffällt,** ist	what is indeed striking here is
die **Aufgabe** von … erfüllen	to fulfil the function of
die **Aufmerksamkeit** des Lesers lenken auf	to draw/to focus the reader's attention to/on
was sofort ins **Auge** fällt, ist	what immediately springs to mind is
wenn man sich vor **Augen** hält, dass	bearing in mind that
wir verschließen unsere **Augen** vor	we shut our eyes to

die **Ausnahme** bestätigt die Regel	the exception proves the rule
ist keine **Ausnahme** von der Regel	is no exception to the rule
was den **Ausschlag** gibt, ist	what tips the balance is
wir sehen der **Aussicht** entgegen, dass	we will face the prospect of
die **Aussicht** scheint erschreckend	the prospect seems frightening
um es drastisch/einfacher/genauer **auszudrücken**	to put it bluntly/more simply/ precisely

B

bedauerlicherweise (was noch schlimmer ist / was jedoch höchst beunruhigend ist)	sadly (worse still/most worryingly, however)
bedeutsam	meaningful
einer Sache **Bedeutung** beimessen	to attach importance to sth.
einer Sache große **Bedeutung** beimessen	to place a premium on sth.
von überragender ↔ geringer **Bedeutung** für	of vital/prime/utmost ↔ slight/ minor/secondary importance to
etw. negativ **beeinflussen**	to affect sth. adversely/negatively
beeinträchtigt sein durch	to be dented by
behaupten, dass	to maintain that
man darf wohl **behaupten,** dass	it is safe to say that
wie zum **Beispiel**	if you take, for example,
ein schlagendes **Beispiel** für … taucht auf in den Zeilen …	a striking example of … occurs in lines …
weitere **Beispiele** für … sind	further examples/instances of … are
es gibt **Belege** dafür, dass	there is some evidence to suggest that
dies lässt sich **belegen** in den Zeilen …	proof of this can be found/this can be traced in lines …
was (noch) **bemerkenswert**(er) ist	(more) significantly
es ist **berechtigt,** zu sagen, dass	it is justified/fair to say that
etw. präzise/im Detail/ anschaulich ↔ ungenau/unpräzise/ unzureichend/sehr ausführlich **beschreiben**	to describe sth. precisely/ accurately/in detail/vividly ↔ vaguely/imprecisely/ at great length
seine **Besorgnis** ausdrücken, dass	to express one's concern about
es ist (un-)**bestreitbar,** dass	surely it is (un-)arguable that
von außen **betrachtet** würde	to the untrained eye it would

es erscheinen	appear
insgesamt **betrachtet**	on balance
besonders **beunruhigend** ist jedoch	most worryingly however is
es gibt genügend **Beweise,** dass	there is ample evidence that
Beweise dafür lassen sich finden in	evidence of that can be found in
ein ungeschminktes **Bild** von	a stark picture of

D

ins **Detail** gehen bei	to go into particulars / to go to full lengths about
(hin-)**deuten** hin auf	to be indicative of/suggestive of

E

egal ob	regardless of / irrespective of
einfach gesagt	plainly (put)
der wirkliche **Einwand** ist, dass	the real objection is that
in die **Einzelheiten** gehen	to go to full lengths about
wenn man das zu **Ende** denkt	taken to its logical conclusion
wir können nur **erahnen,** ob	we can only guess at
meine eigene **Erfahrung** geht dahin, dass	my own experience tells me that
die **Erfahrung** machen, dass	to learn/to know from experience/ to discover
dies **erklärt**	this accounts for
meine **Erklärung** ist, dass	my explanation is that
es **erinnert** jdn. an	it reminds sb. of
eröffnen mit	to begin by pointing out that
erstaunlicherweise	amazingly/strikingly

F

ein zentraler **Faktor**	a crucial factor
seinen **Fall** darlegen	to lay out his cause
das ist eine klare **Fehleinschätzung**	that is a clear misconception
fortfahren mit	to continue with what can be called
die **Frage** erhebt sich, was	the question arises as to what
dies fordert die **Frage** heraus, ob	this begs the question if
es steht außer **Frage,** dass	it is out of the question that
es scheint außer **Frage** zu stehen, dass	what seems clear is that

man **fragt** sich, ob	one wonders if
etw. **funktioniert** nicht	sth. is unworkable

G

im **Gegensatz** dazu	by contrast/by comparison
ein scharfer ↔ schwacher **Gegensatz**	a sharp/striking ↔ slight/ imperceptible/hardly noticeable contrast
das steht in scharfem **Gegensatz** zu	this stands in sharp contrast to
hier scheiden sich die **Geister**	this is where opinion divides
genauer gesagt	more accurately
gezielt	deliberately, expressly
in etw. **gipfeln**	to culminate in sth.
wenn wir … **Glauben** schenken	if we are to believe
nach etw. **greifen**	to reach out for sth.
etw. **grenzt** an	sth. borders on
die **Gründe** für … sind vielfältig	there are several reasons why / the reasons behind … are many/ complex
ich kann den **Grund** nicht erkennen, warum	I fail to see why
aus (genau) diesem **Grund**	for that (very) reason
ein vorrangiger **Grund** ist, dass	high on the list of reasons is
einen einsichtigen/stichhaltigen/ offensichtlichen/zwingenden/ offensichtlichen/schwachen **Grund** liefern für	to supply a(n) plausible/ solid/apparent/compelling/ obvious/feeble reason for

H

das **hängt** ab von …, kommt an auf …	that depends on
der **Haken** ist aber	the hitch, however, is
die **Hauptlast** tragen von etw.	to bear the brunt of sth.
das **heißt**	i.e./that is to say
das **geht** aus der Tatsache **hervor,** dass	this arises from the fact that
es **kommt** auf dasselbe **hinaus**	it amounts to the same thing
das muss vor dem **Hintergrund** von … gesehen werden	this must be seen against the background/backdrop of
Hoffnungen setzen auf	to pin one's hopes on

I

immer mehr/zunehmend	increasingly
ein **Inbegriff** von … sein	to epitomize/to embody sth.
infolgedessen	as a result
Informationen liefern zu	to provide information (Sg.!) on …
ironischerweise	ironically
das ist **irreführend**	this is misleading

K

klarkommen mit	to come to grips with
klarmachen, dass	to make it clear that
einen **Keil** treiben zwischen	to drive a wedge between
nicht zur **Kenntnis** nehmen	to turn a blind eye on
etw. **klingt** wahr	sth. rings true
etw. **kommt** mir vor wie	sth. strikes me as
in **Konflikt** geraten mit	to come into conflict with/ to be in conflict with
konkret gesprochen	in terms of facts/put in concrete terms
konkret werden, indem	to provide a lot of concrete detail/ to go into particulars/ to illustrate one's view by
konkrete Angaben machen zu	to supply precise/exact data
kreisen um	to revolve around
um es **kurz** zu sagen	to put it in a nutshell
kurzum	the long and short of it is

L

leider	sadly/unfortunately
es **leuchtet** ein, dass	it stands to reason that
es lässt sich nicht **leugnen**, dass	there is no denying that
sich **lustig** machen über	to poke fun at

M

die **Meinung** vertreten, dass	to advocate/to endorse the view that
wir müssen unsere **Meinung** zu … ändern	we need to move away from
der gesunde **Menschenverstand** sagt uns, dass	common sense tells us that

merkwürdigerweise	interestingly/oddly enough
missachten	to turn a blind eye on

N

ich kann das **nachvollziehen,** frage mich jedoch	I can see the point, yet I wonder

P

paradoxerweise	paradoxically
eine **Parallele** ziehen zwischen	to draw a parallel between
etw. **passt** wie angegossen	sth. fits like a glove
passt das zusammen?	does it add up?
nicht **passend** zu	out of character with
eine **Position** ist unhaltbar	a position is untenable
etw. **preisgeben**	to give sth. away
ein **Problem** angehen	to address/to tackle a problem
ein Teil des **Problems** ist, dass	part of the problem is that
das trifft den **Punkt** nicht	this misses the point

R

was mir **rätselhaft** ist, ist	what puzzles me is
einen **Rückzieher** machen	to back out of

S

sich einer **Sache** (schmerzhaft) bewusst sein	to be (acutely) aware of sth.
so wie ich (wir) die **Sache** sehe(n)	from what I (we) can tell
schließlich	finally
was die Dinge **schlimmer** macht (für)	what makes matters/things worse (for)
was noch **schlimmer** ist	worse still
zu dem **Schluss** kommen, dass	to arrive at/to come to the conclusion that
daher lässt sich **schlussfolgern,** dass	hence it may be inferred that
eine **Schlüsselfigur** sein in	to be a key-player in
seltsamerweise	curiously (enough)
sinnlos	senseless/pointless
einen klaren **Standpunkt** beziehen zu	to take a firm stand on
das kann schon **stimmen,** aber wie …?	that may well be but how …?
unter dem **Strich**	subsequently / at the final count

T

man kann in der **Tat** behaupten, dass	in fact one might say that
diese **Tatsache** ist geeignet, zu	this fact tends to
es ist eine schlichte **Tatsache,** dass	it is a simple fact that
relevanter/zentraler ist die **Tatsache,** dass	more pertinent is the fact that
der **Text** gliedert sich in	the text breaks into/divides into
der **Text** ist durchsetzt mit	the text is littered with
der **Textteil** umfasst die Zeilen …	the text part comprises lines …
ein **Thema** ansprechen	to address an issue
den **thematischen** Zusammenhang sichern	to establish thematic coherence by
eine **These** vorstellen	to present/to put forth a thesis
eine **These** entwickeln	to expand/to evolve a thesis

U

es **überrascht** kaum, dass	it is hardly surprising that
überzeugt sein, dass	to be convinced of the fact that
ich bin nicht **überzeugt,** da	I remain unconvinced because
es ist **undenkbar**, dass	there is no way that
ich bin **unentschieden**, ob	I am in two minds about
das **Unmögliche** vollbringen	to square the circle
es ist wichtig zu **unterscheiden** zwischen	it is important to distinguish between
eine klare **Unterscheidung** treffen zwischen	to make a clear distinction between
der **Unterschied** liegt in der Tatsache, dass	the difference lies in the fact that
so **unterschiedlich** sein wie Katz und Hund	to be as different as chalk and cheese
wenn man **unterstellt,** dass …, bin ich der Meinung, dass	given that we know that … I believe that
etw. ist **unübersehbar**	sth. stares you in the face
es ist **unvorstellbar,** dass	it is inconceivable that
wenn man nach … **urteilt**	judging by

V

eine **Veränderung** durchmachen	to undergo a change
etw. **verkörpern**	to epitomize/to embody sth.
es ist zu **vermuten**, dass	it may be suspected that
vernünftigerweise	reasonably enough
versichern, dass	to assert that
so viel **Verständnis** ich auch habe für …, kann ich dennoch nicht verhehlen, dass	sympathetic that I am to … I nevertheless cannot help feeling that
das kann **verstanden** werden als	this can be read/understood as
etw. ist schwierig zu **verstehen**	sth. is difficult to fathom
auf etw. **vertrauen**	to have faith in/confidence in sth.
vor (zeitliche Präposition)	prior to
vorausgesetzt, dass	provided that/on condition that

W

es liegt wahrscheinlich ein Körnchen **Wahrheit** in	there is probably some truth in
jdm. auf halbem **Wege** entgegen-kommen	to meet sb. halfway
etw. nimmt eine unerwartete **Wendung**	sth. takes an unexpected twist/turn
ebenso **wichtig**	equally important
für besonders **wichtig** halten	to attach great importance to
(nicht) **willens** sein, etw. zu tun	to be (not) prepared to do sth.
etw. lässt viel zu **wünschen** übrig	sth. leaves a lot to be desired

Z

ein **Ziel** ansteuern/anstreben	to aspire to/to strive for a goal
ein **Ziel** erreichen/verfolgen	to achieve/to pursue an aim/ a goal/an objective
jdn. **zitieren**	to quote sb. as saying
es ist kein **Zufall**, dass	it is no coincidence that
Zugang haben zu	to have access to
zugegebenermaßen	admittedly
etw. **zurückführen** darauf, dass	to put sth. down to the fact that
zwangsläufigerweise	inevitably
zwar …, aber	it is true (that) … but
es ist mehr als **zweifelhaft**, ob	it is more than doubtful whether
zweifellos	undeniably

B) How to Relate Ideas

Zusatz	Addition
auch	also
darüber hinaus	besides
außerdem	furthermore/in addition/moreover

Logische Folge	Consequence
entsprechend	accordingly
infolgedessen	as a result
daraus folgt	consequently
sonst	otherwise
so dass	so that
somit	thus
daher	hence
as I have said	wie ich bereits gesagt habe
aus diesem Grund	for that reason

Zusammenfassung	Summarizing
alles in allem	all in all
zusammen betrachtet	all things considered
kurz gesagt	briefly/in short
insgesamt	by and large
auf jeden Fall	in any case
im Ganzen	in conclusion/on the whole
auf lange Sicht	in the long run
unter dem Strich	subsequently

Verallgemeinerung	Generalizing
in der Regel	as a rule
generell	generally/generally speaking/usually

Umformulierung	Restatement
mit anderen Worten	in other words
nämlich	namely/that is
das will sagen	that is to say
um es anders auszudrücken	to put it differently

Gegenüberstellung und Vergleich	Contrast and Comparison
ähnlich	similarly
im Gegensatz dazu	conversely/in contrast to/unlike
stattdessen	instead
einerseits … andererseits	on the one hand … on the other hand
jedoch/hingegen	yet/but/however/still
nichtsdestoweniger	nevertheless

Abfolge	Sequence
zunächst	at first/first of all/to begin with
zugleich	at the same time
im Augenblick	for now/for the time being
später	later on
inzwischen	meanwhile
gleichzeitig	simultaneously

Veranschaulichung	Illustration
zum Beispiel	for example/for instance
zum einen … zum anderen	for one thing … for another

Sources

Textnachweise

Unit 1

Elizabeth Montebello Is the Prettiest Girl in School
http://books.guardian.co.uk/shortshortstories/story/0,14414,1270270,00.html (July 27, 2004)

Why Beauty Spas Thank Heaven for Little Girls
Amelia Hill, The Observer (May 1, 2005)

The Tyranny of Slenderness
Susan Bordo, Unbearable Weight. Feminism, Western Culture and the Body, University of California Press, Berkeley 1995, 140–141

Mass Media and the Female Body
http://www.culturebunker.com/columns/angel_mass.php3 (Aug. 30, 2005)

Unit 2

Arriving at the Monopark 5000 Hotel
William Boyd, Stars and Bars, Penguin Books, Harmondsworth 1985, 220–224

G. W. Bush: the Second Inaugural Address, Jan 20, 2005
George W. Bush, http://www.whitehouse.gov/news/releases/2005/01/20050120-1.html (March 10, 2006)

Rhetorical Devices
Thomas H. Neale, Speech Writing in Perspective, http://countingcalifornia.cdlib.org/crs/ascii/98-170 (March 12, 2006)

America's Democratic Deficit
America's Democratic Deficit, New Statesman (Nov. 20, 2000)

Unit 3

The Coming Merging of Mind and Machine
Ray Kurzweil, http://www.kurzweilai.net/meme/frame.html?main=/articles/art0063.html (Jan. 26, 2006)

"Issaquah, Wash. – A 43-year-old man ..."
Ray Kurzweil, http://www.kurzweilai.net/meme/frame.html?main=/articles/art0565.html (March 12, 2006)

Will Computers Ever Achieve a State of Consciousness?
Steven Pinker, The Sunday Times (Jan. 31, 1999)

The Satisfied Customer
Nathan Carter, http://www.sffworld.com/authors/c/carter_nathan/fiction/satisfiedcustomer1.html (March 21, 2006)

Real Fun
Ray Bradbury, Fahrenheit 451, Reclam, Stuttgart 1953, 28–29

On Sports and Practice
Minette Marrin, Slobbed Out and Dreaming of the Body Beautiful, The Sunday Times (Feb. 24, 2002)

Unit 4
Cloning As a Valid Reproductive Choice
James Hughes, http://www.betterhumans.com/error.htm?aspxerrorpath=/searchEngineLink.article.2002-11-06-3.aspx (Nov. 6, 2002)

Cloning and Stem Cell Research
Alison Driver, Biotechnology, www.britishcouncil.org/learnenglish-central-magazine-biotechnology.htm (Jan. 26, 2006)

The Ten Year Old Head
Jimi Five, http://www.nippedandtucked.com/iManuscripts/tenhead.html (March 10, 2006)

"We can make cells immortal …"
Michael Fossel, Is Ageing Irreversible?, www.galaxymagazine.com/Fossel_Michael/aging_part1.html (Jan. 15, 2001)

Happy 150th Birthday? New Era Looms for Ageing
http://msnbc.msn.com/id/11840433/; Reuters(March 16, 2006)

Study („From appearance to reality …)
http://languagelearningresourcecenter.org/anglais/language_db/interpretation/images/appearance_reality.gif (March 10, 2006)

Unit 5
An Exhortation Concerning Good Order and Obedience to Rulers and Magistrates (1547)
M. M. Badawi, Background to Shakespeare, Macmillan Education 1981, Appendix, 130–131

An Age of Invention, Discovery and Exploration
Karl Emunds, The Shakespeare Background Reader, Langenscheidt-Longman, München 1989, 46

Our Present Civilization
Lewis Mumford, The Pentagon of Power, Harcourt Brace, New York 1970

William Shakespeare, Henry V
W. Shakespeare, Henry V, Act 1, Scene 2, ll. 179–213, http://absoluteshakespeare.com/plays/henry_V/a1s2.htm (Jan. 26, 2006)

Honeybees
Ric Bessin, University of Kentucky Department of Entomology, www.uky.edu/Agriculture/Entomology/ythfacts/4h/beekeep/beebio&s.htm (March 12, 2006)

Unit 6
A Neighbourly Visit
Roy Minton, Bovver, New English One-Act Plays, hrsg. P. Pasch, Klett, Stuttgart 1990, 45–50

"Yes," resumed the younger stranger …
Benjamin Disraeli, Sybil, or The Two Nations, http://www.gutenberg.org/catalog/world/readfile?fk_files=6761&pageno=1 (Jan. 26, 2006)

I'll Buy Houses and a Flash Car, Says Yob Awarded £ 567,000
Peter Zimonjic, http://www.portal.telegraph.co.uk/news/main.jhtml?xml=/news/2005/03/20/nyob20.xml (March 12, 2006)

I Know the Hate That Comes With a Mixed-race Marriage
Yasmin Alibhai-Brown, http://comment.independent.co.uk/columnists_a_l/yasmin_alibhai_brown/article281213.ece (March 12, 2006)

Mixed-race Children
Cindi John, The Changing Face of Britain, http://news.bbc.co.uk/hi/english/static/in_depth/uk/2002/race/changing_face_of_britain.stm (Aug. 20, 2005)

Answer Key

"On Sept. 11, 2001, beginning ..."
Roger Nelson, http://noosphere.princeton.edu/terror.html (March 12, 2006)

Die vier erfolgreichsten Boomregionen
Frankfurter Allgemeine Zeitung (19. Jan. 2005)

Artificial Intelligence
http://en.wikipedia.org/wiki/Artificial_intelligence (March 14, 2006)

Turing Test
http://en.wikipedia.org/wiki/Turing_test (March 14, 2006)

Nanobots
http://en.wikipedia.org/wiki/Nanobot (March 14, 2006)

Bildnachweis

S. 8, 19, 28, 30, 31, 37, 71, 96, 122, 125, 151: Corbis GmbH, Düsseldorf
S. 8, 142, 146: Das Fotoarchiv, Essen
S. 15: VISUM Foto GmbH, Hamburg, Impact Photos
S. 20, 56, 89, 91, 134: Cartoon Stock Ltd, United Kingdom
S. 24: Laura Schreiber
S. 39: dpa Picture – Alliance GmbH, Frankfurt
S. 47, 111, 120: Archiv für Kunst und Geschichte, Berlin
S. 59: Advanced Micro Devices GmbH, Dornach b. München
S. 79: Cinetext Bild- und Text-Archiv GmbH, Frankfurt
S. 94: KEYSTONE Pressedienst GmbH, Hamburg
S. 101: Dr. Donald J Davidson
S. 106: Bayerische Staatsbibliothek, München
S. 155: Photothek.net Gbr, Ute Grabowsky, Radevormwald